SCHOOLING and EDUCATION

Basic Concepts and Problems

JOHN A. LASKA
University of Texas at Austin

D. VAN NOSTRAND COMPANY

NEW YORK   CINCINNATI   TORONTO   LONDON   MELBOURNE

For Joey

D. Van Nostrand Company Regional Offices:
New York   Cincinnati   Millbrae

D. Van Nostrand Company International Offices:
London   Toronto   Melbourne

Published by D. Van Nostrand Company
450 West 33rd Street, New York, N. Y. 10001

10   9   8   7   6   5   4   3   2   1

PREFACE

The purpose of this book is twofold: to organize the body of knowledge relating to the educative process and the school system and to present a systematic introduction to the field of educational studies. Instead of borrowing a conceptual and analytical framework from another academic discipline (such as sociology or psychology), the book offers an explicitly educational framework which allows for the identification, analysis, and discussion of major educational policy controversies in schooling and education.

A conceptual and analytical framework for the scholarly study of education has, I believe, long been necessary. It is especially important today, because serious questions are being raised about the relevance of foundations of education courses to the training of prospective teachers. Instructors must recognize the essential part they play in the professional training of teachers. Prospective teachers have not been adequately prepared if their professional competence is confined to the four walls of a classroom. To be a fully qualified professional, the prospective teacher must also know how to function within the larger setting of the school and the school system.

A course in the foundations of education must prepare prospective teachers for the broader dimensions of their professional roles. This broader preparation is no less important than the acquisition of technical skills. In order to fulfill its responsibility, the foundations of education course must deal with all fundamental education questions, as well as examine value judgments, beliefs, and assumptions about education. Prospective teachers must know what their basic educational views are and why they hold them, and they must reach their own decisions about educational policy questions. Instructors, at the same time, cannot be free of value commitments: they must have a point of view on educational issues and be able to indicate to prospective teachers how their professional competence can be enhanced through a consideration of these problems.

This text contains ten chapters, grouped into three parts, designed to demonstrate the scholarly content and potentiality of the field of educational studies. Part One (Introduction) presents and defines the basic concepts and topics essential to a systematic coverage and understanding of the two major questions raised in the book, each of which is covered extensively in Parts Two and Three. Part Two (Who Should Control Education, and in What Way?) deals with control techniques, moderate and radical proposals for control change, and traditional methods of teaching, along with newer ones. Part Three (What Should Be the Goals of Education?) treats the functions of schooling and the school system and what are and what might be the ultimate and/or penultimate goals or ends of education.

Throughout Parts Two and Three, twelve major educational policy issues are identified and discussed, including such controversies as: "Should We Have Increased Parental Control?"; "Should Compulsory Schooling Be Eliminated or Modified?"; "Should We Have Equal Educational Opportunity?"; and "Which Human Behaviors and Capabilities Should Be Developed Through Education?" Parenthetical references in each chapter refer to further explanatory material and related sources listed in the "General Notes and Bibliography" section at the end of that chapter.

In the preparation of this book, I have benefited from the help of several persons. I would like to thank my colleagues in the American Educational Studies Association for numerous opportunities to discuss alternative approaches in the foundations of education. Some of the ideas contained in the book had their genesis in a research project I carried out during 1966–1967 at the Institute of International Studies, Teachers College, Columbia University. To R. Freeman Butts, director of the Institute, I owe a debt of gratitude. Many additional ideas were developed in discussions with students and friends. I would like to acknowledge particularly the contributions of William C. Bailey. For general encouragement and advice, I am deeply grateful to Kristrun Thordardottir. The task of typing the manuscript was accomplished mainly by Stephanie Amsden and Carol Chodur, who have been extremely helpful.

J.A.L.

CONTENTS

v

. . . the anguish
Of the Real and the Seeming in life.

Herman Melville, "Madam Mirror"

The emperor walked in the procession under the beauiful cano-
py. And all the people in the street and at the windows said, "Heavens, how wonderful the emperor's new clothes are! What a lovely train
he has on the robe! What a marvelous fit!" No one wanted it to appear
that he couldn't see anything, for then of course he would have been
unfit for his position or very stupid. None of the emperor's clothes had
ever been such a success.

"But he doesn't have anything on!" said a little child.

"Heavens, listen to the innocent's voice!" said the father, and
then the child's words were whispered from one to another.

"He doesn't have anything on! That's what a little child is saying—he doesn't have anything on!"

"He doesn't have anything on!" the whole populace shouted at
last.

Hans Christian Andersen,
"The Emperor's New Clothes"

INTRODUCTION

PART ONE

BASIC CONCEPTS AND TOPICS IN EDUCATIONAL STUDIES

CHAPTER 1

Education is one of the most important activities in which human beings engage. It is by means of the educative process and its role in transmitting the cultural heritage from one generation to the next that human societies are able to maintain their existence. But education does more than just help us to keep the kind of society we already have; it is also one of the major ways in which people try to change or improve their societies. For example, if a person were asked how we could eradicate war or eliminate the misuse of drugs, he or she might suggest that this could be done through an appropriate form of education.

The school system—which involves the educative process—is one of the fundamental social institutions. In modern industrialized societies, a person may spend up to a fourth of his lifetime as a student. Moreover, as a parent, he or she will undoubtedly be concerned with decisions about the schooling of his or her children for a similar period of time.

Because of the significance of the educative process and the school system, every citizen and certainly every classroom teacher needs to have some basic knowledge about how society carries out its educational activities and what the society is trying to accomplish through its schools. But it is not enough to have this factual understanding about the educative process; the citizen and the classroom teacher also should have an opinion as to whether the existing educational activities of society ought to be continued or whether they should be changed. Only then will the citizen and the teacher be able to make their full contribution to the task of educational policy formulation.

The educative process and the school system are of such importance that a scholarly field devoted to their study has come into existence. This field has been designated by some educationists as the field of *educational studies*; it is comparable to such fields as political science and economics, each of which is also concerned with the study of a vital social process and a major social institution.[1] The purpose of this book is to offer a systematic introduction to the field of educational studies.

There appear to be two really fundamental policy questions that can be raised about education. One of these is the following: What should be the goals of education? This question must be answered every time a person undertakes an educational activity, since the reason for education is to accomplish some objective.

Education constitutes a deliberate attempt to control the learning process. Therefore, the question must also be asked: Who should control education, and in what way? It is important to know *who* should decide educational ends and *how* control over the means of education should be exercised, because these factors obviously can affect the choice of educational goals.

Each of these two fundamental policy questions can in turn be subdivided into several subsidiary questions or issues. There are several controversial educational questions which arise when a society attempts to operate a school system. In fact, twelve major educational issues have been identified here, with a conceptual and analytic framework for dealing with them. Although definitive answers to these controversial questions are not provided, some of the arguments that have been advanced in connection with them are discussed. We shall also try to show how the issues are related to one another, so that the reader will learn to interpret any educational question in terms of the kind of problem it represents and its relationships to other major educational policy questions.

Anyone who expects to be involved in the school system will

[1]Different views on education as a scholarly field of study are presented in John Walton and James L. Kuethe, eds., *The Discipline of Education* (Madison: University of Wisconsin Press, 1963). The nature of the field of educational studies, its value in teacher preparation, and some indications of the direction in which the field is moving are discussed in Margaret Gillett and John A. Laska, eds., *Foundation Studies in Education* (Metuchen, N.J.: Scarecrow Press, 1973).

benefit considerably by gaining a broader perspective on education. Almost daily the classroom teacher must deal with situations that can only be handled on the basis of a deeper understanding of the techniques and purposes of education. For example, a situation might arise in which the teacher must examine his or her assumptions about the role of discipline in the classroom. In an American history course, for instance, the teacher may wonder whether his or her purpose should be to instill patriotic attitudes or to develop the skills of critical thinking. Also, a teacher may reflect on the need to grade students. Only if the teacher has inquired into the fundamental nature of schooling and the educative process will he or she be able to approach these and similar problems adequately.

DEFINITIONS OF BASIC CONCEPTS

If substantial progress is to be made in the scholarly study of education, it is important to be precise in the use of educational concepts and terminology. Terminological precision is essential if the field of educational studies is to reach the level of development of other fields, such as economics and sociology. Most of the concepts used in the latter fields are quite precise, in contrast to the fuzziness and ambiguity which often surround the use of educational concepts.

Therefore, the meanings of the major concepts we employ shall be specified. That a word is defined here in a particular way does not mean, of course, that a given term may not be defined differently by others. All technical definitions are essentially arbitrary; if we say that a particular concept means exactly thus and so, we are stipulating for our purposes what the concept means for us. Although the reader may prefer to use the concept in a different way, he will be able to understand better what is being written about.

Learning

Learning is an essential human process. At birth, the human infant does not have the capability to utilize language or to perform most of the activities that are expected of an adult member of our society. As he or she matures, however, the typical child is exposed to a vast number of learning experiences, which transform a helpless infant into a competent adult. If by some chance the child does not receive these normal learning experiences (for example, reported cases of children abandoned by their parents and raised by wolves), then a human personality does not develop. Without the learning process, therefore, human life as we presently know it could not exist.

As Hilgard and Bower have noted, it is very difficult to give a completely satisfactory definition of learning.[2] Learning is a process that produces the capability of exhibiting new or changed human behavior, and/or it increases the probability that new or changed behavior will be elicited by a relevant stimulus. But there are many human processes or conditions that may result in new or changed behavior, not just the learning process; for example, the process of aging, the loss of an arm or leg, and fatigue. Consequently, a definition of learning must distinguish learning from the other processes and conditions which produce new behavior or behavior change. Our definition shall thus be qualifed in the following way: *Learning* is the process that produces the capability of exhibiting new or changed human behavior (or which increases the probability that new or changed behavior will be elicited by a relevant stimulus), provided that the new behavior or behavior change cannot be explained on the basis of some other process or experience.[3]

It is sometimes argued that memorization (especially rote memorization, in which the person does not comprehend the meaning of what is being memorized) is not really learning. Is this an acceptable contention? Applying our definition of learning, we would have to state that memorization does result in the capability of exhibiting new or changed behavior in a situation such as a school examination, and thus certainly constitutes an instance of learning. However, what the person probably means to say in the argument that memorization does not really constitute learning is that he or she does not consider rote memorization to be a *good* learning outcome. But if this is so, then a value judgment related to the question of what the objectives of learning should be is at issue; definition is not the problem.

---

[2]See Ernest R. Hilgard and Gordon H. Bower, *Theories of Learning* (3rd ed.; New York: Appleton-Century-Crofts, 1966), pp. 2–6.

[3]This definition applies to human behavior, but it could easily be extended to encompass animal behavior. Also, although reference is made to "the learning process," learning may in fact consist of several processes.

Learning experiences may occur inadvertently, or they may be deliberately produced. Every human being acquires a considerable amount of learning in situations which no one has deliberately controlled. A child, for instance, inadvertently touches a hot stove and learns from the experience. However, because of the indispensability of the learning process to the functioning of human societies, human beings have been unwilling to permit all learning to take place by chance. Instead, they have sought to exert at least some degree of control over the learning process, in order to increase the probability that certain vital learning outcomes will actually be attained, and in the most efficient way. Education—the process of attempting to control learning—is thus an essential process in its own right.

Education

The central concept in this book is "education." For our purposes, education shall be defined in the following way: *Education* (or the *educative process*) is the deliberate attempt by the learner or by someone else to *control* (or *guide*, or *direct*, or *influence*, or *manage*) a learning situation in order to bring about the attainment of a desired *learning outcome* (*goal*). It is from this definition, of course, that the two fundamental policy questions about the control and goals of education are derived.

To apply this definition of education, it must be determined whether the element of deliberate control is actually present in a given learning situation. Consider as an example the showing of a motion picture in the usual commercial theater. Ordinarily this is probably not an instance of education, although most of the viewers of the film will learn from it inadvertently. If the producer and the exhibitor of the film do not consciously intend that learning take place (let us assume that their objective is only to provide entertainment and derive a monetary return), and if the members of the audience do not have a learning objective in mind in attending the motion picture, the activity must be classified a nondirected learning situation rather than as education. However, it is conceivable that the producer of the film may have had a conscious "message" to impart. If this were true, the showing of the motion picture would then constitute an instance of education. Similarly, if some members of the audience deliberately go to see the film for the sake of acquiring certain learning outcomes, the experience is classifiable as an instance of education (for example, if the film were made in a foreign country, a person might attend in order to learn more about the culture of that country).

As the preceding example makes clear, the boundary between a nondirected learning situation and education is usually an extremely flexible one. In two learning situations in which all other elements are identical, it is the presence or absence of *intention* which requires that one be classified as education and the other as a nondeliberate learning experience. Because the element of deliberate control is often forthcoming, however, as soon as someone becomes aware of the advantages to be gained by guiding a particular learning situation, most inadvertent learning situations must be considered as potentially educational ones. This point is admirably illustrated by the attention now given to the portrayal of the activities of girls and boys in primary school reading textbooks. A few years ago little or no attention was given to the manner in which sex roles of girls and boys were depicted, with the result that students were inadvertently acquiring the traditional expectations of how girls and boys should behave (for example, that boys rather than girls should aspire to be athletes). But now a deliberate attempt is being made to present a more balanced view of children's roles. In this manner, an inadvertent learning situation has been transformed into an educational situation.

Another problem in the application of our definition concerns the amount of deliberate control that needs to be exercised before a learning activity can be classified as an instance of education. The amount may be considerable or very limited—it is only necessary that some direction be present. Certain educational activities may be highly controlled. In a television advertisement, for example, the learning objectives the advertiser seeks to achieve are simple and explicit, and much effort is exerted to make the advertisement as effective as possible. But, on the other hand, the learning experiences provided by means of the daily American newspaper (through the "news" section of the newspaper and not through advertisements or editorials) are probably guided to a much lesser extent. Nevertheless, the editorial policy of the newspaper publisher to some degree dictates the selection of items to be printed and the emphasis to be given, and among the newspaper staff a general and diffuse goal such as "the development of informed citizens" may exist. Therefore, as long as someone intends through the publication of a newspaper that some learning take place, then the newspaper must be classified as a means of education.

If the learning outcome that a person intends to bring about is not actually achieved, should his activities still be called "education"? Our answer is "yes"—as long as this person had a learning outcome in mind and was making some effort to accomplish the learning objective. To use an analogy, if a fisherman casts a line into a river and yet is unsuccessful in catching fish, we would still say that he is really trying to catch fish. Indeed, even if he catches only a discarded automobile tire, his activities would nevertheless be characterized as fishing! Therefore, we shall regard every guided learning activity as an instance of education, even if the desired learning outcome is not achieved, or if another learning outcome is inadvertently produced. If it should be necessary to indicate whether the intended learning outcome is actually accomplished in a particular educational situation, that situation shall be regarded as either *successful* or *unsuccessful* education.

In everyday speech statements such as these are frequently heard: "She is well educated," "He has a good education," and "That experience was very educational." The use of the term "education" in these statements does not accord with our definition. In the first two statements "education" is represented as a product, whereas in our definition "education" is regarded as a process. The principal product of the educative process is a set of learning outcomes. Hence, instead of saying "She is well educated" or "He has a good education," it would be more appropriate (although admittedly more cumbersome) to say "She (or he) has acquired a good set of learning outcomes as a result of her (his) educational experiences." The person making the third statement is probably referring to an *inadvertent* learning situation from which something valuable was nevertheless learned, which is antithetical to our definition!

Some writers have defined "education" as the attempt to manage the learning process in order to bring about a *desirable* learning outcome ("desirable" refers to a good outcome, as opposed to one that is merely desired or intended). But such a stipulation would appear to introduce an unnecessary subjective element into the definition of education. If someone considers a given learning outcome to be desirable and someone else does not, whose value judgment are we to accept for the purpose of the definition? Therefore, rather than restrict the definition of education in this way, it would seem much more useful for purposes of study and analysis to include all kinds of learning objectives in the definition (whether we personally feel they are desirable or not), as long as they meet the general requirement of being desired by someone. (Note 1)[4]

Socialization

The term "socialization" (a sociological concept) refers to the process through which persons learn the behaviors required for the performance of social roles. The socialization process encompasses both deliberate and nondeliberate learning. In this respect, at least, socialization is a more inclusive process than education. On the other hand, education is not restricted to the acquisition of behavior required for social roles. A person may study history in his leisure time, for example, for the enjoyment of learning about the past rather than to improve his performance in a particular social role. In this case, then, the activity would be classified as education but not socialization.

The relationship between socialization and education, therefore, may best be described as follows: Some activities are both education and socialization; some activities are socialization which are not education; and other activities are education which are not socialization.

"Teaching" and Related Terms

Most persons consider teaching to be a specialized form of educational activity—the formalized type of education found in a school or comparable setting, in which there are relatively well-defined roles for the person doing the educating, as well as for the learner. This is the way we shall define *teaching*. This term would thus be comparable to such terms as "advertising" and "propagandizing," which also designate specialized forms of guided learning activities (although, of course, these specialized types of education take place outside the schools).

---

[4]At various points throughout the book, reference will be made in this manner to numbered Notes contained in the "General Notes and Bibliography" section at the end of each chapter.

We shall use the terms "instruction" and "training" as synonyms for "teaching." Since "teaching" and "instruction" are often used as equivalent words, there is no problem for us in saying that they shall be treated as synonyms. But some educational writers insist on making a distinction between teaching and training, and even between education and training. These writers take the position that teaching and education are concerned only with the development of understanding. Since the development of attitudes and skills may not involve much need for understanding, these writers prefer to label this type of activity as "training" rather than as "teaching" or "education." But if we were to examine several examples of what might normally be called education or teaching, we would probably find that these labels are applied interchangeably to both the development of understanding and to the development of attitudes and skills. For instance, the usual goal in seeking to develop a learner's skills of arithmetic, speaking a foreign language, or swimming is to obtain automatic responses from the learner rather than to have him consciously reflect upon what is to be done before making a response. Yet we customarily say we "teach arithmetic," "teach a foreign language," and "teach swimming." On the other hand, we also refer to the "training" of medical doctors, lawyers and teachers, although the preparation of these professionals entails the development of understanding. Hence we shall use "teaching" and "training" as synonyms in this book, rather than try to make an invidious distinction between these terms. (Note 2)

"Schooling" and Related Terms

At this point it is necessary to make one of the most important distinctions that we shall offer in this book: the concept of schooling and the concept of education must be differentiated. In common parlance these two concepts are often used interchangeably. For example, we may ask someone how much education he or she has had when we really mean to ask how many years of schooling he has accomplished. However, it is important that these two terms be differentiated.

We shall define a *school* as a relatively permanent organization which includes teachers and students (that is, some of the members of the organization are specialists in education and their roles are defined that way; other members of the organization are learners and their roles are defined accordingly.[5] Teaching is the principal designated activity of a school. It is called the principal *designated* activity because, while most people probably think that schools have been set up for the purpose of providing learning experiences to students, other activities may in fact be of greater actual importance. For example, some persons may decide to attend a university primarily to engage in social activities rather than to study. In fact, if a survey of college students were conducted in which they were asked which was more important, learning or getting a degree, a majority would probably say that obtaining a degree was the primary reason for their being in the university.

We shall define a *school system* as a set of schools whose scope is that of an entire society.[6] As in the case of a school, the principal declared task of a school system is to provide learning experiences for students. In the United States the school system comprises both public and private schools and includes kindergartens as well as universities and technical schools. All of these schools have some degree of functional interdependence in fulfilling the educational responsibilities allocated to them by society.[7]

We shall use the word "schooling" to refer to the experience of attending a school. Thus schooling encompasses the various things that happen to people in school and the various activities in which people engage while in school. These activities include: teaching, informal education, inadvertent learning, and a number of others which do not necessarily involve learning, such as obtaining a diploma or degree, being graded (evaluated), meeting friends or even a prospective marriage partner, keeping children off the streets and thus providing mothers with a free "baby-sitting" service, providing free health care to some students, and so forth.

What is the relationship between education and schooling? It

[5]An *organization* may be defined as a group of two or more persons that exists to carry out specified purposes. It may be as small as a family or as large as the entire society. Both a school and the school system, therefore, constitute organizations. (Note 3)

[6]In the United States the term "school system" is often used to designate the group of schools in a local school district as well as the national system. Misinterpretations can be avoided if it is remembered that our definition is restricted to the national system.

[7]It should be noted that in the United States a university is considered to be a "school." Such a generic use of the term accords with our purposes. This is a broader usage than that of many Europeans, however, who limit "school" to places of less than university standard.

should be apparent that education is, in one sense, a much broader concept than schooling. Education is provided by many agencies in addition to the schools. The family, churches, the mass media, libraries, advertisers, the government, and many employers are all concerned with the educative process. Guided learning activities occur, moreover, in many informal situations that most persons encounter daily (such as conversations among friends). Educational experiences may also be obtained through various means of self-education (reading books to learn from them, for example).

Thus the school system is only one of several means of education available to a society. In fact, although every society has education, not every society has needed schools. Many so-called "primitive" societies have existed without a system of schools. The guided learning activities essential for the maintenance of these societies are provided by such educational agencies as the family, rather than schools. (Note 4)

On the other hand, in those societies in which they are found, schools do more than just educate; in this sense, therefore, the concept of schooling is broader than that of education. Non-directed learning experiences as well as directed learning activities occur in schools (students copy the dress styles of other students, for instance, without anyone's telling them to do so). Furthermore, as previously indicated, the school system is involved in activities which do not necessarily involve learning at all.

After we have had a chance to examine in more detail the nature of the relationships between the educative process and the school system, we shall introduce a new concept: the *educational system* (see Chapter 10). For the time being, however, the term "school system" shall be used to discuss the specialized social institution whose principal declared role is the provision of learning experiences to students.

FOCUS ON EDUCATION OR SCHOOLING?

The selection of topics for consideration is especially difficult because of the difference between schooling and education. Should we deal primarily with the schools or with the educative process? Our focus will be on the school system, although we shall try to view the schools in the general context of the educative process.

The reasons for this approach are threefold. First, the school system is one of the basic social institutions, comparable in importance to the churches, the governmental system, the legal system, and the economic system. Second, although the schools are only one of the educational agencies found in modern societies, they seem to be the principal instrumentality available to these societies for the accomplishment of educative tasks not being adequately fulfilled elsewhere. Third, in deciding which tasks the schools should perform, the members of society must in any case give thought to all of the society's educational activities. They must decide which educational responsibilities should be assigned to the schools and which should be allocated elsewhere. For example, it must be decided whether religious beliefs should be fostered by the school system as well as by the church, and whether knowledge about sex should be provided by the school system as well as by the family. Members of the society must even decide whether the existing school system is the most appropriate means for attaining those educative tasks assigned to it, or whether more effective means of education can be devised.

FOCUS ON FACTS OR POLICY?

A second basic decision about topics to be covered involves the problem of whether we should focus on the facts of education or on educational policy questions. We shall define a *policy question* as one which explicitly or implicitly utilizes the word "should" in its prescriptive sense. Sometimes a "should" question or a "should" statement (the answer to a "should" question) employs a synonym for the term "should"—for example, a word or expression such as "ought," "we need," "we must have," or another term which has fundamentally the same meaning as "should." On the other hand, some statements containing the word "should" are not policy statements. For example, "The sky is getting cloudy, hence it should rain today" uses "should" in the predictive sense of "will be," rather than in the prescriptive sense.

If we were to focus on the facts of education, our principal task would be to provide information on how the school system works (including relevant explanatory theories), data on the nature of the educative process, and so forth. If, however, the focus were on educational policy questions, our main concern would be with the problem of deciding what should be done in education.

Both topics are, of course, very important to understanding the educative process and the school system. We shall, however, focus on the policy questions of education, for the following two reasons: first, the educative process is an intentional activity. By its very nature, each time it is utilized we must know what the ends *should* be, and we must know what means *should* be used to attain these ends. In view of this situation, therefore, the field of educational studies is primarily a *policy science*.[8] Second, a knowledge of facts is necessary before an attempt is made to justify the answers to policy questions. Thus, in dealing with educational policy questions, the obligation to consider educational facts relevant to those questions cannot be avoided. On the other hand, focusing on the facts of education would not necessitate an examination of policy questions. Therefore, the focus on educational policy questions will allow for a more comprehensive treatment of education.

SUMMARY

This book is intended to be a systematic introduction to the field of educational studies—that field concerned with the scholarly study of the educative process and the school system.

Learning is a basic human process; without it, human societies could not exist. *Learning* is defined as the process which produces the capability of exhibiting new or changed human behavior (or which increases the probability that new or changed behavior will be elicited by a relevant stimulus), provided that the new behavior or behavior change cannot be explained on the basis of some other process or experience.

Education or the *educative process* is defined as the deliberate attempt by the learner or by someone else to *control* a learning situation in order to bring about the attainment of a desired *learning outcome (goal)*. The term *teaching* refers to the formalized type of

[8]For a recent affirmation of the view that the "should" questions of education are of paramount importance, see William D. Rohwer, "Children and Adolescents: Should We Teach Them or Let Them Learn?" in *Changing Education: Alternatives from Educational Research*, ed. M.C. Wittrock (Englewood Cliffs, N.J.: Prentice-Hall, 1973), pp. 103–123. See also Harold B. Dunkel, "Wanted: New Paradigms and a Normative Base for Research," in *Philosophical Redirection of Educational Research*, ed. Lawrence G. Thomas (Chicago: National Society for the Study of Education, 1972), p. 79.

education that takes place in a school or similar setting, in which there are specified roles for the educators and learners; *instruction* and *training* will be used as synonyms for "teaching."

An important distinction must be made between the terms "education" and "schooling." The term *schooling* refers to the process of attending a school; thus it encompasses all of the activities which take place in a school, some of which are educational and some of which are not. By a *school* we mean an establishment whose principal declared task is teaching. A *school system* is a set of schools which serves an entire society. In one sense education is a broader concept than schooling, since education is carried on by a number of agencies (such as the family, churches, and so forth), not just the schools. In another sense, however, schooling is a broader concept than education, since schooling includes various other activities (such as granting of degrees and diplomas, the provision of recreational activities, the custodial care of children, and so forth) in addition to teaching.

The focus of this book is the school system as viewed in the context of the educative process. Our major concern is with an examination of two fundamental policy questions of education: (1) Who should control education, and in what way? and (2) What should be the goals of education?

GENERAL NOTES AND BIBLIOGRAPHY

1. CONCEPT OF EDUCATION. The problems involved in formulating definitions have been extensively discussed by philosophers. For a useful introduction to this topic, see John Hospers, *An Introduction to Philosophical Analysis* (2nd ed.; Englewood Cliffs, N.J.: Prentice-Hall, 1967), pp. 18–62.

Many educational writers have offered brief definitions of "education." More recently, however, several have provided extended analyses of the concept. See, for example, R. S. Peters, ed., *The Concept of Education* (New York: Humanities Press, 1967), which contains an article by Peters entitled "What Is an Educational Process?" See also Jonas F. Soltis, *An Introduction to the Analysis of Educational Concepts* (Reading, Mass.: Addison-Wesley, 1968), pp. 2–16. Another helpful source is Israel Scheffler, *The Language of Education* (Springfield, Ill.: Charles C. Thomas, 1960), which contains a discussion of various types of definitions in education. It should be noted that the views expressed in these sources do not always coincide with those in Chapter 1.

2. "TEACHING" AND RELATED TERMS. A number of writers have attempted to explicate the concept of teaching and indicate its relationship to other terms such as "training." A useful collection of articles is contained in C. J. B. Macmillan and Thomas W. Nelson, eds., *Concepts of Teaching: Philosophical Essays* (Chicago: Rand McNally, 1968). Included in this source are the following articles: B. Othanel Smith, "A Concept of Teaching"; Israel Scheffler, "The Concept of Teaching"; and Thomas F. Green, "A Topology of the Teaching Concept." See also P. H. Hirst and R. S. Peters, *The Logic of Education* (New York: Humanities Press, 1971), pp. 74–105.

3. ORGANIZATION. The term "organization" has been defined in several ways. According to Barnard, an organization is a "system of consciously coordinated activities . . . of two or more persons." Chester I. Barnard, *The Functions of the Executive* (Cambridge, Mass.: Harvard University Press, 1938), p. 73. Udy recognizes both a broad and a narrow definition of the concept. In its broadest sense, he regards an organization as "any group of persons plus the system of roles defining their interactions with one another." The narrow definition refers to what sociologists have called a "formal" or "complex" organization: it is one "with objectives which are explicit, limited, and announced." See Stanley H. Udy, "The Comparative Analysis of Organizations," in *Handbook of Organizations*, ed. James G. March (Chicago: Rand McNally, 1965), p. 678. The characteristic of explicit goals is also present in Stinchcombe's definition; he views an organization as a "set of stable social relations deliberately created, with the explicit intention of continuously accomplishing some specific goals or purposes. These . . . are generally functions performed for some larger structure." Stinchcombe excludes from his conceptualization "many types of groups which have multiple purposes (or which perform multiple functions for larger systems, whether these are anyone's purposes or not), such as families, geographical communities, ethnic groups, or total societies." See Arthur L. Stinchcombe, "Social Structure and Organizations," in *Handbook of Organizations*, ed. March, p. 142. For our purposes,

however, it will be sufficient to recognize that by at least one of the above definitions a school and the school system may be regarded as organizations.

4. STUDIES OF THE EDUCATIVE PROCESS. The available literature on the educative process is abundant, but it has been accumulated under many disparate categories. One of the most important topics under which studies of the educative process have been conducted is *socialization*. Research on this subject and the related topics of *enculturation* and *culture and personality* is extensive. For a comprehensive survey, see David A. Goslin, ed., *Handbook of Socialization Theory and Research* (Chicago: Rand McNally, 1969), and Edward Zigler and Irvin L. Child, "Socialization," in *The Handbook of Social Psychology,* eds. Gardner Lindzey and Elliot Aronson (2nd ed.; Reading, Mass.: Addison-Wesley, 1969), 3:450–589. Illustrative of available book-length treatments of these topics are the following: Herbert H. Hyman, *Political Socialization* (Glencoe, Ill.: Free Press, 1959); Talcott Parsons, *Family, Socialization and Interaction Process* (Glencoe, Ill.: Free Press, 1955); John J. Honigman, *Culture and Personality* (New York: Harper and Bros., 1954); and Francis L. K. Hsu, ed., *Psychological Anthropology: Approaches to Culture and Personality* (Homewood, Ill.: Dorsey Press, 1961).

Another topic under which research pertaining to the educative process has been accomplished is *attitude change*. For a general overview of this research, see William J. McGuire, "The Nature of Attitudes and Attitude Change," in *Handbook of Social Psychology*, eds. Lindzey and Aronson, 3:136–314.

Related to the topic of attitude change are the topics *communication, public opinion, propaganda*, and *advertising*. For representative works on these topics, see Colin Cherry, *On Human Communication: A Review, a Survey, and a Criticism* (2nd ed.; Cambridge, Mass.: MIT Press, 1966); Leonard W. Doob, *Public Opinion and Propaganda* (New York: Holt, 1948); Daniel Lerner, ed., *Propaganda in War and Crisis* (New York: Stewart, 1951); Bruce Lannes Smith, Harold D. Lasswell and Ralph Casey, *Propaganda, Communication, and Public Opinion: A Comprehensive Reference Guide* (Princeton, N.J.: Princeton University Press, 1946).

Certain forms of nonschool educational activities or agencies are closely related to the school system. Examples of these are adult education programs and libraries. A considerable body of research exists on the various types of non-school educational agencies that might profitably be consulted by a student in the field of educational studies. This research could be especially helpful in attempting to understand the basic factors involved in the educative process. It also provides, of course, a fuller appreciation of the educational forms that serve as potential alternatives or as complements to the school system. For a guide to this research, see Rolland G. Paulston, *Non-Formal Education: An Annotated International Bibliography* (New York: Praeger, 1972).

The research accomplished relative to the educational institutions of societies which do not have school systems also needs to be mentioned. While some of this research is included in the studies of socialization referred to above, other studies have focused even more directly on the educational agencies involved. Representative of this research are the following: Margaret Read, *Children of Their Fathers: Growing Up Among the Ngoni of Nyasaland* (London: Methuen, 1959) and John W. M. Whiting, *Becoming a Kwoma: Teaching and Learning in a New Guinea Tribe* (New Haven: Yale University Press, 1941).

JUSTIFICATION OF POLICY STATEMENTS

CHAPTER 2

Before examining the two fundamental educational policy questions, how to provide an acceptable answer to a policy question needs to be considered. Since the answer to a policy question consists of a policy statement, the problem is: How do we *justify* (support in a convincing manner) a policy statement?

METHODS OF JUSTIFICATION

A person trying to justify a policy statement may rely on one of three methods. For instance, the person may appeal to a higher *authority*. Let us suppose that a person has been asked to justify the policy statement "We should do X" (the term X refers to the action required by the policy). The person might respond as follows: "We should do X because the eminent philosopher John Dewey said so." If asked "So what?" the person might then say: "Don't be silly. We should always do what John Dewey says." In this case the justification is based on the authority of John Dewey.

Another approach is to base the justification on *intuition*. For example, a person affirming "We should do X" might justify this policy statement with "We should do X because I just know we should." If pressed for a further justification, the person might say something like: "I believe that human beings can have a mystical experience that goes beyond the power of reason. I have had such an experience, and as a result I know we should do X."

But it is apparent that if a justification is based on an appeal to authority or to intuition, then it will be acceptable to a second person only if the second person believes in the same authority or respects the first person's intuition. Fortunately, however, there is another method of justification which has a greater chance of being acceptable. This type of justification is based on an assessment of *consequences*.

The use of this third method of justification is illustrated in the following dialogue. President Smith: "We should do X." Senator Adams: "Why?" President Smith: "Because X will result in Y." President Smith has argued that we should do X because it will produce Y. He assumes that Senator Adams will agree with him that Y is a desirable outcome and that X is an appropriate means for achieving it. If, however, Senator Adams should also raise doubts about the desirability of Y, President Smith can specify the additional consequences that will follow from the achievement of Y—and so on until Senator Adams accepts the justification or until no further consequences can be specified.[1]

The advantage of a justification based on consequences is that it is formulated in such a way that the views of the person we are trying to convince are recognized as being just as important as our own. In presenting the argument it is hoped that the other person shares our views on the desirability of the consequences and the efficacy of the means for achieving them. If this is so, then it may be possible to convince him or her that our policy statement is acceptable. This procedure is quite different from justification by intuition (where it is *our* intuition that matters) and justification by authority (which is dependent upon *our* conception of the proper authority). Accordingly, when dealing with the justification of educational policy statements in this book, justification by consequences shall be regarded as our basic approach. (Note 1)

[1]Sometimes a justification may involve reference to a moral rule. For example, if we were to ask someone why we should X, he might say: "Because X is good, and we should do good things," or "Because it is right, and we should do the right things." These responses do not, however, constitute another basic method of justification. For if we were to ask why we should do good or right things, the person offering the justification would have to give a further justification of the rule—and such a justification would be on the basis of authority, intuition or consequences. It might be shown, for instance, that following the rule invariably leads to desirable outcomes (a justification by consequences).

JUSTIFICATION BY CONSEQUENCES: PROCEDURES AND PROBLEMS

Means–Ends Chain

A justification by consequences utilizes what is known as a *means-ends chain*. A means-ends chain depicts a series of cause-effect relationships that leads to a desirable outcome. To illustrate what is involved in a means-ends chain, let us assume that the means to the end of reading ability is reading instruction. This may be diagrammed as follows, with the symbol M representing the means, E representing the end, and the arrow signifying that M causes E:

$$M \longrightarrow E$$
(Reading instruction)   (Ability to read)

But for what purpose does a student learn to read? A student may wish to acquire the ability to read in order to earn a university degree. If this is the case, the ability to read must also be regarded as a means to the end of obtaining a university degree, as well as the end of reading instruction. These relationships may be diagrammed as follows:

$$M \longrightarrow E \quad (M) \longrightarrow E$$
(Reading   (Ability   (University
instruction)   to read)   degree)

Note that by using the symbols E (M) it is indicated that from one perspective something may be an end, but from another perspective it may also be a means.

Extending this idea, we may ask whether the university degree is also a means to some other end. Assuming that the student's purpose in acquiring a degree is to use it as a basis for securing high-salaried employment, the means-ends chain would then need to be diagrammed as follows:

$$M \longrightarrow E \quad (M) \longrightarrow E \quad (M) \longrightarrow E$$
(Reading   (Ability   (University   (High-salaried
instruction)   to read)   degree)   employment)

If the required effort were made, this chain could be carried still further beyond the end of high-salaried employment; similarly, we could also proceed in the other direction and identify a means such as hiring a reading teacher, which would have reading instruction as its end.

How far does a means-ends chain continue? Is it infinite? Presumably there is some final or ultimate end that a means-ends chain is expected to reach. For instance, in the case of the student's securing high-salaried employment, the high-salaried employment might be a means to obtaining the end of a specified way of life, which in turn is the means to a still further end such as happiness. Beyond the end of happiness, however, it is not possible to go, because happiness does not seem to be a means to anything else. Thus happiness can be called an *ultimate* end, while the specified way of life which leads to it is a *penultimate* (next to the last) end. The test of whether an end is an ultimate one is to inquire whether the end is sought for itself or because it leads to something else. Such ends as happiness, enjoyment, and satisfaction appear to meet this test and, thus, are generally considered ultimate ends.

Some educational ends may be extremely remote and are achieved indirectly through a long means-ends chain. An example of this would be the creation of an improved type of society through the use of education. On the other hand, such individual ends as acquiring a sense of competence, a feeling of mastery, or a feeling of enjoyment might be realized concurrently with the educational activity—as in the case of a person being taught to play a guitar. Both the distant and the immediate ends of education are equally capable of giving someone a reason for carrying on educational activities, however.

Disagreements Over Ultimate and Penultimate Ends

As has already been suggested, if a means-ends justification (that is, a justification by consequences) is to succeed, then the person to whom the justification is directed must have an evaluation of consequences that is similar to that of the person who has advanced the justification. If the person to whom the justification is directed does not share the same basic value judgments as the person advancing the argument, then there can be no hope for reaching agreement.

Most persons seem to agree in their conception of an ultimate end, however. They probably would concede that the attainment of happiness or a similar outcome constitutes an acceptable description of an ultimate end. But when different persons are asked about their penultimate end (the end which is the means to the ultimate end), serious disagreements may exist. For some people the private accumulation of wealth is the means for achieving happiness; for others it might entail religious contemplation, and for still others it might involve ample amounts of leisure time.

In a practical situation in which two persons discover that their penultimate ends are different, they may decide to re-state them in such a way as to arrive at a compromise version that both can accept. For example, if the penultimate end were to be defined as the attainment of a society in which everyone obtains those things that are personally satisfying but which do not harm others, we would probably find that many persons would be willing to express agreement. Such a compromise is brought about because the persons involved in the argument believe that it is better to have some basis for agreement rather than to continue to disagree.

Nevertheless, it is clear that such a compromise could not cover those situations in which the achievement of one person's penultimate end would entail the negation of another person's penultimate end—for example, in the case where one person favors the conservation of natural resources and the other believes in using them without restraint; or where someone desires a free enterprise economic system and someone else wants state ownership of the means of production. In these instances a disagreement over penultimate ends will persist which cannot be resolved through rational discussion, since it arises from fundamental value preferences of the individuals involved in the dispute.[2]

Costs–Benefits Problem

Let us assume that we have a situation in which two people agree that a certain end is desirable and both agree that a given

[2]Our primary concern here is with the possibility of using rational arguments to justify a policy statement. Other processes (such as coercion and irrational means of persuasion) may be used to resolve issues when group decisions are actually made, of course.

means is a way of reaching that end. Yet one of the persons may be unwilling to accept a policy statement offered by the other person in which the use of this means is advocated. Such a disagreement may arise if there are differing interpretations of the *costs* and *benefits* involved in carrying out the proposed policy. By "costs" and "benefits" reference is made to both the monetary and non-monetary advantages and disadvantages of doing something, including such factors as psychic costs and benefits.

The question of whether children should be bused in order to achieve racially integrated schools affords a good illustration of the costs-benefits problem. Let us assume that two persons are discussing this issue and they both agree that racially integrated schools are desirable, because such schools are a means to the penultimate end of a racially integrated society, which they both accept. We shall further assume that both persons believe that the mandatory busing of children would be an effective means for achieving racially integrated schools. Yet it is nevertheless possible that one person might favor a busing policy while the other opposes it.

If such a disagreement should occur, it may be explained by the fact that the implementation of the busing policy entails costs: the economic costs of operating the buses, the loss of time on the part of students who ride the buses, and the psychic costs to parents and children who may be compelled to do something they prefer not to do. Accordingly, one may consider these costs to be so great that they would more than offset the benefits to be gained by achieving the penultimate end of a racially integrated society. For another person, however, the costs of busing may be regarded as minimal compared to the benefits derived from this policy.

This example brings out the point that implementation of a means-ends chain usually produces *side effects*. Frequently the side effects are negative in character, although sometimes positive side effects do result. Thus, in considering how to achieve an agreed-upon ultimate or penultimate end, it is possible for two persons to disagree about the relative costs and benefits of using a given means-ends chain. Rather than adopt a policy that is too costly, an *alternative* means-ends chain based on a different policy might be preferred. As far as the busing question is concerned, some of the policies from which an alternative means-ends chain might be developed are the following: retention of the "neighborhood school," voluntary busing, new zoning laws to change the racial composition of residential areas, and so forth. It should be stressed, however, that this issue is being used for illustrative purposes only at this point (the substantive merits of the busing question will be dealt with in Chapter 8).

As in the case of disagreements about ultimate or penultimate ends, there is little that can be done to resolve disagreements over relative costs and benefits of using alternative means-ends chains, since the determination of what is a cost and what is a benefit involves a value judgment. The person offering the justification can, however, point out what he or she considers to be the desirable side effects of using the means being proposed if any exist. It can also be indicated why other side effects are not considered representative of significant costs. If the person he or she is trying to convince is not aware that the proposed means involves these side effects, then the person presenting the justification may be successful in persuading the other to accept his argument—provided that the person he is attempting to convince shares his value judgments about these side effects and provided that this person agrees the proposed means does, in fact, entail these side effects.

Disagreements Over Relationships of Means and Ends

There is still one other problem that may arise in connection with the use of a means-ends justification. It involves, of course, the possibility that the person we are trying to convince may share our conception of what constitutes a desirable penultimate or ultimate end and acceptable side effects, but may not agree that a particular means will lead to that end or those side effects. To take the busing question again as an illustration, two persons might agree on the desirability of a racially integrated society and they both might be prepared to accept the costs of mandatory busing, yet they might disagree as to whether this policy will achieve the intended outcome. One person might contend that it will, while the other might argue that it will bring about "white flight" or that racial hostility will result, rather than racial harmony.

The likelihood that such disagreements will arise is increased by another factor: the existence of complex means-ends chains. Thus far in the discussion only simple means-ends chains have been considered. In actuality, however, most educational policies entail complex means-ends chains, in which there may be several sets of means and intermediate ends that converge at various points. In the example depicted above, reading instruction is a means that leads to a university degree. This is obviously greatly simplified, since in order to achieve the intermediate end of a university degree, several additional means-ends chains (for instance, those involving instruction in other relevant fields of study) would need to be implemented before a person acquired his degree. In effect, all of these additional means-ends chains converge to bring about the intermediate end of a university degree.

Similarly, a university degree will not lead to the intermediate end of high-salaried employment unless several other converging means-ends chains are also implemented. The accomplishment of a given means-ends chain, therefore, depends upon or influences the accomplishment of other means-ends chains. As a result of these complex interrelationships, the possibilities increase that two persons may disagree on whether a particular policy will actually achieve an agreed-upon end, or they may disagree about the exact nature of the side effects that will be produced when a complex means-ends chain is implemented.[3]

Something can be done, however, to resolve disagreements over the relationships between means and ends. Fundamentally, the person we are trying to convince must be provided with evidence that the means in question does in fact lead to the designated end and/or side effects. To obtain this evidence we shall need either to engage in empirical research or to utilize the results of empirical research that has already been accomplished by someone else. (Note 2)

EMPIRICAL RESEARCH: BASIC CONCEPTS

Before considering the methods of empirical research, it is necessary to discuss what is meant by the term "empirical." It is also important to know how to differentiate an empirical statement from the other types of statements which commonly appear in discussions about education: analytic statements, metaphysical statements, and normative statements.

[3]The possibility does exist that two persons with different views about the ends of education or acceptable side effects might agree on a particular policy proposal because of a mistaken belief that the policy in question conforms, respectively, to their differing views. Thus even erroneous knowledge about means-ends relationships might conceivably bring about an agreement on policy!

What Is an Empirical Statement?

An *empirical statement* is one which in principle can be confirmed or disconfirmed through the use of one or more of the five senses (the senses of sight, hearing, smell, taste, and touch). An example of an empirical statement is the following: "This room is thirty-feet wide." This statement is empirical because it may be confirmed or disconfirmed by using a measuring instrument and observing whether the instrument indicates thirty feet or not. A second example is "This milk is sour." This statement means that the milk has the same taste as another glass of milk which had previously been identified as sour; we can confirm it by comparing the taste of the present glass of milk with the other glass. In a similar way, other empirical statements can be confirmed or disconfirmed through the senses of smell, touch, and hearing.

Empirical statements may refer to the past or the future, as well as to the present. While it may not actually be possible to obtain the data necessary for confirmation or disconfirmation, it is necessary only that this be possible *in principle*. Thus the statement "There were 1,807,296,313 fish in the Atlantic Ocean on January 1, 1534" cannot in actuality be confirmed or disconfirmed; but it is possible in principle, since someone living in 1534 who had the capability of counting the fish could have done so. Although we cannot now confirm or disconfirm the statement "There is a green plant growing on Mars," we can in principle do so—for example, if a spacecraft could be sent to the planet.

Is the statement "Teaching method A is more effective than teaching method B" an empirical statement? Yes, because the word "effective" is a synonym for the term "productive of desired outcomes."[4] Presumably, therefore, we could confirm or disconfirm this statement by observing whether the desired outcomes (these outcomes might be measured, for example, by scores on an achievement test) are present to a greater extent among students who have been exposed to method A than a comparable group of students exposed to method B.

Is the statement "Abraham Lincoln delivered his Gettysburg

----

[4]It should be noted that the word "desired" is used instead of the word "desirable" in this term. Using the word "desirable" would make the term a normative one, not an empirical one. (See section on "Other Types of Statements," this chapter, for a definition of "normative.")

Address in 1970" an empirical statement? Yes, simply because it is a statement which in principle can be confirmed or disconfirmed through the use of one or more of the five senses. The point of this example is that a statement does not have to be one that seems true for it to qualify as an empirical statement; a statement that appears to be clearly false may be as much an empirical statement as one that is thought to be true (provided it meets the criterion of confirmability or disconfirmability by means of sense experience).

Some empirical terms may be extremely vague or ambiguous. For example, in the statement "The school system promotes the general welfare" the term "promotes the general welfare" is an ambiguous concept, yet it is empirical because we can presumably determine through sense experience whether the general welfare of a given society has been promoted. (The problem of ambiguous terms shall be discussed further in connection with our treatment of operational definitions. See section on "Confirmation of Empirical Statements," this chapter.)

What about concepts such as intelligence, motivation, or for that matter, the concept of learning itself? Are these concepts empirical entities? No one has ever seen intelligence, motivation, or learning—therefore, how do we know they exist? These concepts, which are usually called *constructs*, represent empirical entities, even though they cannot be observed directly. Their existence is inferred by the presence of certain indicators (such as scores on tests), but we do more than make an inference. For example, if we have inferred on the basis of test scores that a particular individual has a high intelligence, we can then proceed to validate the original inference by hypothesizing how that individual will act in other situations. If the inference is useful in making such predictions, we have obtained indirect empirical evidence for the existence of the construct. (It is in this way, of course, that physicists confirm the existence of such invisible entities as electrons.)

Other Types of Statements

At least three other types of statements may be used in the justification of answers to policy questions. It is necessary, therefore, to be able to distinguish these statements from empirical statements and from each other.

An *analytic* or *tautological* statement is one that depends upon the analysis of words for the determination of whether it is true or false (for example: "All black cats are black") or which arbitrarily stipulates a definition. Our definition of "education" as the deliberate attempt to control the learning process represents the meaning that we have assigned to this term; thus for our purposes the definition is a true one, irrespective of whether it can be established empirically (by conducting a survey, for instance) that all or most writers on education have also defined "education" this way.

A *metaphysical* statement is one that refers to first principles or to the ultimate nature of things. Such a statement is similar to an empirical statement in that it attempts to say something about reality and is not analytic; however, it is different from an empirical statement in that it cannot be confirmed or disconfirmed through sense experience. Metaphysical statements thus may be classified as *factual* statements (together with empirical statements), but they are not confirmable in the same way as empirical statements. For example, consider the statements "The soul of man is a part of the Infinite Soul" and "The universe is pervaded by an ever-changing, life-giving force." These statements would seem to be factual ones that are either true or false, yet how would we confirm them? A possible answer might be that the mind has a "built-in" capability which can apprehend the truth of such statements, or that we can know them to be true by intuition; but we certainly cannot confirm these statements by sensory data. It will suffice to say here that the correctness of metaphysical statements is very difficult or impossible to establish.

A *normative* statement is one that expresses a value judgment. The following are examples of normative statements (the normative words have been italicized): "He is a *good* teacher," "This is a *beautiful* picture," "This is the *right* thing to do," "These learning outcomes are *desirable*," "We *should* have integrated schools," "His teaching method is *very* effective," and "Mary's teaching method is more *efficient* than Margaret's." Note that a "should" statement (policy statement) is normative. Note furthermore that while "effective" is an empirical concept, use of the evaluative term "very" in the example above makes the statement a normative one. Also, note that the term "efficient" expresses a judgment about the relationship of benefits to costs. Since benefits and costs are ordinarily normative concepts, a statement about their relationship is normative.

Although the preceding examples are easy to classify, it may sometimes be difficult to distinguish between empirical and normative statements. Consider the following pairs of statements: "Today is an unpleasant day" and "Today most of the people that I saw on the street were wearing raincoats"; "This desk is beautiful" and "This desk is made of mahogony"; "She is a likeable person" and "She is a person who is liked"; "This is a desirable educational outcome" and "This is a desired educational outcome." In each of these pairs a normative statement is followed by an empirical one. Why in the third pair, for example, is "likeable" normative and "liked" empirical? The term "liked" is empirical because it can be agreed what sort of evidence could be used to confirm a statement about whether someone is liked by other people. For example, a questionnaire survey would be one way of finding out whether the person was liked or not. While there might be differences of opinion over whether a favorable response rate of a given percentage is sufficient to indicate that someone is liked, or whether personal interviews are a more appropriate means than questionnaires for collecting data, everyone would probably agree that in principle data obtained through one or more of the five senses could be used to establish that a person is liked. On the other hand, the term "likeable" is normative because it can always be asserted as a value judgment that someone is or is not likeable, irrespective of any empirical evidence that may be accumulated about the person.

Confirmation of Empirical Statements

In the preceding discussion of the nature of empirical statements, the word "confirm" is used rather than "prove"; and rather than call an empirical statement "true" or "false" we have referred to such a statement as having been "confirmed" or "disconfirmed." The reason for this choice of words is that it can never be established whether a given empirical statement is absolutely true or false; there is always at least the remote possibility that our observations have been faulty and, therefore, that the inference based on them is wrong. For example, if someone reports that the object in front of him is ten-feet high, it may be that he is making an inaccurate measurement or that he is experiencing some sort of hallucination. Even if several persons agree with the first observer, they may all be experiencing similar difficulties—or it may even be that the first observer has paid them to report their agreement with his statement.

Yet the example concerning the ten-foot-high object involves a statement that is relatively easy to confirm, since it is what may be called a *particular* empirical statement; that is, a statement referring to a specific observable phenomenon (either past, present, or future). Much more difficult to confirm are what may be called *general* empirical statements or *empirical generalizations*, which refer to a non-specific class of observable phenomena—for example, "Water at the pressure of sea level boils at 212 degrees Farenheit" or "Stones always fall to the earth when dropped." How can we be sure that these statements are now correct everywhere, or that they will be correct a thousand years from now, or that they were correct a million years ago? Thus, the best we can do is to obtain evidence that will confirm (support) an empirical statement; but the statement can never be proved in the sense that there is absolutely no possibility of its being incorrect.

Of the two types of empirical statements that we have mentioned (particular and general), well-confirmed empirical generalizations have a special value to mankind. Such statements are usually called *laws*. Science is concerned with the discovery of laws, not with the confirmation of particular empirical statements. It is by means of laws that predictions about future events can be made, or that the reason for past events can be explained. For example, if a well-confirmed empirical generalization about teaching stated "Instructional Method M always produces Result R," then we would be able to predict that Ms. Jones, who is now using Instructional Method M, will obtain Result R in her classroom. Similarly, if we wanted to explain why Ms. Jones has obtained Result R in her classroom, we could point out that Ms. Jones used Instructional Method M yesterday, and this method always produces Result R.

To confirm empirical statements containing vague or ambiguous terms, *operational definitions* must be provided for the questionable concepts. An operational definition of a term is one in which the observations that provide evidence about the term are specified. For example, we might define the concept "gifted student" as a student who obtains a score of 130 or above on a specified test.

For an operational definition to be valid, however, it is essential that there be general agreement that the observations specified in the definition constitute at least one way of defining the term. To illustrate, suppose that we were trying to confirm the empirical statement "Teaching Method A is more effective than any other method for the purpose of getting people to learn arithmetic." One of the terms in this statement that we would need to define operationally is "learn arithmetic." We might specify that by "learn arithmetic" we mean the scores obtained on a particular thirty-minute test of multiplication and division. There would no doubt be general agreement that the operational definition we have given represents one way of determining whether a person has learned arithmetic, although some persons might claim that other operational definitions are more appropriate (for example, a definition which explicitly included addition and subtraction, or which explicitly included fractions and decimals, or which was one hour instead of thirty minutes, and so forth).

Cause–Effect Statements

Empirical generalizations such as "Instructional Method M always produces Result R" and particular empirical statements such as "Rousseau wrote *Emile*" represent a certain kind of statement— what is usually referred to as a *cause-effect statement*. In technical discussions of empirical research, the terms "cause" and "effect" are often replaced by the terms "independent variable" and "dependent variable." What would normally be regarded as the causal factor is called the independent variable; what we would usually think of as the effect (of an independent variable) is called the dependent variable. Any characteristic or condition that can vary or change is a *variable*. In statements about education the variables might be such factors as test scores, personality characteristics of teachers, teaching methods, or the ages of the students. Even the sex of the students can be considered a variable, since a given student differs from another by being either male or female.

The relationship between a means and an end is a causal one. If we are offering a means-ends justification and someone has questioned whether a given means actually leads to a particular end, then evidence which confirms our cause-effect statement must be provided.

What research techniques can be used to confirm empirical statements, particularly cause-effect statements? Several procedures are available, which brings us to a consideration of the methods of empirical research.

METHODS OF EMPIRICAL RESEARCH

Let us say we wish to confirm that, for a particular teacher, the discovery method of teaching mathematics is more effective than the telling method as the means (the independent variable) of bringing about the learning (the dependent variable) of mathematical concepts. But exactly what should be considered to be an instance of each of the two different methods? And how are we to know whether someone has learned mathematical concepts? The first step, therefore—regardless of the research technique that we decide to use—is to provide operational definitions for our key variables. Operational definitions enable someone else to make his own investigation if he does not accept our findings. They also permit someone else to make a judgment as to whether our operational definitions have adequately reflected the generally understood meanings of the terms used for our independent variables ("discovery method" and "telling method") and for our dependent variable ("the learning of mathematical concepts"). Operational definitions are essential to most methods of empirical research, especially where constructs are involved.

The next step is to observe the learning of students in relation to the two teaching methods. Our object is to find out whether we can accept the hypothesis that students learn more mathematical concepts when taught by the discovery method. However, to make an accurate assessment of this hypothesis, we must be certain that the outcomes observed are really the results of using the two teaching methods, rather than the effects of other independent variables. In other words, we must be able to eliminate other plausible competing interpretations or hypotheses that could be used to explain the results we observe.

For example, let us assume that the teacher instructs a class of thirty students using one method, and then soon after instructs the very same class by means of the second method. If we gave the class the identical test following the use of each method we would probably find that the students obtain a higher average score after the second method has been used than after the first. But it could plausibly be hypothesized that the learning acquired from the first method or the experience gained in taking the test the first time carried over and influenced the result observed in the second test. If, however, the second administration of the test resulted in a lower average score, one might just as plausibly argue that the use of the second method interfered with the learning acquired from the first method; the students became confused and hence made a lower score. Alternatively, it could be hypothesized that the students became bored when the second method of instruction was used. The students may have assumed they had acquired the desired learning outcomes already when actually they had forgotten some of them; therefore, when they took the test the second time they made a lower average score. Obviously, to confirm our original hypothesis, we must try to eliminate such competing hypotheses.

Experimental Method

The most rigorous procedure available for the elimination of competing hypotheses is the *experimental method.* In an experiment the independent variable to be investigated can be manipulated and randomly assigned to the subjects of the experiment. "Manipulation" means that the experimenter is able to choose freely which subjects will receive the variable and, usually, that the experimenter may change the values of the variable. The manipulated independent variable is called the *experimental* variable or the *treatment* if it consists of a combination of variables that act as a unit.

To apply the experimental method to the study of the effectiveness of the two teaching techniques in the circumstances we have just described, we could randomly divide the class of thirty students into two groups of fifteen, one of which would be exposed to the discovery method and the other of which would be taught by the telling method. The random assignment of the students to the two groups eliminates any suspicion that there might be systematic differences between the two groups. Using appropriate statistical techniques, the magnitude of chance variations between the two groups can be estimated, thus allowing for elimination of the competing hypothesis that one group of students may learn more because they are academically superior to the second.

In an experiment the other independent variables which could have an effect on the dependent variable can also be controlled. In some cases control takes the form of actually removing from the experimental situation some of the independent variables that might contaminate the result. For example, in an experiment to determine the relative effectiveness of two different teaching methods, the investigator would probably not allow the students to read any textbooks during the course of the experiment, since if the students believed they were not learning with one of the methods being used by the teacher, they might nevertheless seek to acquire the necessary information themselves from their textbooks.

Some independent variables cannot be removed from the experimental situation. They are still controlled, however, if they are allowed to act in an unbiased manner upon all of the subjects involved in the experiment. In our present example it is not feasible to eliminate changes in atmospheric conditions, room temperature variations, the aging of the students, and other such factors which might conceivably affect the learning outcome; but if these factors are permitted to act on the two groups in the same place at the same time, they are presumed to have an equivalent effect on the two groups.

In the illustrative experiment we are describing, each of the two groups would be taught by a different teaching procedure, preferably in different parts of the same room so that the teaching activities would not interfere with each other while allowing the other conditions in the room to be the same for all students. If the experiment continued for several days, the teacher would teach one group first one day and then the other group first the next day, thereby helping to eliminate the competing hypotheses that the students taught earlier were more highly motivated (or less so) and that the teacher was more energetic (or less so) with the earlier group.

At the end of the experiment the average (mean) achievement scores of the two groups would be measured and the difference calculated. Then, if it were found that there was a difference between the means of the two groups, by the application of appropriate statistical techniques the probability that this difference was due to chance factors would be estimated. If there were a difference between the two groups which was larger than that which could reasonably be accounted for by chance variations between the groups, then that difference could be attributed to the effect of the experimental treatment, either by itself or through an interaction between the treatment and some other factor in the experimental situation.[5]

---

[5]In educational research a difference is often accepted as being statistically significant if the probability that a difference of that magnitude could result by chance is five times out of a hundred: the result is thus referred to as being significant at the .05 level of significance. A more strin-

Our discussion of the experimental method has been concerned with the basic principles of this research technique. It should be noted, however, that many variations on this procedure exist. For example, instead of comparing the effects of different amounts or types of the experimental variable (as in our illustration of the comparison of the two methods of teaching), the researcher may investigate the effects on the dependent variable of simply the presence or absence of the experimental variable. In this situation one group would receive the experimental variable (this group is traditionally called the "experimental group") while the other group would not receive the experimental variable (traditionally called the "control group"). But as in the example discussed above, an experiment may be conducted with two groups that receive different values of the experimental variable. In such a case both groups are in a sense "experimental," and each group serves as a "control" on the other group. Much more sophisticated refinements of the experimental method also exist, but a discussion of these refinements would take us beyond the intended scope of this chapter.

Correlation Method

Because of its logical rigor and the precise interpretation that can be made of its results, the well-conducted experiment has a significant place in educational research. Unfortunately, many independent variables are difficult or impossible to manipulate experimentally. For example, a researcher cannot take a group of students and decide on a random basis that some members of the group will become blacks and the remainder will become whites in order to test the effects of race on school achievement. The characteristic of race is one that a person is born with; it is not a variable that can be manipulated at will by the researcher. A similar situation exists with such variables as sex, age, birth order, national origin, and so forth. Still other variables, while not absolutely impossible to manipulate, cannot be conveniently varied by the researcher. For example, a group of babies cannot, under normal circumstances, be randomly assigned by a researcher to a variety of families representing differ-

gent standard—the .01 level of significance—is also used (in this case, the probability that the difference would occur by chance is only one out of a hundred times).

ent levels of social stratification, in order to assess the effects of social class on school performance.

Yet these nonmanipulable variables are among the most important ones the educational researcher might wish to consider. If he wishes to investigate them, therefore, research techniques that are inherently less rigorous than the experimental method must be employed. One of the most useful nonexperimental research methods that can be used for the study of the effects of these variables is what shall be referred to as the *correlation method.*

When this method is used, the researcher attempts to discover the existence of a correlation between an independent variable and a dependent variable. The term "correlation" is used here in the general sense of a relationship or association between two variables. A correlation exists between two variables if, when the value of one variable changes, the value of the other variable also changes. If two variables are causally connected, they are also correlated. But although a causal relationship entails a correlation, not every correlation is indicative of a causal connection between the variables: a third variable may be related to both of the variables and thus account for their joint variation. For example, ice cream sales are positively correlated with the number of serious cases of sun burn, although they are not causally connected; it is a third factor (the summer season) which is causally related to both variables and thus brings about their correlation.

The possible existence of a third variable that may be the factor actually responsible for the observed correlation between two variables is the major source of difficulty in the use of a correlation as evidence for a causal relationship between two variables. For example, we might study the relationship between IQ scores and success in school and discover that a positive correlation exists between IQ score and the likelihood that a student will obtain a university degree. But is the IQ score the causal factor? IQ scores are also positively correlated with socio-economic status; the actual factor responsible for college graduation, therefore, may be the greater ability of the parents with high-IQ children to afford to send these children to college. Or high IQ may be genetically associated with high energy levels; thus high energy may be the factor that accounts for success in obtaining a university degree.

Therefore, unless the independent variable can be manipulated and randomly assigned to the subjects of our research, we must always accept the possibility that some third factor is correlated with both the independent variable and dependent variable we are investigating, and that it is this third variable which is in fact responsible for any correlation discovered between the two variables.

Is there any way that a correlation can be analyzed to increase our confidence that the existence of a causal relationship has been discovered? Rosenberg shows how a given correlation can be tested through the explicit introduction of a third variable into the analysis.[6] As an illustration he cites the relationship between the variable of age and the habit of listening to religious programs on the radio, which was reported in a particular investigation. It was found in this study that, of those surveyed: 17 per cent of the young persons surveyed listened to religious programs, compared to 26 per cent of the old persons surveyed. Thus it would seem that old people are more likely to listen to these programs than young people—that the variable of age is responsible for a certain kind of radio listening habit.

But we also know that old and young people differ in many ways; is it possible that one of these other variables is the causal factor, rather than age? Perhaps the causal factor is really schooling. If this were the case, people with similar scholastic backgrounds should have similar radio-listening habits. The factor of schooling can be held constant by comparing the radio-listening habits of young and old persons with equivalent amounts of schooling. We then find among those persons with considerable schooling, 9 per cent of the young and 11 per cent of the old listen to religious programs; but among those persons with little schooling, 29 per cent of the young and 32 per cent of the old listen to these programs. Because the variable of age is not significantly correlated with radio-listening habits when schooling is held constant, the presumed causal relationship between age and radio-listening habits is no longer tenable. On the other hand, the variable of schooling would now seen to be causally related to the difference in radio-listening habits. If the same mode of analysis (which constitutes a statistical control of plausible independent variables analogous to experimental control) were repeated using other "third" variables, and if the relationship between schooling and listening habits *did not disappear* as the relationship between age and listening habits had disappeared, then our confidence would increase that we had discovered a

[6]Morris Rosenberg, *The Logic of Survey Analysis* (New York: Basic Books, 1968), pp. 24–25.

valid causal relationship between schooling and radio-listening habits. However, we can never be certain unless all other plausible independent variables have been considered, which is not usually feasible.

There is still another major problem, however, with the use of correlations to study causation. Even if there is reason to believe that a causal connection is present, merely knowing that there is a causal relationship between two variables does not allow us to infer the *direction* of causality between the two variables—in other words, we do not know which is the cause and which is the effect. For example, if a positive correlation is found between the average length of time that teachers have served in the different schools of a particular community and the quality ratings of these schools, should this relationship be interpreted to mean that long tenure of teachers brings about a high quality rating, or that high quality schools induce teachers to remain in them for a long period of time? To help eliminate this kind of difficulty it is necessary to give attention to the time sequence of the variables. "Since something that happened later cannot be responsible for what happened earlier, it follows that the variable which is temporally prior must always be the determinant or independent variable."[7] In many instances, of course, this rule will be useful; but as in the case of correlation between teachers and school quality, the rule may be difficult to apply and the problem is still unresolved as to which is the cause and which is the effect.

Thus far we have been concerned only with the general principles involved in the analysis of correlations for the purpose of ascertaining causal relationships, without reference to the actual statistical techniques that may be used. However, before concluding this topic, we shall discuss briefly one of the most commonly used mathematical expressions of the degree of association between variables: the *product-moment correlation coefficient*, represented by the symbol r. Values of r may range from $+1.00$ to -1.00, with $+1.00$ indicating perfect positive correlation, 0.00 indicating no correlation, and -1.00 indicating perfect negative correlation. Obviously, therefore, the closer the coefficient is to 1.00 (either positive or negative) the stronger the relationship is between the variables.

The correlation coefficient may be subjected to statistical tests of significance in the same way as the results obtained in an experi-

[7] Ibid., p. 11.

mental study. Even a relatively large correlation coefficient may not be statistically significant if a small sample is used. On the other hand, with a large sample, a statistically significant correlation between certain variables will probably be found; then we must make a judgment as to whether the degree of association represented by the correlation coefficient seems important or not.

A good way of interpreting the strength of a product-moment correlation coefficient is to square it. The resulting number (r^2) represents the degree to which a knowledge of one variable enables us to predict or explain the magnitude of the second. For example, if a particular correlation coefficient is .70, after squaring it we obtain .49; this means that one variable explains or accounts for about 49 per cent of the variation in the second. On the other hand, a correlation coefficient of .20 would have rather low explanatory power, since after squaring it we obtain only .04, or 4 per cent.

The correlation method may entail the use of complicated research designs involving many variables and statistical techniques of much greater sophistication than the calculation of product-moment correlation coefficients. However, regardless of the complexity of the study, we should never lose sight of the two problems of interpretation: the possibility that another variable may actually be the cause of the relationship observed between a particular dependent variable and a presumed independent variable, and the difficulty at times of knowing the direction of causation between variables.

Other Methods

Experimental studies and correlation studies do not represent the only ways of investigating causal relationships between variables. A very common technique, for example, is the *historical method*, with which anyone who has ever read a history book is probably familiar. Another frequently used technique is the *case study*, which involves the detailed examination of one or more individual cases. This latter technique is often used by educational researchers in the study of a particular school system or even a single school; it may also be used to study small numbers of particular types of students (for example, those with learning difficulties). The problem with both historical and case studies is that it is much more difficult to eliminate plausible alternative hypotheses in these studies than it is with experimental investigations or even correlation studies (since correlation studies generally utilize a sample that is large enough to permit statistical tests of significance).

Still other types of empirical research are of importance in the study of education, but these approaches do not attempt to discover causal relationships between variables. These research techniques include those that are often labeled "merely descriptive": for example, surveys to discover the attitudes of parents toward schools or the availability (in a certain area) of school facilities of different kinds. Another frequently encountered type of non-causal research study is what may be called the *predictive study*. In this type of investigation, the researcher attempts to discover the existence of correlations between variables in order to use knowledge about one variable for the prediction of other variables (for example, whether scores on a certain achievement test can be used to predict success in college). It is recognized in this type of study that some third variable probably accounts for the relationship between the predicting and the predicted variables, but the information contained in the study is nevertheless often valuable for making practical administrative decisions.[8]

Generalizations from Empirical Research

A final caution is in order concerning the generalizability of the findings obtained through empirical research. The distinction between particular empirical statements and general empirical statements which was made earlier needs to be recalled.[9] The research methods that have been discussed can confirm or disconfirm particular empirical statements, and can also disconfirm general empirical statements. For example, if we should use Instructional Method M and discover that it does not produce Result R, then we have disconfirmed the empirical generalization "Instructional Method M always produces Result R"—or at least it would have been made necessary for the generalization to be rewritten in such a

[8]A knowledge of the causal laws pertaining to a given variable is, of course, the best basis for making predictions about that variable (see section on "Confirmation of Empirical Statements," this chapter), but such laws are often not available.

[9]See section on "Confirmation of Empirical Statements."

way that it would specify the conditions under which it does hold. But while a single research study may disconfirm an empirical generalization, such a study obviously does not confirm a general empirical statement; only through a number of replications of the study can we begin to acquire the necessary evidence to support the generalization.

It is also important in attempting to provide evidence for a general empirical statement to carry out research in situations representative of those to which the generalization applies. If, for example, a research investigation is conducted in a school that is very different from the average, with students that are also atypical, the results of the study will provide little support for a generalization pertaining to the school system as a whole. But even if a more representative situation is selected for research, the fact that a study is being undertaken in that situation may alter the situation sufficiently that the results obtained are still unrepresentative.[10] (Note 3)

CONCLUDING COMMENTS

While at least one suitable technique for the justification of policy statements exists (the justification by consequences), the use of this technique does not guarantee a successful outcome. If we and the person we are trying to convince already share the same basic value position with respect to ultimate and penultimate ends, then the prospects for obtaining agreement on a particular educational policy statement would seem to be excellent, assuming that any empirical disagreements over means-ends relationships that might exist can be resolved and that our assessments of the costs-benefits of carrying out the proposed policy are similar. If we disagree on our basic value position or have a divergent evaluation of costs-benefits, then our chances for reaching a consensus are extremely limited. But in those instances in which the disagreement is over the means-ends chain—an empirical rather than a normative matter—we can be more optimistic, since in principle empirical statements can be confirmed. The problem here, of course, is that valid empirical gen-

[10]For a discussion of these points, see Donald T. Campbell and Julian C. Stanley, "Experimental and Quasi-Experimental Designs for Research on Teaching," in *Handbook of Research on Teaching*, ed. N. L. Gage (Chicago: Rand McNally, 1963), pp. 171–246.

eralizations that deal meaningfully with the educative process in all of its complexity may require many years before they are forthcoming, if ever.

Is there nothing to do, then, except to deplore the situation we are in? Is it even worthwhile to attempt to study the school system and the educative process?

There is much that the field of educational studies can contribute. After all, difficulty in resolving policy debates is common to all of the policy sciences (economics, government, religious studies, and so forth), not just to educational studies. In fact, because educational studies is a newly emerging field and therefore relatively undeveloped, proportionately much more remains to be done to give us the kinds of insights and understandings about education that are so urgently needed.

Specifically, through an attempt to arrive at answers to educational policy questions, at least three significant things may be accomplished. First, much can be done in the way of *clarification*. The identification of the basic policy questions and sub-questions requiring answers can help us to gain a better appreciation of what is involved in educational decision making. Also, by attempting to define our concepts with some precision, a better means of communicating about educational issues can be provided. This will help in avoiding the wasted effort that occurs when people think they disagree about an issue but in reality are talking about different issues. Most importantly, in examining the basic educational policy questions we may expect to clarify the nature of the controversies that exist. We need to know what the arguments on each side of the important issues are, and why an agreement has not been reached. Does the disagreement involve differing conceptions of ultimate and penultimate ends? Does it involve differing views about the costs and benefits of carrying out the proposed policy? Is the disagreement over matters subject to empirical research?

Second, we may achieve an increased understanding of what the *focus of empirical research* should be. Although, as we emphasized, empirical research can make only a restricted contribution to the justification of policy questions, it is nonetheless vital to obtaining satisfactory answers. By knowing what the basic educational policy questions are and where the deficiencies in the empirical knowledge pertaining to these questions exist, educational researchers will be able to guide their efforts accordingly.

Finally, the attempt to justify answers offered to the principal educational policy questions will enable us to become much more *sensitive to existing limitations* in the available knowledge about education. Instead of exhibiting a misplaced confidence in unexamined assumptions about education, a more accurate conception of what we know and do not know will have been acquired, with respect to the educative process.

Society cannot defer its obligation to answer the basic educational policy questions. As long as our society conducts educational activities, it must decide how education should be controlled and for what purpose. But the answers to the fundamental educational policy questions that have already been provided may not be the most appropriate ones; if they are good, it would be reassuring to know this is the case. By helping to clarify educational policy controversies, focus empirical research efforts, and make us aware of the extent of our knowledge about education, the field of educational studies can make a vital contribution to educational decision making.

SUMMARY

There are at least three possible ways in which to *justify* (support in a convincing manner) a policy statement. A justification can be based on an appeal to higher *authority*, on *intuition*, or on a knowledge of the *consequences* that would follow from carrying out the proposed policy. Because of the advantages of the latter method, justification by consequences shall be regarded as our basic approach.

The means-ends chain is the essential element in justification by consequences (which shall also be referred to as a means-ends justification). The "links" in a means-ends chain are brought about by the fact that an end can usually be the means to another end; only an ultimate end cannot be a means to something else.

There are three problems in the use of a means-ends justification: (1) We and the person we are trying to convince may disagree over ultimate or penultimate ends. (2) We may disagree whether a particular means-ends chain is the most efficient (least costly in relation to benefits) way of reaching a given end. (3) We may disagree whether a particular means does in fact lead to a given end.

While there is little that can be done to resolve the first type of disagreement, the methods of empirical research can be used to: (1) help identify the side effects of a given means-ends chain; and (2) help determine whether a given means leads to (is the cause of) a given end. Empirical research is important to justification by consequences, therefore, because it represents a reliable way of obtaining evidence about cause-effect relationships.

An *empirical statement* is one which in principle can be confirmed or disconfirmed through the use of one or more of the five senses. Care must be taken not to confuse empirical statements with three other types of statements frequently encountered in writings about education: analytic or tautological statements, metaphysical statements, and normative statements.

The most rigorous procedure that can be used for the confirmation of cause-effect statements is the *experimental method*. When an experiment is conducted, the researcher is able to assign the experimental variable freely to the subjects of the experiment. The researcher either removes other relevant independent variables from the experimental situation or allows them to act in an unbiased manner on all of the subjects in the experiment. A simple form of experiment involves two groups of subjects, divided on a random basis. The researcher allows the experimental variable to act on one group of subjects and withholds the experimental variable from the other group. Then, if at the end of the experiment he observes a difference between the groups that is statistically significant, the researcher may attribute that difference to the effect of the experimental variable, since his procedures were intended to eliminate other plausible competing interpretations or hypotheses that might account for any differences between the two groups.

But not all important independent variables can be freely assigned by the researcher to the subjects of an experiment. To study cause-effect relationships involving these variables, a research method that is less rigorous than the experimental method must be employed. The *correlation method* is an approach frequently used for this purpose. Two variables that are causally related are also correlated, but every correlation does not represent a causal relationship. A third variable may be related to both of the variables and thus account for their joint variation. It is possible, however, to analyze a correlation in terms of a third variable. If the correlation between the original variables does not disappear when the third variable is introduced into the analysis, then our confidence is increased that a valid causal relationship has been discovered. However, because not all possible third variables can be tested, the correlation method does not allow for the elimination of all other plausible competing hypotheses which might account for the observed correlation.

Establishing valid empirical generalizations is very difficult to do, even with the most satisfactory research techniques. One of the difficulties is the need to replicate a given study a number of times in different places before we can begin to have some assurance about the generalizability of the findings. Also, the very act of conducting research may alter the situation being investigated, so that we cannot be sure that our conclusions would apply to other situations.

Is it possible, therefore, to provide an adequate justification of a policy statement? The chances are extremely limited if the person we are trying to convince does not share our value position about ultimate and penultimate ends, or if he has a different evaluation of the costs and benefits entailed in reaching an end. Even if the disagreement is confined to the matter of cause-effect relationships, it is not certain that we will be able to obtain adequate empirical evidence.

But these difficulties in the justification of policy statements are common to all policy sciences (economics, government, religious studies, for example); they are not unique to the field of educational studies. Through an examination of attempts to justify educational policy statements we can hope to: (1) clarify the nature of the disagreements that exist; (2) indicate where empirical research is most needed; and (3) increase our awareness of what is and is not known about the educative process.

GENERAL NOTES AND BIBLIOGRAPHY

1. METHODS OF JUSTIFICATION. An examination of the topic of justification from an educational point of view may be found in many books written by educational philosophers. The following are representative: D. J. O'Connor, *An Introduction to the Philosophy of Education* (New York: Philosophical Library, 1957); R. S. Peters, *Ethics and Education* (Glenview, Ill.: Scott, Foresman, 1967); Louis A. Reid, *Philosophy and Education: An Introduction* (New York: Random House, 1965). For a general discussion of the relevance of philosophy to educational studies, see L. M. Brown, *General Philosophy in Education* (New York: McGraw-Hill, 1966).

2. BASIC REFERENCE SOURCES. There are two encyclopedias with which every student in the field of educational studies should be familiar. One of these is the *Encyclopedia of Education*, ed. Lee C. Deighton (10 vols.; New York: Macmillan, 1971). This is a general encyclopedia, covering a variety of topics related to the school system. Included are descriptions of the school systems of foreign countries and biographies of some of the more important figures in education. Bibliographies are provided in conjunction with most of the articles, although their coverage is limited primarily to major books and is not as complete as that of the bibliographies in the *Encyclopedia of Educational Research*, ed. Robert L. Ebel (4th ed.; New York: Macmillan, 1969), another basic encyclopedia. A new edition of this source is published approximately at ten-year intervals. Each new edition of the *Encyclopedia of Educational Research* is mainly concerned with assessing the research produced from the time of publication of the preceding edition. The 1969 edition is approximately 1,500 pages long and contains about 200 survey articles on a variety of topics in the field of educational studies. It is produced by the American Educational Research Association.

The *Review of Educational Research* (Washington: American Educational Research Association, 1931–date) is a journal that may be regarded as a supplement to the *Encyclopedia of Educational Research*. Five issues of the *Review of Educational Research* are published each year. Until June, 1970, each issue had been devoted to a single topic. Since that time, however, each issue has provided survey articles on several different topics in the same issue.

In 1973, the American Educational Research Association issued the first volume in a projected series of annual assessments of educational research: *Review of Research in Education*, ed. Fred N. Kerlinger (Itasca, Ill.: F. E. Peacock, 1973). The policy of this publication is "to cover a variety of educational fields. Areas and topics significant and influential in the immediate past, at present, or potentially in the future will be favored. Certain areas, however, such as learning and instruction, will always be favored because of their functional significance in education. . . . The *Review*'s larger function is to probe a field, bring out its strengths and weaknesses, and point the way to enlargement and improvement; only second-arily is its purpose bibliographic" (pp. v-vii).

There are two principal subject indexes for current journal articles in education: *Education Index* (New York: H. W. Wilson, 1929–date; monthly, except July and August, with annual cumulations) and *Current Index to Journals in Education* (New York: CCM Information Corporation, 1969–date; monthly, with annual cumulations). In discussing the *Education Index*, it is necessary to distinguish between the issues published prior to 1961 and the issues that have appeared since that date. From 1929 to 1961 the *Education Index* covered all educational books published in the United States (except school texts) and many yearbooks, book reviews, pamphlets, reports, and government publications, as well as journal articles. But after 1961 the coverage was considerably curtailed, so that now the *Education Index* is basically a subject index to educational journal articles. The *Current Index to Journals in Education* commenced publication in 1969. In comparison with the *Education Index*, it covers a greater number of publications (over 700, compared to about 250 in the *Education Index*). The *Current Index* also provides a brief abstract for most materials indexed.

3. EMPIRICAL RESEARCH. The characteristics of empirical statements and the problems entailed in their confirmation are discussed on an elementary level in John Hospers, *An Introduction to Philosophical Analysis* (2nd ed.; Englewood Cliffs, N.J.: Prentice-Hall, 1967), pp. 101–128. For more advanced treatments of these topics, the following works may be consulted: Richard B. Braithwaite, *Scientific Explanation* (London: Cambridge University Press, 1953); Robert Brown, *Explanation in Social Science* (Chicago: Aldine, 1963); Richard S. Rudner, *Philosophy of Social Science* (Englewood Cliffs, N.J.: Prentice-Hall, 1966). A discussion of the problems involved in formulating operational definitions is provided in Lise Wallach, "Implications of Recent Work in Philosophy of Science for the Role of Operational Definition in Psychology," *Psychological Reports* 28 (1971): 583–608.

The nature of normative statements is dealt with extensively in the field of ethics. Two books by R. M. Hare provide useful introductions to this subject: *The Language of Morals* (London: Oxford University Press, 1952) and *Freedom and Reason* (London: Oxford University Press, 1963). Another helpful source is Stephen E. Toulmin, *An Examination of the Place of Reason in Ethics* (London: Cambridge University Press, 1950).

Research methods in education are covered in a number of general surveys. The following books are particularly recommended for their coverage of the experimental and correlation methods, as well as other research techniques: Fred N. Kerlinger, *Foundations of Behavioral Research* (2nd ed.; New York: Holt, Rinehart and Winston, 1973); Deobold B. Van Dalen, *Understanding Educational Research* (rev. ed.; New York: McGraw-Hill, 1966); John W. Best, *Research in Education* (2nd ed.; Englewood Cliffs, N.J.: Prentice-Hall, 1970).

An excellent, nonstatistical discussion of the advantages and limitations of different types of experimental designs may be found in Donald T. Campbell and Julian C. Stanley, "Experimental and Quasi-Experimental Designs for Research on Teaching," in *Handbook of Research on Teaching*, ed. N. L. Gage (Chicago: Rand McNally, 1963), pp. 171–246. Equally useful is the treatment of the basic principles of the correlation method (although the method is not explicitly identified as such) in Morris Rosenberg, *The Logic of Survey Analysis* (New York: Basic Books, 1968).

The basic assumptions which underlie contemporary empirical educational research are examined in Harry S. Broudy, Robert H. Ennis and Leonard I. Krimerman, eds., *Philosophy of Educational Research* (New York: Wiley, 1973) and Lawrence G. Thomas, ed., *Philosophical Redirection of Educational Research* (Chicago: National Society for the Study of Education, 1972).

WHO SHOULD CONTROL EDUCATION, AND IN WHAT WAY?

PART TWO

MODERATE PROPOSALS FOR CONTROL CHANGE

CHAPTER 3

The idea of control is of fundamental importance in education. In discussing "education" in Chapter 1, the educative process is defined as the deliberate attempt to control learning situations in order to accomplish desired learning outcomes. This control may be exercised by the learner or by someone else, and may pertain to the anticipated ends of education and/or the means for accomplishing these ends.

Control exists if someone or something has an effect on someone or something else. Thus, in our use of the term, control does not mean that the person being controlled must act completely in accord with the wishes of the person exerting control. Rather, it merely means that the person exerting control must be able to have some effect on the other person. But this effect might be simply to cause the other person to act in a different manner, or even to act contrary to the wishes of the person exerting control. Control may be exercised deliberately or, as in the case of the control exerted by the weather, there may be no conscious direction. However, we shall confine our attention (unless otherwise indicated) to those control techniques which entail a conscious attempt to have an effect on someone or something; hence, in using the word "control," it should be understood that reference is made to deliberate control.

There is another important point which needs to be mentioned before going further. For many persons, the word "control" carries strong negative connotations. These persons think of control as something undesirable, the opposite of being free. But for our purposes, the term shall be regarded in a neutral sense. For us control is neither good nor bad as such; it is simply a basic condition of human life. Some control techniques in certain situations may be preferable to others in the same situations; but the reader will have ample opportunity to make his own value judgments concerning the appropriateness of using particular control techniques in specified situations. (Note 1)

The basic question "Who should control education, and in what way?" has not, to date, been satisfactorily answered for the American school system. The problem of who should control the educational means-ends chain is one of the major questions confronting us, since the nature of the ultimate and/or penultimate end selected depends on the value judgment of the person who makes the decision. If children were to choose their educational objectives, they might decide on very different goals from the ones their parents might choose. The problem of the way control over the ends and means of education should be exercised is also important. Are some ways of exerting control over learning situations more effective and/or less costly than others?

Until recently, there has been general agreement that someone other than the student should control the ends and means of education, at least until the student has reached the age of sixteen. The major issues, therefore, have been concerned with the problem of who other than students should control the school system—the government, the teachers, or the parents—and the problem of how to make the existing control structure more accountable through a more effective exercise of motivational control over teachers and school administrators.

Several proposals relative to who should control the school system and how to make the existing control structure more accountable have been advanced. Because the adoption of these proposals would not affect the way students are motivated, and thus would not bring about a fundamental change in the control of education from the point of view of the student, we shall label them the *moderate proposals* for reform.

Moderate proposals can nonetheless be highly controversial. For convenience the major recommendations may be grouped under the following headings: (1) change in the locus of governmental control, (2) increased teacher control, and (3) increased parental control. The principal arguments that have been advanced for and against these proposals shall be identified in this chapter.

Should the Locus of Governmental Control Be Changed?

Issue 1: _____

Who has the basic formal responsibility for control of the American school system? The answer to this question is specified in most countries in the national constitution, the document which prescribes the fundamental allocation of authority within the governmental structure of the society. The Constitution of the United States does not give the federal government any explicit authority over education (in fact, the terms "education" and "school system" are not mentioned in the Constitution), and by virtue of the Tenth Amendment powers not granted to the federal government are reserved to the states. Therefore, in the United States the fifty states have the formal responsibility for the control of the school system.

But if we accept the foregoing interpretation, how is the role of the federal government to be accounted for in the control of the American school system? It is well known that the national government gives money to the schools and also provides information and other guidance. Is this assistance unconstitutional? The federal government is permitted to provide financial resources and similar assistance to the schools through the "general welfare" clause of the Constitution, since such assistance is regarded as pertaining to promotion of the general welfare. However, the power granted by this clause does not permit the federal government to pass a law stipulating a mandatory curriculum, for example. Such laws remain the prerogative of the states.[1]

In 1970 the financial aid provided by the federal government amounted to about 10 per cent of the operating costs of public primary and secondary schooling. The federal government also has direct control over certain schools, such as schools for Indians and the national military academies. The federal executive agency with primary responsibility for the school system is the U.S. Office of Education, which is located within the Department of Health, Education and Welfare.

[1]This decentralized approach to the control of schooling is relatively unusual as far as the rest of the world is concerned. In most countries the basic formal responsibility for the school system is vested in the national government; among those countries which have decentralized control are Australia, Canada, India, and West Germany.

With the exception of Hawaii, the states have chosen to delegate much of their responsibility for the control of public primary and secondary schools to local school districts. The school district is controlled by a governing board, which usually has the right to collect taxes, appoint teachers, determine the types and locations of new school buildings, and within the framework of state law to make decisions concerning the curriculum.[2] The members of a school board may be appointed or elected. In about one-half of the local school districts that operate schools, the school board employs a chief executive officer, who is usually designated the superintendent of schools. An administrative hierarchy generally exists between the superintendent of schools and the classroom teacher. Each school is ordinarily headed by a principal, who has supervisory authority over the teachers, who in turn have authority to control student behavior. (Note 2)

While many persons are satisfied with the existing arrangement of the states' delegating much of the responsibility for the control of the public primary and secondary schools to the local school districts, two quite different views have also been expressed. One position is that the educational means-ends chain would be more effective and/or less costly if there were more centralized direction of the school system (that is, control by the federal government). The contrasting position is espoused by the advocates of community control. They argue that if local control is considered to produce desirable outcomes, then the benefits of local control should be extended even further by having more decentralization of policy-making authority.

The issue, therefore, is: Should the locus of governmental control be changed? Should we have more national control of schools? Or should we have more local control? In discussing this issue, we shall assume that whether or not the U.S. Constitution actually allows us to make the change is not a relevant consideration—if the change were unconstitutional, we will assume we could amend the Constitution as necessary. Also, we shall assume that the decision

[2]The responsibility for providing financial resources to the public primary and secondary schools is presently shared mainly between the states and the local school districts. In 1970 the states provided about 50 per cent of the operating costs of these schools, and the school districts contributed about 40 per cent (with the federal government as previously noted giving about 10 per cent). The costs of land and buildings, however, are the responsibility of the school districts.

to change or retain the present locus of governmental control will be based on factors other than the financing of schools (this topic is dealt with in Chapter 8 in connection with the goal of equal education). Thus, the major factors to consider are who should have curricular control, control over the employment of teachers, and control over the locations and types of new school buildings, but not who should be responsible for funding the schools. (Note 3)

Arguments Concerning National Control

A major argument for more national control of schools rests upon the contention that locally controlled schools are not necessarily responsive to national needs and, hence, are not as effective in meeting societal educational goals as a federally controlled system might be. These arguments have been expressed by Myron Lieberman in his book, *The Future of Public Education*. Lieberman identifies four major reasons why he believes local control of schools in the United States has outlived its usefulness. "In the first place," he notes, "mobility and interdependence have completely undermined the notion that local communities ought to have a free hand in educating their children. Second, national survival now requires educational policies and programs which are not subject to local veto. Third, it is becoming increasingly clear that local control cannot in practice be reconciled with the ideals of a democratic society. Finally, local control is a major cause of the dull parochialism and attenuated totalitarianism that characterizes public education in operation."[3]

Lieberman states that the most important argument against a nationally controlled system of public schools "is the notion that any such system would be 'totalitarian' or 'undemocratic.' We are warned that a centralized system would provide an opportunity for one particular group, say a political party, to seize control of the schools, and by indoctrinating its point of view, maintain itself in power. . . . Those who think along these lines usually point to Soviet Russia to illustrate the dangers of a centralized system of education. But it should be obvious that one cannot assume that a cen-

[3]The quotations in this paragraph and in the two which follow it are from Myron Lieberman, *The Future of Public Education* (Chicago: University of Chicago Press, 1960), pp.34, 37–39, 52.

tralized system per se is more likely to be totalitarian than our own. England, France, and the Scandinavian countries all have national systems. In all of these, there is less political interference with teachers than there is in the United States. Put positively, there is more freedom to teach and to learn in all of these national school systems than there is in the overwhelming majority of schools in the United States."

Lieberman goes on to criticize what he regards as the "totalitarianism" of local control. "Our present system of local control," he insists, "is far more conducive to totalitarianism than a national system of schools would be. . . . At the local level, it is relatively easy for a preponderant group to enforce a policy of intellectual protectionism for its sacred cows. . . . Communities in which fundamentalist sects predominate exclude instruction [favorable to] evolution. Some communities have prohibited the study of the United Nations or of UNESCO. Ours is a heterogeneous country, but in most communities the predominant racial, religious, economic, or political groups are able to veto whatever in the school program displeases them. . . . We do not readily recognize the totalitarianism implicit in our situation because not all schools protect the same dogmas."

The proponents of the existing system of local control reject Lieberman's position and maintain that the residents of the local community know better than the national government what kind of schooling the community requires. They also argue that the present system of local control permits those who care deeply about matters involving their schools to have direct contact with the persons who make the important decisions for the schools. There is thus an opportunity for individual initiative and a flexible response to local needs. As a result, locally controlled schools are considered by their defenders to be more effective and/or less costly in achieving the educational goals of the community than would be a system of federally controlled schools.

Arguments Concerning Community Control

A very different attack on the present system of local control has been mounted by the advocates of community control. They point out that several large American urban centers have populations that exceed those of some of our states. Hence to talk about the merits of local control in a metropolitan school district is meaning-less—the bureaucratic inefficiences and distance of the school ad-ministration from the average citizen are nearly as great as they would be in a national system of control. Moreover, in some smaller school districts there may be groups of parents resident in specific geographic areas who believe their views not to be adequately reflected in the decisions of the school boards. The solution proposed by the proponents of community control is to divide the original school district into smaller units or sub-districts, each of which would encompass a single identifiable community (for example, an area that is populated mainly by a particular ethnic group or that is demarcated by special geographic features might qualify as such a community). Financial resources available to the original school district would be distributed in an equitable manner to the various community sub-districts. Each community sub-district would be governed by its own policy-making body, which would be permitted to use the funds allocated to it to operate the schools of the sub-dis-trict in the way deemed most appropriate for the needs of the com-munity. A community sub-district would have the right to manage its own budget, to recruit its own teachers, to develop special cur-ricula, and to determine the types and locations of new school buildings.

Some of the basic arguments for community control have been presented by Maurice R. Berube. He contends that "schools will best help children learn when they strengthen pupils' feelings of control over their destinies. That is at the heart of community control of city schools. Big city school systems, unaccountable and isolated, generate feelings of powerlessness and alienation among parents and pupils. Only when these city schools are operated by their vari-ous communities can an educational 'system' even begin to dispel this powerlessness. And students, developing a greater sense of self-worth, would correspondingly develop a greater motivation to learn. . . . The first step to better education in city schools is to transfer educational power to a series of autonomous, community controlled local school districts. The rest will follow."[4]

Berube addresses the counter-argument that community con-

---

[4]The quotations in this paragraph and in the one which follows it are from Maurice R. Berube, "Achievement and Community Control," in *School Policy and Issues in a Changing Society*, ed. Patricia C. Sexton (Boston: Al-lyn and Bacon, 1971), pp. 226, 229, 231, 233.

trol of schools will prevent the attainment of racially integrated schools. He suggests that the movement for community control of schools received its impetus from the failure of the white majority to provide effective school integration: "The trouble with local control of the schools, critics maintain, is that such an arrangement closes off the possibility of school integration—what these critics view as the most beneficial educational condition for the black poor—thereby raising the 'threatening' spectre of black power separatism. . . . According to census patterns, most American cities are increasing in racial segregation, and within a generation will have a majority black population. School integration simply is neither feasible nor foreseeable in the near future. The movement of parents for community control was based on this default of the white community. . . .That is not to say our society should continue on its present segregated course. It is to say, however, that the black ghetto can develop its own values and rationale for success. And it is to say that the black power ideology is 'extremist' only to those who are themselves psychologically unable to tolerate black citizens who have the equal opportunity to determine their own fates."

Additional Comments

It seems clear from the preceding discussion that before we can answer the question of whether the locus of governmental control of public primary and secondary schools should be changed, we must consider the ultimate/penultimate ends of education as well as the effectiveness and/or costs of the educational means-ends chain. Some who advocate increased national control of the school system may do so because they believe that this initial means will lead to the penultimate end of a more homogeneous society, whereas others who favor community control may do so because they believe this initial means will result in a more pluralistic society.

The more local control we have, the more effective the schools will be in meeting locally determined educational objectives. Hence a greater amount of pluralism will be fostered. But the attainment of pluralistic local objectives (no matter how efficiently arrived at within the local school district) necessarily involves a less effective achievement of national homogeneity, unless it should happen fortuitously that all locally determined goals be consonant with national goals. When the goal of national homogeneity is important, societies are willing to tolerate the inefficiency that usually accompanies centralized bureaucracies, because there is no other way to achieve national objectives as effectively. Although some administrative decentralization may be appropriate, basic policies must originate at the national level if we wish to achieve national goals.

Thus an important question for us is: To what extent do we want a pluralistic society? This problem shall be encountered once again when we consider Issue 3 (the question of whether public funds should be provided to private schools). This problem is also dealt with in Chapter 8, where we shall try to decide whether the educative process should result in attainment of equal outcomes.

Should We Have More Teacher Control?
Issue 2:

Teachers in the public primary and secondary schools have much less autonomy and decision-making authority than their counterparts in the university. The exercise of authority within colleges and universities has historically been of what may be termed the "collegial" type. The university professor, in Burton Clark's view, "occupies a role that has much in common with the position of other experts in other organizations, particularly the scientist in industry and the physician in the hospital, where the demands for extensive personal and group autonomy are high. . . . In short, faculty authority tends toward professional authority in federated form."[5]

At the primary and secondary levels, according to Clark, "the authority structure takes a markedly different form from that just described. There is less expertness, less impulse toward federated professionalism protective of teacher autonomy. The public school systems are more characterized by a vulnerable bureaucracy. The authority structure of the school takes the form of a single hierarchy . . . with teachers as employees under supervision of administrators. The critical feature of this authority [structure] is its amenability to external control."[6]

The question has arisen, therefore, whether steps should be

[5]Burton R. Clark, "Sociology of Education," in *Handbook of Modern Sociology*, ed. Robert E. L. Faris (Chicago: Rand McNally, 1964), pp. 759–760.
[6]Ibid., p. 760.

taken to grant nonuniversity teachers an increased amount of control over the school system. Two problems related to increased control by public primary and secondary school teachers will be examined: (1) teacher strikes, and (2) the professional status of teachers. Whether teachers should be held more accountable for the effectiveness of their teaching shall also be discussed. (Note 4)

Should Teachers Have the Right to Strike?

Primary and secondary school teachers have sought to increase their policy-making authority in the school-system organization. They have created organizations of teachers on the national, state, and local levels. The two major national organizations of teachers are the National Education Association (NEA), with about 1.7 million members (most of whom are teachers), and the American Federation of Teachers (AFT), with a membership of 450,000. Teachers have tried to induce the school system to accept their proposals regarding conditions of employment, school facilities, and teacher salaries. One of the means that teachers can use to increase their influence on school system decisions is to threaten to withdraw their services (*strike*). Should teachers resort to this technique?

The strike is one of the most extreme forms of teacher activism. Other ways in which teachers seek to realize their objective of an enhanced role in educational policy making include lobbying, participation in school board and state election campaigns, publication of policy statements and criticisms of school policies, work slowdowns, professional holidays, and mass resignations.

Some questions surround the legality of strikes and similar activities on the part of teachers. In some states laws have been passed which deny public employees (including teachers) the right to strike. In other states, however, teachers have gained a qualified right to strike (for example, in Hawaii and Pennsylvania). The right of a teacher organization to negotiate with a school board and enter into a binding agreement (*collective bargaining*) also differs from state to state.

The case for greater teacher militancy has been presented by David Selden. "What America needs is more teacher strikes," he declares.

> Instead of putting work stoppages by teachers in the same category as matricide and spitting on the flag, school board members and superintendents should be delighted when they have a group of educa-

tors who care enough about the schools and their own professional status to lay their jobs on the line in order to bring about improvements. . . . What is so terrible about a strike by teachers? The traditional answer is, "Think of the children!" Yet it is often more harmful to the children for teachers *not* to strike than it would be to close down the schools for a while. . . . During the course of a year schools are closed for a dozen holidays of varying significance, and they are shut down for two weeks at Christmas time, a week at Easter, and two to three months in the summer. No one thinks of these "work stoppages" as harming the children. But let teachers close the schools for even one day, for the purpose of making the schools better, and the pillars of society tremble. . . . It is time teachers were released from their conformist bondage. Anyone who really worries about education ought to kick, prod, cajole, wheedle, and exhort teachers to far greater militancy. When teachers are willing to stop work rather than continue under substandard conditions, they will have gone a long way toward attaining the professional status to which they have given lip service for so many years.[7]

One of the principal arguments against giving teachers the right to strike is the view that the school board against whom the strike is directed is not comparable to a private employer, who is concerned with monetary costs and profits. The school board is concerned with the public welfare, thus making the teacher strike a threat to society. Another major argument is the view that teacher strikes are harmful to children. Both of these arguments are expressed by Arthur Corey:

> In private employment the strike imposes financial losses on both the employer and the employe. In public employment the strike imposes financial losses only on the employe while the employer actually saves money. An extended strike can break a private employer while a public employer could at least theoretically finance sizable salary adjustments with the money saved during an extended work stoppage. In most school districts enough reserve could be accumulated through a two-week strike to finance a 5 per cent raise for the following year. In private employment the strike is an economic weapon, while in public employment, it becomes a social weapon. When a strike occurs in public employment, the losses incurred by the employer must be measured in the peril and possible catastrophe which may accompany a cessation of public service. A strike in any segment of the public service depends for its effectiveness not on the possibility of enforced economic loss to the employer but on the threat to the public welfare or a breakdown in law and order. . . . It is rather pathetic to note the attempts made by proponents of the strike to argue that a

[7]David Selden, "Needed: More Teacher Strikes," *Saturday Review*, May 15, 1965, p. 75. (Emphasis in the original.)

forced vacation for children really does them no harm. If this be true, it would be wise not to let the public *in* on the secret. If the idea that a day of school (every day) is important to the child is merely an unsophisticated concept indulged in by simple-minded N.E.A. members, the future of teaching in America is indeed precarious. Whatever dramatic impact the strike may have depends upon the fact that the public is thoroughly convinced that an interruption in children's schooling is terribly important. If this were not true, the strike would have no impact—it simply wouldn't matter. Any attempt to argue that a teachers strike is not against children is pure sophistry.[8]

As Selden pointed out, however, schools are closed for holidays during various times of the year and for a summer vacation of two or three months, yet "no one thinks of these 'work stoppages' as harming the children." Although Corey in his statement refers to the question of whether students are harmed by a teacher strike, he focuses his argument on the importance of schooling—which is a very different matter.

It has also been argued that it is "unprofessional" for teachers to strike. Yet it should be noted that in some countries in which medical doctors are paid by the government, these doctors have had strikes. "Professional codes of ethics," Lieberman and Moskow contend, "not only permit but obligate professional workers to withdraw their services under certain conditions. For example, doctors are not supposed to serve where they cannot take responsibility for the outcome. Lawyers are supposed to withdraw from the service of clients who insist upon unethical means to achieve favorable verdicts. Even when a person's eternal salvation is at stake, a priest will not perform services for him if he has not met the conditions set by the church itself. The professional groups in these situations have made a collective decision that the client must meet certain conditions in order to receive professional services. Whether the professional is employed individually or by a community is irrelevant; professional ethics still obligates him to withdraw his services under certain conditions. Teacher strikes usually arise and are discussed in the context of teacher welfare, but nothing is more clear than this: If teachers followed the policy and practice of the ac-

[8]Arthur F. Corey, "Why Teacher Strikes Must Be Rejected by the Profession and Why 'Sanctions' Should Be Considered," *Nation's Schools*, September, 1962, pp. 69–70. (Emphasis in the original.)

knowledged professions, teacher strikes would occur much more frequently than they do."[9]

The professionalism argument presupposes, in any case, that
teaching actually constitutes a profession. If teachers were professionals, the argument goes, they would derive considerable economic and other benefits from their status in society and hence might
not require the right to strike. They would also enjoy professional
autonomy. But it has already been indicated that primary and secondary school teachers lack such autonomy, and this is one reason
that they might wish to have the right to strike. Hence we need to
discuss whether teaching really is a profession, and if it is not,
whether it has the potential of becoming one.

Is Teaching a Profession?

Whether we regard teaching as a profession depends on how
we define the term "profession." Taking the professions of medicine
and law as our standard, we may establish two basic criteria by
which the professional status of an occupational field can be evaluated. First, there is a specialized body of knowledge that must be
mastered before a person can become a professional. This body of
knowledge is generally quite difficult to acquire and rather esoteric
in character; without it, therefore, a person is a layman rather than
a professional. And second, because of the need to master an esoteric
body of knowledge before a person can become a professional, the
professionals themselves must control admission to the profession.
In a sense, only those who are already professionals are able to
make relevant judgments concerning the qualifications of an aspir-
ant to a profession.

If these two criteria are applied to the occupation of teacher,
we might conclude that primary and secondary school teachers are
not professionals in quite the same way that doctors and lawyers
are. The principal reason is that a specialized body of knowledge relating to the act of teaching does not yet exist. It often is taken for
granted, in fact, that anyone can teach. For example, most university teachers have had no formal training in the methodology of

[9]Myron Lieberman and Michael H. Moskow, *Collective Negotiations
for Teachers* (Chicago: Rand McNally, 1966), p. 297.

teaching. (University teachers are thus not professionals when considered in their role as teachers, although they may be thought of as professionals in their various fields of expertise—such as historians or economists.) And since teacher training does not yet include the mastery of an esoteric body of knowledge, it has not yet been possible for teachers to assert the right to determine who will be allowed to become a teacher. Therefore, teaching does not fulfill our criteria for a profession.

This does not mean, however, that teaching does not have the potential of becoming a true profession. Indeed, it is quite conceivable that a specialized body of knowledge about the teaching process can be developed. To effect the professional transformation of teaching, however, teachers will need to conceive of their roles very differently than they presently do. Instead of mainly being disseminators of information (instructional stimuli), teachers must become *managers* of the instructional process. Currently, most of a teacher's time in the classroom is devoted to talking to students, and much of the talking involves the presentation of information. Yet virtually all of the information offered by the teacher could be disseminated through mechanical means—books, films, television, teaching machines, audio tapes, mimeographed handouts, and so forth. If such mechanical devices were used for the presentation of information, the teacher would then be free to do the things that are based on an esoteric body of knowledge. For example, the teacher could spend much more time assessing student performance, diagnosing learning difficulties, and prescribing the appropriate learning situations for the attainment of desired learning outcomes. To be done competently, all of these activities would require a specialized body of knowledge about the teaching process. It would not be possible any longer to insist that "anyone can teach." True, it might be possible for almost anyone to present information, but only a person who had been trained in the requisite diagnostic and prescriptive skills could be a manager of the instructional process.

The manager of instruction would not hesitate to make use of available mechanical devices if they would facilitate the performance of his role, just as the medical doctor is not reluctant to make use of X-ray equipment, antibiotics, and other products of medical technology. The manager of instruction would still retain personal contact with students, and in fact would be able to have much more relevant contact, simply because the routine task of disseminating information would have been allocated to a mechanical device. He would also probably make extensive use of teacher's aides and other ancillary personnel, just as the medical doctor relies on the help of nurses, medical technicians, and hospital orderlies.

While the body of esoteric knowledge about the teaching process that would be necessary for the establishment of the manager of instruction role has not yet been produced, it seems reasonable to expect that it will be created as soon as an adequate demand exists. Thus, when teachers are sufficiently interested in becoming true professionals, it will probably be feasible for them to do so. Yet the technology that would permit teachers to change their role from disseminators of information to managers of instruction has been with us since the invention of the printing press. Why, then, has no basic change taken place in the role of the teacher?

One explanation might be that professional competence is not really required of teachers, because of the function they currently perform in the school system. Teachers in primary and secondary schools spend much of their time enforcing discipline, because the students they teach are compelled by society to be in school; most students are not in school as a result of their own free choice. When it comes to teaching activities, school authorities usually do not ask the teacher to help each of his students achieve a specified set of learning outcomes, regardless of the length of time involved. Instead, the teacher is asked to evaluate the progress of his students over a specified period of time (a school term) and to provide school authorities with a rank-ordering of students on the basis of their quickness to learn. Since excessive teaching competence is not required to produce this rank-ordering, it is understandable that teachers have little incentive to obtain the professional expertise that would be necessary if instead they had been given the task of assisting each student to attain a specified set of learning outcomes.

In advancing this explanation, matters that pertain to radical criticism of the school system have been touched upon. Full treatment of these topics shall be deferred until we encounter them again in Chapters 5 and 6. But it is very important to be aware of the additional perspective on the school system and its problems that can be gained from an understanding of the radical criticism. Indeed, it may be advisable to withhold final judgment on the moderate proposals for change in the control of education until we have had an opportunity to examine the radical proposals.

Let us assume for the time being, however, that either through the right to strike or by becoming true professionals (or both), teachers acquire greater decision-making authority within the school system. Can we be certain that teachers would use this power for the benefit of students, or would they use it primarily to secure benefits for themselves? This raises the question of whether teachers should be made more accountable, which is the next problem we shall consider.

Teacher Accountability

The concept "teacher accountability" entails holding a teacher responsible for his teaching performance. If the teacher were to do well, he would receive additional remuneration. But if the teacher were to do poorly, he would receive less pay or even lose his job.

To some extent, of course, public primary and secondary school teachers in the United States are already accountable to principals, superintendents and school boards for the quality of their performance. Yet many people believe that the school system harbors incompetent teachers. Moreover, teacher salaries in the public primary and secondary schools are usually based on years of service and academic qualifications; teachers who are comparable with respect to these factors are paid the same salaries, regardless of whether they are outstanding or mediocre in their work.

It has been suggested that primary and secondary school teachers would be more accountable if a system of merit pay for teachers were introduced. Under a merit-pay system the highly competent teacher could expect to receive a higher salary than the less capable teacher, irrespective of years of service or academic qualifications. The incompetent teacher would face the prospect of a reduced salary, or termination of employment.

Many persons accept the principle of merit pay for teachers; however, they have been unable to agree on how merit pay can be successfully implemented. There are two possible bases for a workable merit-pay system. The performance of a teacher could be assessed either on the basis of what he or she does, or on the basis of what his or her students do. The former procedure, however, is the one presently being used, and it is considered to be inadequate. The problem with trying to assess the competency of a teacher by observing his actions is that it has not yet been agreed what constitutes an outstanding teacher. If teaching were a true profession, presumably it would be possible to judge the performance of a teacher in accordance with generally accepted professional standards. But since teachers are not now expected to act on the basis of an esoteric body of knowledge, this method of assessing teacher performance cannot be used at the present time.

The task of the teacher is to help the student to learn. If we cannot evaluate teacher performance satisfactorily on the basis of what the teacher does, it would seem that we might be able to judge his or her competency on the basis of what happens to the students. This procedure, however, is also beset with difficulties, since several factors have a bearing on whether the student learns or not. As examples, the student's home background, his quickness to learn, and his motivation must be considered. Thus it would be unfair to hold a teacher responsible for the learning outcomes attained by his or her students if the teacher happened to be assigned students who were slow learners, poorly motivated, or who came from home backgrounds unconducive to academic achievement. Unless *all* students were randomly assigned to all classes, a teacher could plausibly argue that his class did not score as well as another class of the same type because the students were not as quick at learning, rather than because he was deficient as a teacher.

Is it to be concluded, therefore, that an adequate merit pay system cannot be established? Our response is a qualified "no." In the conventional school system, students are held accountable (by means of examinations) for their performance as students. It would seem that this requirement could be utilized in making teachers more accountable for their performance as teachers. To do so, however, the present method of evaluating students (norm-referenced testing with fixed time limits), which results in rank-ordering, would have to be transformed into a system that would permit each student to attain a prescribed set of learning outcomes (criterion-referenced testing with no fixed time limits).[10] Under this new system of student evaluation a teacher would presumably have more incentive to help his students achieve stipulated learning outcomes, while both the students and the teacher's supervisor would have more information by which to judge the teacher's performance. Under the present system of norm-referenced student evaluation, all teachers—regardless of their effectiveness—are able to produce a rank ordering of their students. With criterion-referenced testing,

[10]These concepts will be discussed more fully in the section on "Grading," Chapter 5.

however, it would be apparent to all concerned how effective a teacher would have been in assisting his students to achieve the prescribed set of learning outcomes. Of course, there would still be variations in the amount of time individual students might spend in acquiring these learning outcomes. However, it would be much easier to make appropriate allowances for student differences under a system of criterion-referenced grading than under a norm-referenced system.

We might even consider allowing students to choose their own teachers, instead of assigning students to teachers, as is now generally the case. It seems reasonable to assume that a student would select a teacher who would be of the greatest assistance to the student in his preparation for a prescribed examination. It would seem logical that the student would seek the teacher who could help him most in attaining the desired learning outcomes. If teachers were to be compensated for the number of students they served, we would have the basis for a viable system of merit pay for teachers. In fact, it would be similar to the present system for the compensation of medical doctors and lawyers. And, since it would encourage teachers to become managers of the instructional process, this system of merit pay would also contribute to the further professionalization of teaching.

Before the proposed merit-pay system could be implemented, numerous problems would need to be carefully examined—for example, whether very young students would be capable of selecting appropriate teachers, and whether students would be sufficiently motivated to study for prescribed examinations. Several of these problems will be considered when the radical proposals for change in educational control are discussed in Chapters 5 and 6; for this reason, it does not seem appropriate to begin to discuss them here. In particular, in Chapter 6 the concept of the teacher as instructional manager will be more fully developed, when we shall be able to give further consideration to the implications for teaching of using criterion-referenced evaluation without fixed time limits instead of norm-referenced evaluation with fixed time limits.

Also, in discussing the next issue, we shall have an opportunity to give greater attention to the free market principle that underlies the merit-pay proposal. As we shall see, the free market principle is the central feature of one of the proposals to give parents increased control of education (the voucher proposal).

Should We Have Increased
Parental Control?
Issue 3:_____|

There are several ways in which parents might achieve a greater amount of control over the school system. Parents can take a more active part in the political process by becoming better informed about the educational views of candidates for public office, and by supporting the candidates of their choice. Parents can work through existing organzations, such as the PTA, to bring about changes in their schools, or they can create new groups to exert pressure on local and state educational policy makers. But the most feasible ways of giving each parent maximum control over primary and secondary schooling would be to eliminate the financial barriers which presently restrict the use of private schools, or to allow parents to decide in which schools the public funds available for their children's schooling are to be used (instead of allocating these funds directly to the public schools).[11]

Thus, in asking the question "Should we have increased parental control?" we must consider whether public funds should be provided for the support of private schools, including church-related schools. If public funds are provided directly to private schools, parents will have a choice between available public and private schools. This will certainly increase the amount of parental control, but perhaps not greatly. On the other hand, if public funds were to be given to parents to spend for the schooling of their children, parents would be in a much stronger position to determine the type of schooling their children would receive. Both of these means of increasing parental control over the schools shall be examined. (Note 5)

Arguments Concerning the Direct
Public Support of Private Schools

The United States Supreme Court in 1925 (*Pierce* v. *Society of Sisters*) decided that parents have the right to enroll their children

[11]Issue 3 has been stated as if it involved only an increase in parental control; in fact the proposals to be discussed would also increase student control, since younger students may be expected to have an influence on their parents, while many students who have completed secondary school

in private primary and secondary schools rather than public schools, although the Court recognized the right of the state "reasonably to regulate all schools, to inspect, supervise and examine them, their teachers and pupils; to require that all children of proper age attend some school, that teachers shall be of good moral character and patriotic disposition, that certain studies plainly essential to good citizenship must be taught, and that nothing be taught which is manifestly inimical to the public welfare." This decision of the Supreme Court invalidated a law of the state of Oregon that required all school-age children to attend public schools.

There are two basic types of nonpublic schools in the United States: sectarian and nonsectarian. The sectarian primary and secondary schools may be divided into three principal categories: Catholic schools, Lutheran schools and Jewish schools. The greatest sectarian school enrollment is found in Catholic schools (approximately 90 per cent). Included among the nonsectarian schools are the independent schools (which include such socially exclusive schools as Andover, Groton and Choate), and the laboratory schools maintained by certain colleges and universities.

The states exercise varying degrees of control over the nonpublic primary and secondary schools. Campbell, Cunningham and McPhee describe this control as follows: "[The] regulatory rights [of the states] include the privileges of inspection for the purposes of determining the adequacy of the curriculum and teaching staffs, the enforcement of compulsory attendance laws, and the fulfillment of state expectations in regard to some aspects of pupil achievement, especially good citizenship. Although there is agreement on the regulatory rights of the states on these matters, there are widespread differences among the states in the stipulation and enforcement of those rights."[12]

While the number of students presently enrolled in private primary and secondary schools constitutes only a relatively small proportion (about 10 per cent) of the total enrollment in these two levels of the American school system, this proportion has been de-

---

would probably themselves make most of the basic decisions about their further schooling. Similarly, the proposals to be discussed would also increase private control over the schools. For convenience, however, this issue shall be examined from the perspective of increased parental control.

[12]Roald F. Campbell, Luvern L. Cunningham and Roderick F. McPhee, *The Organization and Control of American Schools* (Columbus, Ohio: Charles E. Merrill, 1965), p. 496.

clining. At the college and university level a similar situation prevails, although the total proportion of students enrolled in private schools is somewhat higher (about 30 per cent). Since a major reason for the declining numbers of students in private schools is financial (increased operating costs for the schools and increased tuition fees), it has been suggested by those who favor private schooling that increased public financial support be made available to private schools.

As far as church-related private schools are concerned, however, this request for public assistance faces a legal question: does the U.S. Constitution permit the allocation of public funds to such schools? But the primary issue in the question of public support for private schools is not the legal one. If such assistance were not regarded as constitutional, then an amendment to the Constitution could be added. The real issue, therefore, is whether public support for nonpublic schools is warranted.

A major argument against public support of private schools is the contention that private schools foster cultural heterogeneity instead of cultural homogeneity. This view has been offered by A. Stafford Clayton, who uses the separatist experience of the Netherlands as the basis for his argument. Clayton points out that in the Netherlands "the Primary Education Act of 1920 provided for equal support of private as well as public schools. . . . Since 1920, private primary schools have been founded automatically upon application of a certain minimum number of sponsoring enrollments. Privately controlled secondary schools of a variety of types may also be completely supported from public funds. . . . In the last half of the nineteenth century between 70 and 80 per cent of primary students were in public schools. After 1900 the percentages change, after 1920 more radically, so that in 1958, 28 per cent were in public primary and 72 per cent in private primary schools. Similar changes occurred in secondary schools and in infants' schools. More than 90 per cent of vocational schools are private; four out of eleven universities and technical universities are private."[13]

Clayton also points out that "these changes in the patterns of Dutch schooling are associated with the structure and organization of Dutch society. In the Netherlands the organization of social life is

[13]The quotations in this paragraph and in the two which follow it are from A. Stafford Clayton, "The Effects of Public Support of Church-Related Schools," *Phi Delta Kappan* 47 (1965): 22–24.

dominated by membership in and distinctions between Roman Catholic, Protestant-Christian, and general or neutral associations. Not only do private schools fall into these categories but the organizations and institutions of social life are marked off so that people of the same religious group interact with each other rather than with members of other religious ideologies. Dutch society is organized less in terms of socioeconomic class or ethnic group than in terms of columns of ideological (ultimately theological) belief and doctrine. A column, or pillar, is a block of social organizations encompassing the entire range of group activity—churches, schools, employment, trade unions, professional and occupational organizations, stores, hospitals, sports and leisure time activities, newspapers, radio and television, political and civic activities—so that an individual may spend practically his whole life in contacts with members of his own religious group. Basically, the entire range of group life is organized on a denominational basis. The columns cut across practically all of the areas of social life so that 'to each his own,' in the sense of loyalty to members of his own religious orientation, characterizes the entire range of institutions and associations."

Although Clayton is reluctant to draw any firm conclusion, he notes that "certain forces in American life seem, either intentionally or through lack of attention to the full range of consequences, to encourage the growth of columns based on religious ideologies in this country. . . . The public schools are called 'godless,' frequently in response to efforts to keep the inculcation of ecclesiastical doctrines out of the schools. It is not clear that countervailing conditions in American life are sufficient to resist the weight of forces encouraging the columnizing of our society."

In presenting a counter-argument to this position, Ernest van den Haag concedes that "private schools contribute to cultural heterogeneity; at least that often is their purpose. . . . But, even if the case for cultural homogeneity were quite appealing, should we use financial pressure—be it effective or not—to achieve it? Permitting or persuading is one thing, but attempting to coerce people into a public school when they would prefer private ones is quite another matter. But let that go. Grant, too, that public education helped in bringing American culture and society to their present development. (Other possibilities existed to be sure; the Swiss fared pretty well without using a melting pot.) Do we still need that emphasis on cultural homogeneity and these means? Would the generation or perpetuation of some cultural heterogeneity be bad now? . . . The secular forces of cohesion in the United States are overwhelming. It seems to me that conservation and support of what diversity of cultural tradition remains is likely now, and ultimately, to strengthen them more than insistence on further homogenization. If there is a weak spot in our cohesion, it is not our heterogeneity but our cultural homogeneity; not our religious differences, but the insufficiently transcendent nature of our cohesion, which is influenced by the American standard of living as much as by the idea of America. This is perhaps more likely to be remedied by private than by public schools."[14]

Van den Haag also refers briefly to some of the benefits that may be attributed to private schools. "Their very independence," he writes, "permits them to be more various in their methods, less uniform in their curricula, more adaptable to the needs of minorities, and more experimental than public schools can afford to be. And taxpayers will continue to profit financially from the existence of private schools: whatever subsidy is granted them is not going to cover costs—nor do proponents demand this."

Another argument for the direct public support of private schools is based on the fact that private schools are permitted to exist, and parents are permitted to choose to send their children to these schools. Now, if private schools are inferior to public schools, owing to lack of public support, then the education provided by them may be expected to be inferior to that provided by the public schools. Should children who attend private schools be penalized for decisions their parents make? Since society allows private schools to exist, does it not have a responsibility to insure that these schools are as adequate as the public schools, even if only for the sake of the children who have no choice but to attend them?

R. Freeman Butts has succinctly summarized the dilemma in the issue of direct public support of private schools. "Public schools," he observes, "have a commitment to elevate the civic goal of unity above the particularist goals of special and self-serving interests in the society. This is one of the most sensitive and complicated of all the tasks of public education, for it is extremely difficult to draw the line between the values of diversity (which a democratic society prizes) and of divisiveness (which may threaten the very society it-

[14]The quotations in this paragraph and in the one which follows it are from Ernest van den Haag and Oscar Handlin, "Federal Aid to Parochial Schools: A Debate," *Commentary*, July, 1961, pp. 5–6.

self). Most modern school systems in the world are torn by two conflicting drives: on the one hand, to help build national unity out of diverse racial, cultural, ethnic, religious and linguistic groups, and, on the other, to honor the drive of particularist groups that demand their own schools for the teaching of different languages, religious beliefs, ethnic customs or regional aspirations."[15]

Increased Parental Control Through Vouchers

The present-day American school system is mainly financed by public funds and operated by administrators and teachers who are public employees. As we have already indicated, about 90 per cent of primary and secondary level enrollments are in public schools. Parents of children who are of compulsory school age have little or no choice concerning which schools their children will attend, unless in addition to their school taxes the parents are able to afford the tuition fees for private schooling. As Levin has noted, "the continued existence of [public primary and secondary] schools derives from the fact that they do not have to be effective to survive. In most cases they perform for a captive audience. Pupils are assigned to them for better or for worse, and each school can retain most of its students because the majority of pupils have no other alternatives."[16]

Even if public support were provided for the operation of private primary and secondary schools, the range of individual parental choice would be limited to the types of schools that public and private authorities decided to establish. An innovation that promises to greatly increase parental influence over the schools is the adoption of a system of educational vouchers. A *voucher* is a document (such as a food stamp) that authorizes the purchase of a specified value of goods or services. Thus an educational voucher would be restricted to the purchase of educational services. Under the educational voucher proposal, public funds available for schooling would be given to parents/students in the form of educational vouchers, rather than channeling these funds directly into the operation of public schools or the support of private schools. It would then be the responsibility of parents and/or students to decide where the vouch-

[15]R. Freeman Butts, "The Public Schools: Assaults on a Great Idea," *Nation,* April 30, 1973, p. 558.
   [16]Henry M. Levin, "The Failure of the Public Schools and the Free Market Remedy," *Urban Review,* June, 1968, p. 32.

ers would be spent. Depending on the nature of the specific regulations governing a voucher system, an educational voucher could be spent in a profit-making private school, a nonprofit private school, or in a public school (but the public school would be dependent for its funding on the vouchers it received, rather than on direct public financing, which is presently the case).

The advocates of educational vouchers assume that public support of a school system is in the public interest, but they believe that direct public support of schools is unwarranted. Many proponents of the voucher proposal recognize that a set of regulations would need to be provided to govern the use of the vouchers. Thus it would be possible to have either compulsory or noncompulsory education under the voucher system. If the regulations called for compulsory education, for example, parents would be legally required to send their school-age children to a school eligible to receive vouchers or to engage a competent tutor. The regulations might also specify the racial composition to be maintained in eligible schools, or vouchers of varying amounts might be given to parents of different racial backgrounds to make the vouchers of one ethnic group more attractive to the schools than the vouchers of another ethnic group. Through this procedure of "reverse discrimination" it might be possible to encourage the integration of schools, with the use of positive rather than negative incentives. In addition, the regulations might stipulate that vouchers could be supplemented by private payments, or they might state that no eligible school could accept such supplemental payments.

The basic argument for the voucher plan is that the adoption of the free market principle would probably stimulate competition among schools, thereby improving the quality of education in all schools. Instead of the public schools having, as at present, a monopoly on the provision of publicly supported instruction, the availability of indirect public funding for private schools would encourage the establishment of a variety of new schools. To attract pupils, both private and public schools would make a greater effort to improve the effectiveness of their instructional programs. The proponents of educational vouchers also argue that the schools would be much more willing to try new educational techniques. Parents who wanted to send their children to innovative schools would be much more likely to find such schools available to them if educational vouchers were used. On the other hand, if some parents wanted to send their children to traditional schools, these would also be much more likely to be available. "Here as in other fields," Milton Friedman has written, "competitive private enterprise is likely to be far more efficient in meeting consumer demands than either nationalized [publicly run] enterprises or enterprises run to serve other purposes."[17]

One of the criticisms of the voucher proposal is that it places the burden of choice on parents and students, some of whom may lack the ability to make the best decision. It is argued that the schools may resort to misleading advertising in order to attract students. The answer that has been offered to this objection is that the guidelines for the voucher system can specify which schools are entitled to receive vouchers. If some schools should resort to fraudulent practices or provide totally inadequate instruction, they could be removed from the list of approved institutions.

A much more fundamental argument against the voucher proposal is that it will decrease social cohesion. By providing members of various ethnic and religious groups with the financial capability of sending their children to the private schools of their choice, it is quite conceivable that group loyalties would be fostered at the expense of loyalty to the society as a whole. A defense of the present system of publicly operated schools that expresses this point has been provided by R. Freeman Butts:

> The general quest for "alternatives" to the existing system [such as the voucher proposal] is in part deliberately designed to weaken public education, in part unaware that it may have that effect. It is the convergence and mutual reinforcement of so many forces—political, social, economic, racial, religious and intellectual—that makes the search for "alternatives" so beguiling. But if the American people should become disenchanted with he idea of the public school and turn in significant numbers to other means of education, they will weaken, perhaps beyond repair, a basic component of democratic American society. . . . Achieving a sense of community is the essential purpose of public education. This work cannot be left to the vagaries of individual parents, or small groups of like-minded parents, or particular interest groups, or religious sects, or private enterprisers or cultural specialties. . . . The public schools [should] concentrate as they never have before on the task of building a sense of civic cohesion among all the people of the country. This should become the chief priority for educational planning, curriculum development, organization, research and experimentation. I am not calling for a new patriotism of law and order, nor for loyalty oaths, nor a nationally imposed curriculum in "civics," nor flag salutes, nor recitation of prayers or

[17]Milton Friedman, "The Role of Government in Education," in *Economics and the Public Interest,* ed. Robert A. Solo (New Brunswick, N.J.: Rutgers University Press, 1955), p. 129.

pledges of allegiance. But I do believe that we require the renewal of a civic commitment that seeks to reverse and overcome the trend to segmented and disjunctive "alternatives" serving narrow or parochial or racist interests. . . . We can no more dismantle our public schools, or let them be eroded, than we can dismantle our representative government, or our courts or our free press. This is not to say that important changes are not necessary; it *is* to say that undermining free public education is tantamount to undermining the free society itself.[18]

It is certainly true that some proponents of educational vouchers have not been overly concerned with the divisive effects that might well result from the implementation of the plan. Friedman, for example, believes that if his voucher proposal (which has a minimum of restrictions) were to be accepted, "it would permit a variety of schools to develop, some all white, some all Negro, some mixed. It would permit the transition from one collection of schools to another—hopefully to mixed schools—to be gradual as community attitudes changed. It would avoid the harsh political conflict that has been doing so much to raise social tensions and disrupt the community. It would in this special area, as the market does in general, permit cooperation without conformity."[19]

But other advocates of the educational voucher idea have recognized the possibility that uncontrolled use of vouchers might exacerbate social class and ethnic divisions. Levin, for instance, has suggested that the value of educational vouchers might be "inversely related to family income and wealth. Disadvantaged children might be given vouchers which are worth two or three times the value of the maximum grants given children of the well-to-do. Such a redistributive system of grants would overcome many of the initial market handicaps faced by slum families. Thus, differences in tuition would be based upon relative needs, costs, and the family resources for fulfilling those needs."[20]

Christopher Jencks has proposed a similar solution: Jencks would also require that schools accept any applicant, provided space were available. If the number of applicants exceeded the number of places available, at least half the students accepted in the school

[18]Butts, "The Public Schools: Assaults on a Great Idea," pp. 533–534, 559–560. (Emphasis in the original.)

[19]Quoted in Mark Blaug, *An Introduction to the Economics of Education* (London: Allen Lane The Penguin Press, 1970), p. 312.

[20]Levin, "The Failure of the Public Schools," p. 35.

would be randomly selected from among the total number who applied. The rest of the applicants accepted would be chosen in such a manner as to avoid ethnic discrimination.[21]

Another counter-argument to the position that a publicly operated system of schools is essential for the continued existence of a unified society and a democratic form of government is the view that, under the voucher system, all schools approved to receive vouchers could be required to provide various instructional activities that would impart common societal values. Such a requirement, in fact, is often imposed on private schools within the present-day American school system. Blaug has made the point that if public schools are so vital to social cohesion, then why should any parents now have the right to send their children to private schools? And if wealthy parents are generally the ones who take advantage of this right, why can't it be extended to the less affluent members of society who desire it? In Blaug's view, "to continue to permit the rich to opt out [of the public school system] as they now can is to imply that they stand in no need of being assimilated in the community. It is not enough to say that they have paid their taxes for 'free' state education and to prevent them from paying twice by buying private education out of their own resources would be an intolerant interference with personal liberty. If that is true for them, it is true for everyone, and we are led straight to the proposal to tax everyone for education vouchers. . . . If [the voucher] idea is rejected because it would destroy social solidarity by producing more 'separatist' schools, the implication is that we must deny everyone choice outside the State sector. To advocate State provision of education, while tolerating private education for those who can afford it, is to add insult to injury."[22]

Butts might respond to Blaug's contention, however, by maintaining that as long as the overwhelming majority of students are in public schools, the needs of society will be achieved. Considered as a matter of practical politics, the existence of a relatively small number of private schools can be tolerated as a "safety valve" to accommodate those members of society who are the most dissatisfied with public schooling.

[21]See Judith Areen and Christopher Jencks, "Education Vouchers: A Proposal for Diversity and Choice," in *Education Vouchers: Concepts and Controversies*, ed George R. LaNoue (New York: Teachers College Press, 1972), pp. 48–57.
[22]Blaug, *Economics of Education*, pp. 313–314.

And would a regulated system of vouchers work as well as the voucher advocates claim? George LaNoue has argued that the voucher proposal would not succeed. In the following excerpt he suggests that, in the first place, the coalition of interest groups which might favor the voucher idea and strive to get it adopted is a coalition that wants an unregulated voucher system, not a system regulated in the idealistic manner recommended by Jencks and others: "Those who advocate ideal or model vouchers don't seem to fully recognize the true nature of the voucher constituency. There is a latent coalition prepared to support vouchers, and it won't be led by the gentlemen scholars from Cambridge and Berkeley. . . . It is composed mainly of Southern Protestant nativists and Northern Catholic ethnics—plus, I would add, a touch of the far right and the far left. . . . The danger is, then, that while the intellectual debate focuses on ideal vouchers, the true voucher coalition will rise up to take command of the idea. Once united, that coalition might be able to bring about the kind of unregulated, noncompensatory, constitution-free vouchers that would lead to . . . social disaster."[23]

LaNoue also questions the applicability to schools of the assumption behind the voucher plan that competition based on profit motives will improve education. He believes that the "public schools are not a noncompetitive monopoly like the postal service. They are highly decentralized and they do compete, both with private schools . . . and with each other. . . . Competition in the private school sector does not correspond to market theory either. With the possible exception of the housing industry, most profit-making firms will sell their products to anyone with cash or credit regardless of his race, religion, social background, manners, intelligence, or skills. Private schools, however, generally prefer to be exclusive based on one or more of the above factors. They do not view increasing their share of the market in the same way corporations do."

LaNoue's arguments can be answered, at least to some extent. It may be hoped that if a voucher plan is ever adopted, the desires of the American people to maintain a unified society will be reflected in the regulations of the voucher system. Regarding LaNoue's comments on the inapplicability of the free market principle to the schools, it may be suggested by way of counter-argument that (as

[23]The quotations in this paragraph and in the one which follows it are from George LaNoue, "The Politics of Education," *Teachers College Record* 73 (1971): 314, 318.

LaNoue admits) sufficient evidence is not yet available. To draw conclusions from the present situation may indeed be too risky. Although there are a number of private schools in the present school system, these schools do not seem to compete very much with each other and with the public schools as far as teaching effectiveness is concerned. The reason for this—as was suggested in the discussion of Issue 2—would seem to be that the schools presently utilize a system of student evaluation which results in a rank-ordering of students (norm-referenced grading) instead of assisting all students to attain a specified minimum set of learning outcomes, without fixed time limits. It seems that the free market principle might have a significant effect if the second approach were used, but not with the first.

CONCLUDING COMMENTS

The arguments for and against the moderate proposals have been presented on the assumption that the student motivational control features of the present school system will be retained. But would the cogency of these arguments be altered if compulsory schooling and school system credentialing were abolished or modified, and a planned, society-wide system of reinforcements introduced?

As has already been suggested in the analysis of Issues 2 and 3, different solutions to these questions might indeed be developed if the conventional school system were changed. With respect to Issue 1—although the validity of the arguments pertaining to the locus of governmental control would probably not be affected if compulsory schooling and/or school system credentialing were abolished or modified—the establishment of a planned, society-wide system of reinforcements would entail at least some degree of national control of education. Hence, favoring this radical proposal would probably also entail favoring a change from the present system of local control to more national control.

Chapters 5 and 6 examine more thoroughly the proposals of the radical critics. The comments offered on the radical proposals in this chapter are intended to demonstrate in a preliminary way the major reorientation in our thinking about education that can be expected when the conventional school system is no longer taken for granted.

SUMMARY

Control over education may be exercised by the learner or by someone else; this control may pertain to the ends and/or the means of education. The problem of who should control education is particularly important where the goals of education are involved, since the value judgments of different persons and groups may be expected to differ. The problem of the way education should be controlled is also important, because some procedures may be more effective and/or less costly than others.

Although control may be deliberate or nondeliberate, our concern is with deliberate forms of control. The term "control" shall refer to a situation in which someone has a deliberate effect on someone or something else.

According to the Tenth Amendment to the U.S. Constitution, the formal responsibility for control of the American school system rests with the fifty states (since the authority to control education has not been specifically given to the federal government in the Constitution). With the exception of Hawaii, however, the states have chosen to delegate much of their authority for the control of public primary and secondary schools to local school districts.

One of the moderate proposals for change in the school system control structure involves changing the locus of governmental control over the schools. Some persons favor increased national control rather than local control so that the school system can become more effective in accomplishing national purposes. Others favor an extension of local control in large cities in order to permit community control by smaller and more homogeneous groups (*pluralism*).

Increased teacher control is the focus of the second moderate proposal. One way to accomplish this objective would be to grant public primary and secondary school teachers the right to strike. Those who argue for this right contend that the overall effectiveness of the school sysyem will be improved by giving teachers more control. Those who oppose the right to strike take the opposite point of view. Another solution to the issue of whether teachers should have increased control over the schools is to transform the occupation of teaching into a true profession. But if teachers were to acquire increased control over education, would they use their power for the benefit of students? This raises the question of whether new procedures to increase the accountability of teachers should be instituted. Although some critics of this proposal do not believe a workable system of merit pay for teachers can be devised, greater teacher accountability could probably be achieved if a different method of student evaluation were adopted, and if students were free to select their teachers on the basis of which would be most helpful to them in preparing for prescribed examinations (the free market principle).

A third moderate proposal pertains to increased parental control of the schools. One means of increasing the options open to parents is through the provision of direct public financial support to private schools. The supporters of this idea believe that as long as we permit private schools to exist, we are obligated to insure that their quality is commensurate with the quality of the public schools; otherwise we are harming the children who are required by their parents to attend private schools. The opponents of direct public financial support of private schools contend that this would destroy the public schools, which have a special responsibility for promoting societal cohesion. Another way of increasing parental control over the schools is through the establishment of a system of educational vouchers. This proposal is viewed by its supporters as a way of improving the effectiveness of teaching by requiring schools to compete for students (again, the free market principle). The critics of educational vouchers object to the indirect public financial support for private schools that the adoption of the voucher proposal would provide. These critics also have doubts about whether the benefits claimed for the free market would in fact be realized. Perhaps, however, a change in the present system of student evaluation might increase the feasibility of the voucher proposal.

GENERAL NOTES AND BIBLIOGRAPHY

1. BASIC CONCEPTS. *Power* comes from two sources. Some roles in an organization confer upon their occupants the right to exercise power over others on behalf of the organization. Power that derives from an organizational role ˙(for example, the right of a policeman to use force in order to apprehend law breakers) is usually called *authority*. Power may also be obtained from *nonauthority sources*; for example, a person may have money and use it to influence the behavior of other persons. The occupant of a role in an organization may draw upon nonauthority sources of power; the head of a government, for

example, may have a special talent as a public speaker, which he might use to influence voters to support him.

Some roles in a large organization carry with them the authority to make basic policy decisions (*policy making*). Other organizational roles are primarily concerned with the implementation of these decisions. However, the implementors of policy to some extent also formulate it. For example, a teacher in a classroom must give his own interpretations to the policy directives he receives; these interpretations constitute a form of policy making by the teacher.

The concepts "power" and "authority" are discussed in several sources. For definitions of both terms, see, for example, Arnold M. Rose, *The Power Structure* (New York: Oxford University Press, 1967), pp. 43–53, and Richard A. Schermerhorn, *Society and Power* (New York: Random House, 1961), pp. 1–14. For an extended discussion of the concept of power, see, for example, Adolf Berle, *Power* (New York: Harcourt, Brace and World, 1969) and John R. Champlin, ed., *Power* (New York: Atherton Press, 1971).

2. CONTROL OF THE SCHOOL SYSTEM. The five human behavioral control techniques discussed in Chapter 4 are used in the exercise of control over the school system, with the usual exception of the technique of direct physical/physiological control. There are a number of different ways of conceptualizing the use of these techniques. For example, the policy-making process may be referred to as the process of administration, the political process, and so forth. Similarly, there are a number of ancillary activities related to the exercise of control. For example, data collection and the preparation of plans are activities which facilitate the use of the control techniques. Finally, there are contextual factors pertaining to the school system organization that affect the use of control techniques: types of personnel recruited; interpersonal relationships among personnel; and the values and attitudes that develop within the organization.

The formulation of basic policy for the school system and the exercise of deliberate control within the system involve those in positions of authority in the formal control structure. But there are also mechanisms outside the formal control structure that may be used in the control of schools. For example, various interest groups (such as teachers' organizations) attempt to influence members of the legislature when bills affecting the school system are being considered. Also, a private citizen may write a book criticizing the schools.

In addition, there are many nondeliberate factors that influence behavior within the school system. An excellent example of such a nondeliberate factor is the effect of cultural values on educational policy-makers and students. Another example is the operation of the labor market; in most societies the relative attractiveness of different occupational careers (and hence the relative attractiveness of scholastic programs that lead to these careers) is determined by the effects of supply and demand on wage and salary scales. Various groups, such as the Educational Testing Service and textbook publishers, also have an impact on the schools, simply by performing their services, without necessarily having an intent to influence educational policy.

Colleges and universities in the United States have enjoyed a large measure of autonomy in their operation. According to Lyman A. Glenny, each school "has acted as an independent unit and each has determined its policies and programs, established its customs and procedures, and obtained administrative direction from a single board. Governmental controls have been largely limited to legislative action in establishing the public institutions and providing for their financial support, and to chartering the private institutions. The wide variety of colleges and universities and their programs has, in part, been attributed to the many sources of authority and responsibility for the institutions. Some are church related, others secular; some private, others public; some nonprofit, others capital ventures." This excerpt is from "Colleges and Universities—Government," in *Encyclopedia of Educational Research*, ed. Chester W. Harris (3rd ed., New York: Macmillan, 1960), p. 243.

In recent years, however, a trend toward increased state control of public colleges and universities has become apparent. Particularly important in this connection are the activities of the state coordinating agencies for higher education.

Among the sources that may be consulted for further information on the processes of educational policy formulation are the following: James Bryant Conant, *Shaping Educational Policy* (New York: McGraw-Hill, 1964); Nicholas A. Masters, Robert H. Salisbury and Thomas H. Eliot, *State Politics and* the *Public Schools* (New York: Knopf, 1964); and Marilyn Gittell, *Participants and Participation: A Study of School Policy in New York City* (New York: Center for Urban Education, 1967). The following sources may also be consulted: Alan F. Brown and John H. House, "The Organizational Component in Education," *Review of Educational Research* 37 (1967), pp. 399–416; Charles E. Bidwell, "The School as a Formal Organization," in *Handbook of Organizations,* ed. James G. March (Chicago: Rand McNally, 1965), pp. 972–1022.

3. LOCUS OF GOVERNMENTAL CONTROL. A general source on the issue of the locus of governmental control is C. A. Bowers, Ian Housego and Doris Dyke, eds., *Education and Social Policy* (New York: Random House, 1970). A research study on the administrative decentralization of schools is Melvin Zimet, *Decentralization and School Effectiveness* (New York: Teachers College Press, 1973). Other research studies on the general topic of decentralization are summarized in Carol Lopate et al., "Decentralization and Community Participation in Public Education," *Review of Educational Research* 40 (1970): 135–150. See also: Kenneth W. Haskins, "The Case for Local Control," *Saturday Review,* January 11, 1969, pp. 52–54; Leonard J. Fein, "The Limits of Liberalism," *Saturday Review,* June 20, 1970, 83–85, 95–96.

For treatments of the topic of cultural pluralism in relation to education, see Edgar G. Epps, ed., *Cultural Pluralism* (Berkeley, Calif.: McCutchan, 1974), and Richard Pratte, *The Public School Movement* (New York: McKay, 1973).

4. TEACHER CONTROL. Several aspects of this issue (including teacher strikes and the professionalization of teaching) are reviewed in Donald A. Myers, *Teacher Power—Professionalization and Collective Bargaining* (Lexington, Mass.: Lexington Books, 1973).

For extensive analyses of the topic of teacher strikes within the larger context of collective bargaining, see Myron Lieberman and Michael H. Moskow, *Collective Negotiations for Teachers* (Chicago: Rand McNally, 1966), and Stanley M. Elam, Myron Lieberman and Michael H. Moskow, *Readings on Collective Negotiations in Public Education* (Chicago: Rand McNally, 1967). For a discussion of teacher militancy in relation to university professors, see Everett C. Ladd and Seymour

M. Lipset, *Professors, Unions, and American Higher Education* (Berkeley, Calif.: Carnegie Commission on Higher Education, 1973).

The professional status of teachers is discussed in many sources, including Louise L. Tyler, "Is Teaching a Profession?" *Educational Forum* 28 (1964): 413–421; D.D. Darland, "The Profession's Quest for Responsibility and Accountability," *Phi Delta Kappan* 52 (1970): 40–44; J.M. Paton, "Movements Toward Teacher Autonomy in Canada," *Phi Delta Kappan* 52 (1970): 45–49; Helen Bain, "Self-Governance Must Come First, Then Accountability," *Phi Delta Kappan* 51 (1970): 413; James R. Covert, "Second Thoughts About the Professionalization of Teachers," *Educational Forum* 39 (1975): 149–154.

Teachers—especially those at the university level—have considered academic freedom to be their prerogative. This right, according to Sterling M. McMurrin in "Academic Freedom in the Schools," *Teachers College Record,* May, 1964, is generally understood to mean the freedom of teachers (as well as students) "to engage honestly and openly in the pursuit of knowledge, to enlist fully the instrumentalities of reason and critical intelligence in that quest, and to express and communicate their opinions and ideas without liability, forfeit, or penalty" (p. 659).

Similarly, teachers have argued for the right to determine their own hair style and standards of dress. Many school boards, however, have attempted to restrict the public school teacher's freedom in these areas on the grounds that a teacher must provide an adult model for his students; therefore, the school board must be allowed to regulate a teacher's appearance if it is to be successful in maintaining dress codes for students. This right has become a matter of legal dispute, according to Louis Fischer and David Schimmel in *The Civil Rights of Teachers* (New York: Harper and Row, 1973), p. 152: "Some courts protect grooming under the First Amendment as symbolic speech and under the due process clause of the Fourteenth Amendment. In addition, the concept of 'liberty' in the Fourteenth Amendment can be interpreted to include grooming, and unless it can be shown that beards or hair styles interfere with the operation of the school it is arbitrary to prohibit them. Schools can, however, expect beards and hair to be clean and neat, and worn in a manner that does not invite or encourage disruption of the learning process. Thus, bizarre practices can probably be controlled. . . . The law related to a teacher's dress is somewhat different. Generally the courts uphold a school district's right to impose reasonable regulations. The distinction between hair grooming and clothing is reasonable if one considers the fact that after school hours and away from school a teacher is free to follow his personal taste in clothing. Beards cannot be removed for school hours and replaced at 5:00 p.m. the way dashikis, sandals, miniskirts, or capri pants can."

The term "accountability" has been applied in recent years to a variety of proposals for increasing the efficiency of school management. For a general overview of this topic, see Allan C. Ornstein and Harriet Talmadge, "The Rhetoric and Realities of Accountability," *Today's Education,* September-October, 1973, pp. 70–80. See also Robert J. Nash and Russell M. Agne, "The Ethos of Accountability—A Critique," *Teachers College Record* 73 (1972): 357–370; Edward Wynne, *The Politics of School Accountability* (Berkeley, Calif.: McCutchan, 1972); Robert Taggart, "Accountability and the American Dream," *Educational forum* 39 (1974): 33–42; W. James Popham, "The New World of Accountability: In the Classroom," *NASSP Bulletin,* May, 1972, pp. 25–31.

A contemporary approach that makes use of the concept of accountability is the procedure known as "performance contracting." The idea of performance contracting comes from a recognition that it is not really necessary for administrators of public schools to recruit and supervise their own teachers. Just as a school district engages a private contractor to construct a new school building, it is equally feasible for a private contractor to be hired to provide the educational services the district requires. The contract between the school district and the contractor would specify what the contractor must accomplish before he is reimbursed. In this way the school system would know exactly what it was getting for its money. Because a contractor would want to get the contract, he would utilize the most efficient methods to achieve the goals stipulated in the contract. He might, therefore, decide to make extensive use of audiovisual devices and teaching paraprofessionals, in addition to regular teachers. The teachers, of course, would be accountable to the contractor and the contractor would, in turn, be accountable to the school district.

A major obstacle to the success of the performance contracting approach is the opposition that will very likely come from teachers presently employed by the school system: the adoption of performance contracting would undoubtedly mean that some (or many) teachers would no longer be able to find employment as teachers. The contractor would be very concerned with efficiency; his requirements, as far as teachers are concerned, might differ considerably from those of the school districts that now employ the teachers. Thus, teachers' organizations could be expected to oppose performance contracting. On the other hand, if teacher strikes became a problem for school boards, then the school boards might look with increasing favor on performance contracting. See Jeffry Schiller, "Performance Contracting: Some Questions and Answers," *American Education,* May, 1971, pp. 3–5. The results of recent attempts to introduce performance contracting are discussed in P. Carpenter-Huffman, G.R. Hall and G.C. Sumner, *Change in Education: Insights from Performance Contracting* (Cambridge, Mass.: Ballinger, 1974).

5. PARENTAL CONTROL. The legal basis for public support of sectarian private schools in the United States is treated in Herbert M. Kliebard, ed., *Religion and Education in America: A Documentary History* (Scranton, Penn.: International Textbook Co., 1969), and Michael R. Smith and Joseph E. Bryson, *Church-State Relations: The Legality of Using Public Funds for Religious Schools* (Topeka, Kansas: National Organization on Legal Problems of Education, 1972). Besides the sources cited in the chapter, the following items may be consulted on the pros and cons of the public support question: William W. Brickman, "For and Against Public Aid to Religious Schools," *School and Society* 89 (1961): 247–251; Donald A. Erikson, "Public Funds for Private Schools," *Saturday Review,* September 21, 1968, pp. 66–68, 78–79; Bruce Rosen, "Government Funding for Private Schools: The Australian Experience," *Educational Forum* 39 (1975): 317–328.

Recent debate on the voucher proposal is surveyed in Evan Jenkins, "Stand By for Vouchers," *Compact,* November-December, 1973, pp. 7–9. See also Theodore R. Sizer, "The Case for a Free Market," *Saturday Review,* January 11, 1969, pp. 34–42, 90; Edward J. Fox and William B. Levenson, "In Defense of the 'Harmful Monopoly,'" *Phi Delta Kappan* 51 (1969): 131–135.

CONTROL TECHNIQUES

CHAPTER 4

The general problem of how control is exercised must now be considered in some detail. This topic is very important, because a common characteristic of the three radical proposals for change in educational control is their concern with the motivation of students. And, as we shall see, motivation is one of the basic techniques for the control of human behavior.

Another reason the general problem of what it means to control someone requires special attention is that an understanding of control techniques will provide a deeper insight into why control over students is necessary. Also, a better idea can be gained of the alternatives that are available to the control techniques presently being utilized in the school system.

HUMAN BEHAVIORAL CONTROL TECHNIQUES

As Cartwright has pointed out, "anyone wishing to gain a fundamental understanding of the nature of social influence must be prepared to cope with a literature that is scattered, heterogeneous, and even chaotic. Relevant contributions have come from the disciplines of psychology, sociology, political science, economics, anthropology, and philosophy. Theorists who have attempted to impose some order upon this literature have found it to be exceedingly intractable."[1]

Despite these difficulties, a preliminary classification of the techniques for control of human behavior will be presented here. We

[1]Dorwin Cartwright, "Influence, Leadership, Control," in *Handbook of Organizations*, ed. James G. March (Chicago: Rand McNally, 1965), p. 3.

shall use the term "behavior" in a broad sense, to include mental behavior (thinking, feeling, and so forth) as well as overt behavior.
The effect of a control technique may be to elicit a behavior, to maintain an existing behavior, to inhibit or eliminate a behavior, or to
produce a new behavior.

Our classification consists of five categories; it was developed
from a variety of sources and is offered on a tentative basis. It does
seem to accord, however, with several previous attempts to classify
the techniques of control. (Note 1)

It should be emphasized that any single procedure actually
used to control human behavior may exemplify the operation of
more than one of the control techniques in the classification. For example, a stimulus used to motivate may also bring about learning.
Moreover, some of the control techniques are seldom used independently. Motivational control, for instance, is frequently used in conjunction with learning control.

Elicitation and Guidance of Responses

Perhaps the simplest technique for behavioral control is the
provision of a stimulus in order to elicit a response or guide an individual in the performance of a response. For example, the pupils
of a person's eyes may be caused to contract by shining a bright light
into them. In this case, the response is considered to be an innate
reflex—an automatic, unlearned response to a stimulus. If a person
has previously learned to be afraid of the dark, we can elicit the response of fear by placing him in a dark room. The white line painted
along the center of a highway illustrates the use of a stimulus to
guide a previously learned response (driving): the driver is better
able to judge the position of his car on the road by observing the
white line.

In the above examples it is assumed that the individual is sufficiently motivated to respond to the stimulus and that he has already
experienced the relevant learning, if any is required. The function
of the eliciting or guiding stimulus, therefore, is merely to "trigger"
a response or to serve as a guide in the performance of a response.
(Note 2)

Eliciting and guiding responses is widely used as a control
technique in connection with the educative process. Teachers frequently request their students to do certain things; such requests

constitute eliciting stimuli, since the students presumably have already learned how to execute the requests and are sufficiently motivated to do so.

Learning Control

Another technique for the control of human behavior is that of causing someone to learn something (the deliberate management of the learning process). This technique has, of course, already been defined as "education." But it is necessary to include a discussion of learning control (education) at this point, because this is one of the fundamental techniques for the control of human behavior. It also presents a further opportunity to consider the nature of learning.

As stated in our definition, learning may result in either of two outcomes—the acquisition of the *capability* of exhibiting new or changed behavior, or an *increase in the probability* that new or changed behavior will be forthcoming when elicited by a relevant stimulus. From the point of view of human behavior control, the first of these is not in any way certain to affect an individual's behavior in a particular situation in which a relevant stimulus is present. For a person to act in accordance with a capability he has learned, a particular situation must contain the appropriate motivational factors, as well as the relevant eliciting stimulus. Thus successful education would not be sufficient to insure that a new or changed response is elicited by the relevant stimulus. An individual who has, for example, learned a foreign language in school will presumably not utilize this learning in his later behavior unless he is in a situation (such as being in a relevant foreign country) where he will benefit from its use. To take another illustration, a person who has learned a particular moral precept (for example, "Do not lie") may not always apply this precept in his later behavior. It is probable that this person has also learned from other experiences the consequences of acting in a manner contrary to the moral precept (for example, that lying may result in certain benefits, and that if caught, the person may not always be punished). In a given situation, therefore, the individual will evaluate the effects of acting in accordance with, and contrary to, the moral precept; the behavior he or she exhibits will reflect this assessment of consequences. Thus, in a particular situation the person may decide not to act in accordance with the moral precept previously learned, if he or she comes to believe that lying (another capability he has acquired) will produce the greater net benefits.

From this analysis we note that in situations in which the behaving individual is regarded as able to exercise a choice, motivational control (which shall be examined next) must be used in conjunction with the control of learning experiences if we want a person to act in accordance with a specified set of learning outcomes. Yet the context of rewards and punishments in which human behavior takes place is often ignored when the efficacy of education is being considered. If an individual fails to act as expected on the basis of certain controlled learning experiences, the assumption is frequently made that these learning experiences have failed to produce the desired learning outcomes. However, instead of attributing this failure to education, it would seem more correct to view the individual as acting within the prevailing structure of rewards and punishments in such a way as to either improve or minimize any decrease in the net pleasantness of his or her situation (according to the person's own perceptions of these outcomes). The individual draws upon a repertoire of learned behavioral capabilities (some of which are alternatives to each other) and selects the behavior he or she deems most appropriate for the situation.

But the second type of learning outcome—that which results in an increased probability that new or changed behavior will be elicited by a relevant stimulus—must inevitably have an effect upon an individual's behavior when the relevant stimulus is present. Successful education in this case will be sufficient to increase the probability that a new or changed response will be elicited. An excellent illustration of the attainment of this type of learning outcome is found in the learning procedure known as *classical conditioning.* Berelson and Steiner describe classical conditioning as a situation in which, after "a new stimulus is repeatedly paired with another stimulus that automatically elicits a certain response, the new one alone gradually becomes capable of eliciting the same or a similar response." They point out that "the involuntary and automatic character of the conditioned response . . . removes it from conscious control and sometimes even from awareness." The original experiments on classical conditioning were conducted by Pavlov, who used a dog in his most famous experiment. Berelson and Steiner describe this experiment: "A dog is harnessed so that he can be fed and his salivation measured accurately. Whenever he eats, saliva flows automatically as a normal physiological response to food in the mouth. (Food in the mouth is said to be an 'unconditioned stimulus' that elicits the 'unconditioned response' of salivation.) At first the sound of a bell produces no increase in saliva, but after a series of trials in which it rings just before food is delivered, the bell alone will produce salivation. The bell has become a 'conditioned stimulus' capable of eliciting the 'conditioned response' of salivation, and it will continue to do so over a number of trials—even if it is not accompanied or followed ('reinforced') by food."[2]

Several theories have been proposed to explain the learning process (one of these is the Pavlovian theory of classical conditioning, which we have just discussed). A basic point of view about the learning process that is shared by several of these theories is the assumption that a person can be caused to learn through the use of *reinforcements*. (A reinforcement may be defined as something which gives the recipient satisfaction.) Reinforcements may be classified as positive or negative. The provision of a *positive* reinforcement is illustrated by saying the word "good" after someone has done something. If a person is subjected to an *aversive* (unpleasant) stimulus, whatever action taken afterwards to reduce or eliminate the impact of the aversive stimulus will be satisfying. The reduction or elimination of an aversive stimulus is known as *negative* reinforcement.

The use of negative reinforcement is often demonstrated in the laboratory by placing an animal in a cage, the floor of which provides an electric shock. The animal then tries to escape from the cage by pressing various levers. When it presses the appropriate lever the door opens and the animal is able to leave the cage. When returned to the cage, the animal will probably press the appropriate lever immediately, indicating that learning has taken place. The reinforcement that produced this learning was the removal of the aversive electric shock stimulus, following the lever-pressing response of the animal the first time it was in the cage. (Note 3)

A final point must be made concerning the use of the learning process as a technique of behavior control: a learning outcome is not necessarily permanent. Some things we learn we may never forget, but other things learned may be highly transient (for example, a

[2]Bernard Berelson and Gary A. Steiner, *Human Behavior: An Inventory of Scientific Findings* (New York: Harcourt, Brace and World, 1964), pp. 136–138.

telephone number we look up in the directory and remember just long enough to dial). To be sure that a learning outcome once attained is still effective in controlling behavior, it may be necessary to engage in periodic re-education.

Motivational Control

Ordinarily, the use of the learning process to control human behavior requires the individual to be sufficiently *motivated* to participate in the learning situation and/or to make the required responses. The term "motivation" refers to that process which energizes behavior—that is, the process that heightens a person's state of arousal or invigorates his responses.[3] In the example of negative reinforcement given above, it is the electric shock that provides the motivation.

Cofer and Appley, in their comprehensive review of motivational theory, discuss the possible mechanisms through which motivation may be induced. They speculate that stimuli previously associated with a rewarding experience may cause an individual to anticipate a recurrence of this rewarding experience, thereby arousing or invigorating the individual. In the case of hunger, "invigoration occurs, not as an inevitable consequence of [food] deprivation but as an effect of anticipations instigated by stimuli that have accompanied feeding. On the other hand, anticipations may develop or occur in the absence of deprivation: cues [stimuli] associated with a sweet taste or sexual satisfaction may arouse an organism, even though it is sated for food and has not been subjected to prolonged sexual abstinence."[4]

As Cofer and Appley point out, anticipation is brought about by learning. Thus the anticipation mechanism for inducing motivation "can only work *after* learning has occurred. What can we say," they ask, "of cases in which learning is unnecessary for motivated behavior to occur?" They suggest that the internal state of the organism (food deprivation, hormone levels, and so forth) may sensitize it to certain stimuli. Thus "the presence of the appropriate stim-

---

[3]Motivation shall be referred to as a process, although—as in the case of learning—more than one process may be involved.

[4]C.N. Cofer and M.H. Appley, *Motivation: Theory and Research* (New York: Wiley. 1964), pp. 822–823.

uli serves to excite or arouse the animal. This may be an innate effect, probably modifiable by learning. In addition, the stimuli can guide or elicit the responses which comprise the instinctive act sequence. The occurrence of responses from this sequence may contribute further to arousal and to the subsequent unfolding of the later innate acts in the sequence."[5]

Now let us consider how the motivational level of a person may be controlled. The basic procedure involves the use of positive and aversive stimuli. There are three principal ways in which these stimuli may be utilized in order to get someone to do something. One of these procedures makes use of positive stimuli. The positive stimulus may be provided to the person after he or she has done what is desired, or it may be promised or even given before he or she performs the stipulated activity. This procedure shall be called *positive motivation.*

In using positive motivation it is recognized that asking a person to do something may require him or her to do something disagreeable. However, by making the reward very attractive, we hope to do more than compensate the individual for his or her efforts, so that a net improvement in the pleasantness of his situation will result. In effect, when positive motivation is used a person is given the choice of remaining as well off as he or she is (by electing not to act in such a way as to obtain our reward), or of increasing the overall pleasantness of his situation (by deciding to act in such a manner as to earn the reward).

The remaining two ways of motivating human beings involve the use of aversive stimuli. The characteristic that makes these two procedures fundamentally different from each other is the timing of the use of aversive stimuli relative to the actions of the person being motivated. Under the procedure labeled *aversive motivation,* the stimulus is applied or threatened *before* the person has acted, either (1) if it appears that the individual will do something not desired, or (2) if the individual has not yet done something desired. The expectation is that this procedure will induce the individual to act in accordance with our wishes. Under the procedure that shall be termed *punishment,* an aversive stimulus is administered to a person *after* he has acted. The purpose of a punishment is to deter the individual from repeating the action.

The use of aversive motivation is illustrated by a parent or

[5]Ibid., pp. 823–824. (Emphasis in the original.)

teacher's informing a child that love for the child will be withdrawn if the child does not make an effort to learn, or by a teacher's telling a student that he or she is presently failing a course and must work harder to improve. An example of the use of punishment is the scolding of a child for taking cookies from the cookie jar.

When aversive motivation is used, the person being motivated is confronted with two unpleasant choices (the choice of doing something otherwise preferable not to do, or the choice of experiencing an aversive stimulus), and he or she presumably would choose the less disagreeable alternative. Thus, by deliberately making the aversive stimulus extremely unpleasant, it is ordinarily possible to get a person to do something that he or she might otherwise be quite reluctant to do. From the point of view of the person to whom aversive motivation is applied, it may seem that no real choice is being offered, for regardless of the option selected, it is obvious that an overall decrease in the pleasantness of his situation will be the result.

If aversive motivation is perceived unfavorably by the person to whom it is applied, then why is it used instead of positive motivation? There would seem to be at least two reasons. First, under some circumstances, it may be more effective than positive motivation. For example, a patriotic soldier who has been taken prisoner may refuse to give his captors any information, despite positive inducements offered; but if he is tortured or his life is threatened, he may then consent to provide information. Second, the use of aversive motivation under some circumstances may be more convenient and/or less costly than positive motivation. Rather than offer a child a bicycle if he does something, it may seem easier to a parent to threaten the child with, say, the loss of television privileges if the child does not obey.

Punishment—unless it is absolutely certain to follow an action and has negative characteristics that clearly outweigh the benefits to be gained from performing the action—is not a very effective deterrent. The reason for this is that the punishing stimulus does not eliminate the reward the individual accrues from performing the action. Therefore, the individual will probably still desire to perform the action, and attempt to perform the forbidden action when it appears that the punishment can be circumvented. But if a significant punishment always follows the desired action (and is perceived as inevitable by the person who desires to act), then the benefits of the action will probably be counter-balanced and offset by its negative consequences, so that the action will no longer be viewed as desirable. An effective way to get a child to stop stealing cookies from the cookie jar might be to add a large quantity of red pepper to the cookie recipe; a mere possibility of punishment by the mother might lead the child to steal cookies when the mother is away, or when someone else could be blamed for their loss.

For all practical purposes, the stimuli which constitute reinforcements may also be regarded as motivational stimuli. Hence Skinner's analysis of the different effects that are attributed to different schedules of reinforcement may be interpreted in motivational terms. According to Skinner, one way that positive motivational or reinforcing stimuli may be provided is on the basis of the number of times a person exhibits a desired behavior—for example, a reinforcement may be given after every desired performance, or after every five. If such a schedule of motivational stimuli—which Skinner calls *ratio* reinforcement—is utilized, "a very high rate of response" may be generated. "Any slight increase in rate [of performance] increases the rate of reinforcement with the result that the rate [of performance] should rise still further. If no other factor intervened, the rate should reach the highest possible value. A limiting factor, which makes itself felt in industry, is simple fatigue." Another way to provide reinforcements and positive motivational stimuli is on the basis of a fixed time interval. This reinforcement schedule, which Skinner calls *fixed-interval* reinforcement, is utilized by employers who pay employees a monthly or weekly salary. But as Skinner points out, "payment for work at the end of each week would generate only a small amount of work just before pay-time." Therefore, employers who pay salaries (which, it should be remembered, are a form of positive motivation) invariably resort to the use of aversive motivation as well. The employer's "main aversive stimulation is the threat of dismissal. . . . The boss threatens dismissal, or some measure which is effective because it is a step toward dismissal, whenever the employee slows down; he removes that threat when the employee speeds up."[6] (Note 4)

The preceding discussion of ratio and fixed-interval reinforcement schedules is very significant for the operation of the school system. The major rewards offered by the school system are those provided on a fixed-interval basis—the grades given at the end of a

[6]B. F. Skinner, *Science and Human Behavior* (New York: Free Press, 1965), pp. 102, 388.

school term, the school certificate awarded upon completion of a program of study which involves a specified number of school terms. Thus the school system uses fixed-interval reinforcement which, as is pointed out above, is generally much less effective than ratio reinforcement. To make fixed-interval reinforcement work to a reasonable extent, the school system must also utilize aversive motivational control—even in the university, which students are not ordinarily compelled to attend. Much like an employer who pays a salary, university professors find it necessary to threaten students with low grades or dismissal from the university if they do not perform as expected.

Direct Physical / Physiological Control

Unlike the three basic control techniques previously described, this one involves direct physical manipulation of the body or direct physiological intervention. An illustration of direct physical manipulation is the case of a person who undergoes surgery to have parts of his body removed, repaired, or replaced. Surgical procedures invariably have an effect (actual or potential) on behavior. Direct physiological intervention is illustrated by the administration of drugs that affect the functioning of the individual: barbiturates may be given to a person, for example, causing him to go to sleep. (Note 5)

For persons involved in education, the most interesting possibilities in the direct physical/physiological control of human beings are the uses of chemicals to facilitate learning and to bring about the transfer of learning by chemical means. Research conducted on the chemical basis of learning is described by Dingman and Sporn: "The possibility that the phenomena of learning and memory might be reflections of specific chemical events occurring in the brain did not receive serious investigative attention until the mid 1950's. . . . In general, the relevant experiments fall into three categories: those that hunt for alterations in brain metabolism or brain molecules occurring in conjunction with the learning of a new task or conditioned response; those that explore (by means of drug-induced alterations in brain metabolism) those aspects of brain metabolism and function that appear to be necessary for the establishment of memory traces; and those that attempt to transfer a memory trace or traces from one animal to another by means of cell-free extracts of the brain. . . . There is an innate resistance on the part of many investigators to the possibility that memory or learning aptitude for a specific task or conditioned response could be transferred from one animal to another by means of chemical extracts from a trained brain. Therefore, workers pursuing this approach to the problem must make every effort to conduct their experiments critically and to provide numerous controls so as to rule out as completely as possible any positive results of an artifactual nature. Negative results . . . have often been more kindly accepted by the scientific community than positive results. Nevertheless, an increasing number of scientists believe that they are beginning to observe truly positive results."[7]

Access Control

Whenever any one of the four techniques for human behavior control discussed above is employed, it must be made available to the person it is intended to influence. Since some type of effort is usually required to bring a person into contact with one of these four control techniques, whatever is deliberately done to facilitate or restrict access to situations involving these four control techniques shall be regarded as constituting a fifth, indirect form of control. This fifth technique shall be called *access control*.

In fact, access control shall be considered to exist whenever access is intentionally afforded to a deliberate *or* nondeliberate control situation. Thus access control is exercised if a person is deliberately exposed to a learning situation, regardless of whether it is a managed or an inadvertent one. Once access control is used with respect to a learning situation, we shall regard that learning situation as being a managed one (education), irrespective of whether it was guided initially.

There are several procedures commonly involved in the exercise of access control. One is to limit (or increase) the extent of a person's environment by placing (or removing) physical restraints— for instance, by sending someone to prison we restrict his or her environment. Access control may be exerted by providing (or withholding) economic resources—for example, we may give a person ten

[7]C. Wesley Dingman and Michael B. Sporn, "Learning: Chemical Basis of Learning," in *Encyclopedia of Education,* ed. Lee C. Deighton (New York: Macmillan, 1971), 5: 429, 431, 433.

thousand dollars, thus increasing his or her capabilities for doing things. A person's access to social roles can be controlled, which would thereby affect opportunities for experience. Things can be placed in a person's environment, thereby increasing the possibilities for experience, or censorship can be imposed. As Ralph Barton Perry has noted, "whoever determines what alternatives shall be made known to man controls what that man shall choose *from*. He is deprived of freedom in proportion as he is denied access to *any* ideas, or is confined to any range of ideas short of the totality of relevant possibilities."[8] (Note 6)

The technique of access control has a particular significance for the conduct of educational activities. Before a person can learn, he or she ordinarily must have access to a learning situation. Through access control, therefore, control can be exercised over the kinds of learning experiences a person will be able to realize, and thus control can be exerted indirectly over the learning outcomes achieved.

CONTROL OF EDUCATION: THE RADICAL PROPOSALS

The basic elements in the educational means-ends chain and their relationships may be represented as follows:

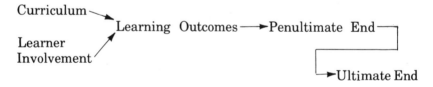

Even in this simplified diagram it is necessary to depict the educational means-ends chain as a complex one, since at least two different means ("Curriculum" and "Learner Involvement") converge to produce "Learning Outcomes." If someone is able to exercise control over the educational means-ends chain, then he has the ability to influence one or more of the elements in the chain; he may, for ex-

---

[8]Quoted in B. F. Skinner, "Freedom and the Control of Men," in *Control of Human Behavior,* eds. Roger Ulrich, Thomas Stachnik and John Mabry (Glenview, Ill.: Scott, Foresman, 1966), p. 15. (Emphasis in the original.)

ample, make decisions concerning the curriculum or learner involvement with the curriculum, determine what learning outcomes should be accomplished, or determine the penultimate and/or ultimate end of education.

The involvement of learners with the curriculum is an element in the educational means-ends chain that is frequently overlooked, yet it is an element in which control techniques play a very important role. The technique of access control is usually necessary to make a directed learning situation available to the prospective learner. In fact, in the case of a naturally occurring learning situation, it is through access control (as noted above) that control is also acquired over the learning situation. For example, we may take a child to the countryside with the expectation that he will acquire an appreciation of the beauty of the landscape. Although we have not created the landscape, we have been able to manage the learning situation through access control. Another basic technique for bringing about learner participation is motivational control. In the school system, positive and/or aversive motivational procedures are extensively utilized to induce students to become passive recipients of learning experiences and/or to make an effort to learn: students may be praised for attaining desired learning outcomes, or they may be threatened with failure if they do not complete their school assignments. For prospective learners who are already motivated, the technique of elicitation and guidance of responses may be used; a teacher may, for instance, tell a student to look at the blackboard, consult a page of the textbook, and so forth.

Participation in a learning situation may also be fostered by a prior use of a controlled learning situation. An example of this would be a parent who tells his child about the benefits that can be derived from attending the university—in this case the parent is causing the child to learn about the advantages of university attendance, in order to increase the probability that the child will decide to participate in the learning situations that are provided by the university. (The parent in this illustration is also resorting to motivational control, but is using learning control as well, which is the point of the example.) Even direct physical/physiological control may be employed to induce a prospective learner to participate in a learning situation, as in the case of students who are given tranquilizers to make them more tractable in the classroom.

In the past decade, however, a number of educational critics have raised strong objections to three important student motivational control features of the existing school system. One of these features is the use of aversive motivation, which is applied to virtually every person in the United States between the ages of six and sixteen, to get them to attend school and to make an effort to learn within the school. This aversive motivation is the result of compulsory school attendance laws or the placement of children in schools by parents, combined with the threat of societal, parental and/or teacher displeasure if the child does not attend school or if he refuses to make an effort to learn within school.

The school system provides positive, as well as negative, reinforcements; but the incentive structure that prevails within the school system has not been systematically correlated with the incentive structure that exists outside the schools. We shall consider the lack of a society-wide, planned system of reinforcements to be a second student motivational control feature of the present school system. A third student motivational control feature of the present school system is its credentialing function, which includes as an ancillary activity the norm-referenced grading of students to determine who shall receive a credential and who shall not (norm-referenced grading results in a rank-ordering of students and is to be differentiated from criterion-referenced grading, which indicates whether the student has achieved stipulated learning outcomes). The degrees, diplomas and other certificates issued by the schools are highly valued by students and thus constitute important rewards; norm-referenced grading may have either a positive or an aversive motivational effect. Since these three student motivational control features are basic to the operation of contemporary school systems, we shall regard them as the defining characteristics of what we shall call the *conventional school system.*

Because the elimination or modification of compulsory schooling and school system credentialing and the establishment of a planned, society-wide incentive system would, for the student, entail a *radical* change in the control of the school system, the advocates of these proposals are generally termed the *radical critics* of education. Chapters 5 and 6 are devoted to a consideration of the radical proposals for the reform of the school system. These suggestions warrant serious and careful attention—regardless of whether they appear to have merit or not—because they will require an examination of some of the most fundamental assumptions about schooling.

The six policy issues discussed in Part II are by no means the only important ones that can be raised about the "who" and the "how" of educational control. For example, basic questions about access control have not been included. Because it is an indirect control technique, however, access control probably can best be discussed in relation to the educational outcomes it is intended to achieve. Hence access control is treated under the "goals of education."

It must be kept in mind at all times that the two fundamental questions about the control and goals of education are inseparable. Decisions relative to the "who" and the "how" of the control of education will, of course, have a profound effect on the educational goals selected and achieved.

SUMMARY

In this chapter brief descriptions of the five major techniques for the control of human behavior are given. The first of these has been labeled the *elicitation and guidance of responses*. When this technique is used, it is assumed that the person is sufficiently motivated to respond, and that he or she has already acquired those learning outcomes (if any) required for the response. The function of this control technique is to "trigger" a response.

A second control technique is that of *control of learning situations*. Learning is a process that produces the capability of exhibiting new or changed human behavior, or which increases the probability that new or changed behavior will be elicited by a relevant stimulus. Some learning outcomes, therefore, have an automatic effect on a person's behavior when a relevant stimulus is present; other learning outcomes, however, may be utilized at the discretion of the learner. In the latter case, the incentive structure in which the learner finds himself is a major factor in determining which behavior he will exhibit.

There are several theories about the learning process, some of which assume that a *reinforcement* after a learner has made the desired response will cause learning to take place. A reinforcement m⌐y be positive (the presentation of a rewarding stimulus) or negative (the removal of an aversive stimulus).

Motivational control constitutes a third control technique. The term "motivation" refers to that process which energizes behavior— that is, the process which heightens a person's state of arousal or invigorates his responses. The principal procedures for the motivation of human beings are the uses of positive motivation, aversive motivation, and punishment. Positive motivation entails the provision of a positive stimulus after the desired behavior has taken place, or the offer of such a stimulus before the desired behavior occurs. Aversive motivation entails the application of an aversive stimulus (or the threat of such an application) before behavior takes place. Punishment involves the presentation of an aversive stimulus after behavior that was not desired has taken place.

A fourth control technique is *direct physical/physiological control*. This technique is illustrated by the use of drugs to control behavior. A fifth technique is *access control*. This technique constitutes an indirect means for controlling human behavior. Access control is the deliberate facilitation or restriction of access to control situations (these situations may involve deliberate or nondeliberate control). It is a control technique of basic importance in education, since a learning situation usually needs to be made accessible to the student if education is to take place.

Several proposals for reform in the present structure for the control of the American school system have been advanced. Some of these proposals do not entail a change in student motivational control features of the existing school system. These proposals, which were called the "moderate proposals" for change, were discussed in Chapter 3. But still others have been directed against the three important student motivational control features of the present school system. These proposals call for: the elimination or modification of the use of aversive motivation in the schools; the establishment of an incentive structure within the school system that is part of a society-wide, planned system of reinforcements; and a discontinuation or modification of the practice of issuing degrees, diplomas, and other school system credentials on the basis of norm-referenced grading. We shall call these the "radical proposals" for changes in the control structure of the school system since, from the point of view of the student, they would involve major changes in the control of schools. The three student motivational control features of the existing school system shall be regarded as defining characteristics of what we shall call the *conventional school system*.

GENERAL NOTES AND BIBLIOGRAPHY

1. CONTROL TECHNIQUES. Although study of the techniques for deliberate control of human behavior is not confined to any one

field, the field of social psychology is probably the most important single discipline, particularly with respect to the topics of learning and motivational control. Thus, as a general supporting field for educational studies, social psychology would seem to deserve a preeminent position.

One of the earliest classifications of the basic techniques for the control of human behavior is Frederick E. Lumley, *Means of Social Control* (New York: Century, 1925). A more recent attempt to synthesize knowledge about most of the control techniques is James T. Tedeschi, ed., *The Social Influence Processes* (Chicago: Aldine-Atherton, 1972). The following sources are also particularly useful for a discussion of more than one control technique: Dorwin Cartwright, ed., *Studies in Social Power* (Ann Arbor: Institute for Social Research, University of Michigan, 1959); Dorwin Cartwright, "Influence, Leadership, Control," in *Handbook of Organizations,* ed. James G. March (Chicago: Rand McNally, 1965), pp. 1–47; William A. Hunt, *Human Behavior and Its Control* (Cambridge, Mass.: Schenkman, 1971); and John Mann, *Changing Human Behavior* (New York: Scribner's, 1965).

2. ELICITATION AND GUIDANCE OF RESPONSES. This control technique is referred to in most psychology textbooks. It is specifically identified as a control technique in *The Social Influence Processes,* ed. Tedeschi, p. 14: "If P is aware that a particular stimulus or cue reliably elicits response x from W, then P can control response W_x by controlling the discriminative stimulus. In effect, by gaining control over the discriminable stimuli, P narrows the range of possible outcomes which W may attain."

3. LEARNING CONTROL. For extended discussions of the concept of learning, see: B. Paul Komisar, "More on the Concept of Learning," in *Psychological Concepts in Education,* eds. B. Paul Komisar and C. B. J. Macmillan (Chicago: Rand McNally, 1967), pp. 211–223; D. W. Hamlyn, "The Logical and Psychological Aspects of Learning," in *The Concept of Education,* ed. R. S. Peters (New York: Humanities Press, 1967), pp. 24–43; and Godfrey Vesey, "Conditioning and Learning," in *The Concept of Education,* ed. Peters, pp. 61–72. The important distinction between how learning outcomes are *acquired* and how *performance* in accordance with these outcomes is induced has been noted by many writers. Goslin, for example, gives special

attention to this point in his "Introduction," in *Handbook of Socialization Theory and Research*, ed. David A. Goslin (Chicago: Rand McNally, 1969).

An excellent survey of the present status of knowledge in the field of learning theory is contained in Ernest R. Hilgard and Gordon H. Bower, *Theories of Learning* (3rd ed.; New York: Appleton-Century-Crofts, 1966). Classical conditioning is thoroughly discussed in Gregory A. Kimble, *Hilgard and Marquis' Conditioning and Learning* (2nd ed.; New York: Appleton-Century-Crofts, 1961). The study of what is known as "vicarious" or "incidental" learning has provided some theoretical explanations of those learning situations in which a person does not respond overtly (as in the case of a student's attending a lecture or watching a demonstration); see, for example, Albert Bandura and Richard H. Walters, *Social Learning and Personality Development* (New York: Holt, Rinehart and Winston, 1963). Most learning theories deal with he phenomenon of learning through practice—that is, with situations in which the learner makes an overt response and learns gradually. For a survey of relevant research on skill learning, see Edward A. Bilodeau, ed., *Acquisition of Skill* (New York: Academic Press, 1966). The phenomenon of learning through insight or discovery is explained by those learning theories which focus on discovery learning. The role of reinforcements in learning has been studied extensively by B. F. Skinner; see his *Contingencies of Reinforcement: A Theoretical Analysis* (New York: Appleton-Century-Crofts, 1969).

4. MOTIVATIONAL CONTROL. Several excellent surveys of the theory and research on motivation have been produced. See, for example, Charles N. Cofer and Mortimer H. Appley, *Motivation: Theory and Research* (New York: Wiley, 1964); J. W. Atkinson, *An Introduction to Motivation* (Princeton, N.J.: Van Nostrand, 1964); Leonard Berkowitz, "Social Motivation," in *The Handbook of Social Psychology*, ed. Gardner Lindzey and Elliot Aronson (2nd ed.; Reading, Mass.: Addison-Wesley, 1969), 3: 50–135; and Dalbir Bindra and Jane Stewart, eds., *Motivation* (2nd ed.; Baltimore, Md.: Penguin Books, 1971).

The role of rewards and punishments in the control of human behavior is recognized in many theoretical formulations in sociology and political science. For a general approach, see J. W. Thibaut and H. H. Kelley, *The Social Psychology of*

Groups (New York: Wiley, 1959). Whereas the ethical aspects of using rewards to control behavior are relatively noncontroversial, this is not the case with aversive motivation and punishment. See B. F. Skinner, *Beyond Freedom and Dignity* (New York: Knopf, 1971); Rudolf J. Gerber and Patrick D. McAnany, eds., *Contemporary Punishment: Views, Explanations, and Justifications* (Notre Dame, Ind.: University of Notre Dame Press, 1972); Stanley E. Grupp, ed., *Theories of Punishment* (Bloomington: Indiana University Press, 1971), and Herbert L. Packer, *The Limits of the Criminal Sanction* (Stanford, Calif.: Stanford University Press, 1968). For an assessment of the empirical research on punishment, see R. L. Solomon, "Punishment," *American Psychologist* 19 (1964): 239–253.

5. DIRECT PHYSICAL/PHYSIOLOGICAL CONTROL. Various aspects of this topic are covered in Seymour M. Farber and Roger H. L. Wilson, *Control of the Mind* (New York: McGraw-Hill, 1961). For a review of the research on learning as a chemical phenomenon, see C. Wesley Dingman and Michael B. Sporn, "Learning: Chemical Basis of Learning," in *Encyclopedia of Education,* ed. Lee C. Deighton (New York: Macmillan, 1971), 5: 424–435.

6. ACCESS CONTROL. As we shall see in other chapters, access control is an important factor in relation to the goals of education. In particular, in Chapter 10 the notion of an "educative society" will be examined and discussed.

A general treatment of access control does not seem to exist. However (as shall be noted in Chapter 10), several works on the "learning society" have been produced. Also (as shall be noted in Chapter 8), the topic of equal access to education is dealt with extensively. Another aspect of access control for which considerable literature exists is the topic of sensory deprivation. See, for example, Philip E. Kubzansky, "The Effects of Reduced Environmental Stimulation on Human Behavior: A Review," in *The Manipulaton of Human Behavior,* eds. Albert D. Biderman and Herbert Zimmer (New York: Wiley, 1961), pp. 51–95.

RADICAL PROPOSALS FOR
CONTROL CHANGE

Chapter 5

Because of the fundamental character of the radical challenge to conventional schooling, and the insight into the educative process that can be gained from an examination of the radical criticism, two chapters are devoted to the radical proposals for control change. As has already been explained (in Chapter 4), the radical proposals for control change are directed against three student motivational control features of the conventional school system: (1) the use of aversive motivation to induce student participation, (2) the lack of a planned, society-wide system of reinforcements, and (3) the issuance of credentials on the basis of norm-referenced grading. This chapter explains what is entailed in the three radical proposals; the following chapter considers the arguments for and against them.

Historically, the first of the three radical proposals to be offered was the one concerned with the elimination or modification of compulsory schooling. This proposal was enunciated by Jean Jacques Rousseau in his book, *Emile,* which was published in 1762. More will be said about Rousseau shortly, but first we need to know something about the traditional methods of teaching that his proposal challenged.

TRADITIONAL METHODS OF TEACHING

Until the publication of Rousseau's *Emile,* a total of three fundamentally different teaching methods had been developed over thousands of years of human involvement with the activity of teaching. These three methods shall be referred to as the *traditional* methods of teaching. There is documentary evidence which shows that each of the traditional methods of teaching was in existence by the time of the ancient Greeks and Romans.

Characteristics of a Teaching Method

Any teaching method is characterized by a unique set of underlying principles or assumptions that govern the behavior of a teacher in consciously attempting to bring about learning in a student.[1] Therefore, a statement in which a given teaching method is described should elucidate the underlying assumptions of the method.

These assumptions would be expected to pertain to (1) the control of learning and (2) motivational control. Since a teaching method is an educational procedure, it is obvious that a statement explaining the method must deal with the control of learning. It is through the provision of particular kinds of learning experiences that a teacher shapes the learning outcome attained by the student. But why must the explanation of a teaching method also encompass motivational control? Because, if a teacher is interested in increasing the effectiveness of his or her control over learning, some form of motivational control must also be used. The function of motivational control is to induce the student to make an effort to learn, or merely to be present in a situation in which he can have a planned learning experience; motivational control thus increases the likelihood that the student will learn something. Just as the experimenter in the laboratory must usually work with motivated (hungry) rats to study the learning process, a teacher must ordinarily be a motivator as well as a provider of learning experiences.

Although the distinction between the teacher as motivator and the teacher as provider of learning experiences is customarily ignored in treatises on education or teaching, it is extremely significant for our analysis of teaching method. And certainly one practical implication for the future preparation of prospective teachers is that they should be as well trained in the art and science of motivation as they are in the art and science of learning control.

[1]For simplicity of treatment in this discussion the teacher and the student are identified as separate persons. However, it would be possible (as indicated in our definition of education) for the student to be his or her own teacher.

A teacher urging a student to sit down and listen would be an instance of the use of motivational control. Then, if the teacher lectured to the student about history, he would be using learning control, since the words he spoke would increase the probability that the student would acquire a particular learning outcome (in this case, knowledge about history) rather than just any learning outcome. If the teacher changed the words he was using from history words to words about mathematics, the probability would be increased that the student would learn something about mathematics. Thus a student learns history in a history class and mathematics in a mathematics class because of the different learning experiences provided in the two classes.

The reason for having different teaching methods is that there are different theories or assumptions about the most effective means of inducing motivation and bringing about desired learning outcomes. These differences are what account for variations among the three traditional methods of teaching, although, as we shall see, they all utilize the same motivational procedure (aversive motivation).

The three traditional methods of teaching shall be called the Telling/Showing Method, the Exercise/Imitation Method, and the Discovery/Restructuring Method.[2] (Note 1)

Telling/Showing Method

The motivational control procedure used with this method, as with the other two traditional teaching methods, is that of aversive motivation. Moreover, this procedure is used *overtly;* that is, the person who is the target of the control technique knows that someone he can identify wants him to make an effort to learn. Since aversive motivation produces a situation in which the person being controlled has no choice but to select the lesser of the two evils (from his perception) being imposed upon him, when the procedure is used overtly the person being controlled is aware of who is responsible for his unpleasant predicament.

The overt use of aversive motivation may be accompanied by

[2]For an earlier discussion of teaching method and a classification of the basic teaching methods, see John A. Laska and Stanley L. Goldstein, *Foundations of Teaching Method* (Dubuque, Iowa: Wm. C. Brown, 1973).

positive motivation, such as would be the case if the student had a teacher who tells jokes frequently, a teacher who is warm and friendly toward his students, or an attractive classroom. But the student also knows that he is expected to listen to the teacher and to be in the classroom, or he will otherwise experience unpleasant consequences. Therefore, it is aversive motivation rather than positive motivation that is the basic means of inducing student effort. (Note 2)

The theory relative to the control of learning experiences which underlies the Telling/Showing Method assumes that the desired learning outcome is achieved through passive participation of the student in the learning situation. The student is expected to learn merely as a consequence of being exposed to certain kinds of stimuli.[3] For example, a teacher may speak to a student (a verbal experience), or a nonverbal experience (such as showing the student a picture, demonstrating a scientific experiment, or taking the student on a field trip) may be provided. (Note 3)

The use of the terms "Telling" and "Showing" in the designation of this method is intended to suggest the dominant role of the teacher and to indicate that either verbal or nonverbal experiences (or both) may be used. A similar use of two terms will be found in the names given to the other two traditional methods of teaching, since it will also be desirable in those designations to indicate that a variety of procedures is subsumed under each method.

Exercise / Imitation Method

This teaching method differs from the preceding method in that the learning theory on which it is based presupposes considerable effort on the part of the student, rather than a passive role. It is assumed that the student will gradually attain the desired learning outcome through practice and repetition. When this method is used, the teacher explicitly stipulates what the student is expected to try to achieve, provides a model that should be imitated, and/or stipulates the specific nature of the learning activity in which the stu-

[3]The learning theories which underlie the Telling/Showing Method and the other teaching methods identified in this chapter are explained in the sources mentioned in Note 3 of the "General Notes and Bibliography" section of Chapter 4.

dent is to engage. This is done, however, without the teacher's believing that the activity will lead to an experience of sudden "insight" on the part of the student. (Note 4)

The difference between the Telling/Showing and the Exercise/Imitation methods is illustrated by the case of a teacher who wants a student to learn how to drive an automobile. One way to do this might be to lecture to the student about the skills of a good driver. The teacher might also supplement the lecture with a motion picture presentation showing a good driver who utilizes these skills, in contrast with a poor driver who does not. This set of procedures would comprise the Telling/Showing Method. On the other hand, the teacher could take a different approach: the student might be put into an automobile and allowed to practice driving it either in regular traffic or in a specially constructed practice area. Alternatively, the teacher might describe to the student which learning outcomes he or she should attempt to achieve through practice. Another procedure might be to demonstrate to the student these learning outcomes (either personally, through another driver, or by means of a motion picture) and then request that the student try to achieve them. This second set of procedures would represent the use of the Exercise/Imitation Method. In the first set of procedures, it is assumed that with the student in a passive role, learning will result merely from a presentation of the appropriate stimuli; in the second set the student is required to make some type of overt response to the stimuli of the learning situation, and based on the student's responding, learning is presumed to take place.

There is an important variation of the Exeircse/Imitation Method (let us call it a sub-type) that should also be mentioned. In modern educational writings, this variation is referred to as "mental discipline" or "formal discipline." The mental discipline view is sometimes advanced today; for example, when a justification of a school subject such as plane geometry is requested. The supporters of plane geometry may agree that the specific learning outcomes derived from studying this subject (skill in proving that two triangles are congruent, for instance) are not important in adult life and will be quickly forgotten; however, they may contend that studying plane geometry also increases the general reasoning ability of the student, which is important in adult life. The mental discipline view likens the student's mind to a muscle that undergoes general improvement and strengthening as the result of certain kinds of exercise. (Note 5)

Discovery / Restructuring Method

This, the third traditional method of teaching, is similar to the Exercise/Imitation Method, in that it requires considerable student effort to attain the learning objective. But the Discovery/Restructuring Method differs from the Exercise/Imitation Method in that the teacher expects the activity of the student to result in an experience of sudden "insight" for the student. As the name given to this method suggests, the student will have the feeling that, whatever learning outcome is achieved, he or she has discovered it, or that he or she has personally restructured previous learnings to obtain the new learning outcome. Thus in using this method it is not possible for the teacher to know in advance (or at least to inform the student in advance) exactly what learning outcomes will be achieved; otherwise the student would not have the sense of personal discovery or restructuring.

Examples of the procedures appropriate to the Discovery/Restructuring Method would be: (1) the teacher's holding a discussion with a student or group of students (or between students under the guidance of the teacher); (2) the teacher's asking questions for the purpose of bringing about discovery or restructuring on the part of the student (this activity is to be distinguished from recitation procedures sometimes used in the Exercise/Imitation Method; recitation is a form of practice intended to help attain a learning objective explicitly established by the teacher and known by the student); and (3) the teacher's putting the student in a position of being required to discover the solution to a problem (this procedure is distinguished from a problem given to the student to allow for practice of a specified skill that he or she is attempting to learn, which would be an instance of the Exercise/Imitation Method). (Note 6)

As these examples indicate, there may sometimes be a fine line between the Exercise/Imitation and the Discovery/Restructuring Methods, since both are based on student activity. The major distinction, of course, is that the Exercise/Imitation Method presupposes gradual learning through repetition and practice, whereas the Discovery/Restructuring Method assumes that learning will be quite sudden (the achievement of an insight).[4]

[4]The purpose of pointing out the fine line between these two methods is to indicate the need for judgment in differentiating the two. Such judgments may, of course, be required for all methods, not just these two.

CHALLENGE TO COMPULSORY SCHOOLING: ROUSSEAU'S STUDENT INTEREST METHOD

As we have seen, the three traditional methods of teaching are based on the assumption that aversive motivation is the appropriate procedure for inducing students to make an effort to learn. In other words, students are compelled to attend school, and once in school they are compelled to participate in prescribed learning experiences. They might even be compelled to attain certain stipulated learning outcomes before being permitted to terminate their period of schooling. Before the widespread enactment of compulsory schooling laws in the nineteenth and twentieth centuries, it was the parents—those who were able to afford schooling for their children—and the teachers to whom they paid school fees who were responsible for applying the aversive motivation procedures inherent in compulsory schooling. Since the passage of compulsory schooling laws, government officials, as well as parents and teachers, have been the sources of overtly provided aversive motivation procedures.

For most children and parents, compulsory schooling probably seems such a natural thing that they do not give it much thought, at least as far as abstract reflection is concerned. Yet the compulsory school system is, in fact, a very unusual social institution. Without intending any pejorative connotation, the only major American social institutions in which a person may be compelled to participate are prisons, mental asylums, the armed forces during times when draft laws are in effect, and the compulsory school system. A person is not compelled to, say, get married or attend a church, and, if his or her economic wants can be provided for without working (for example, by living on an inheritance or by begging), a person is free to live that way. Currently, however, a young child in the United States is obliged to attend school until about the age of sixteen.

It was Jean Jacques Rousseau who, in his book *Emile* (published in 1762), presented the first fully reasoned argument against the practice of compulsory schooling.[5] In Rousseau's view, rather than try to induce student effort by the overt use of aversive motivation (which may not succeed, or which may even engender negative attitudes toward learning), we should rely on positive motivation—

[5]Rousseau was born in Geneva, Switzerland, in 1712, but spent most of his productive years in France. He died in Ermenonville, France, in 1778.

or at least nonovert aversive motivation—to get the student to participate in learning experiences. "There is a better way," he said, than any of the previously developed approaches to instruction. It is "one which is generally overlooked—it consists in the desire to learn. Arouse this desire in your scholar and . . . any method [of providing learning experiences] will serve."[6]

As this quotation indicates, *Emile* is not just an attack on compulsory schooling and the three traditional methods of teaching. It is also an exposition of a new teaching method, which we shall label the Student Interest Method. This and the Reinforcement Method (which shall be discussed later) are the only fundamentally different conceptions of teaching method formulated since the time of the ancient Greeks and Romans. The three earliest methods of teaching were labeled the "traditional" ones; these two more recent approaches will be designated the *modern* methods.

Characteristics of the Student Interest Method

In *Emile* Rousseau describes the educational procedures that he believed would be most suitable for a ficticious boy named Emile. To give the reader an opportunity to appreciate both Rousseau's style of writing and the literary excellence of *Emile* (even in the English translation), three segments from the book follow.

> When I . . . get rid of children's lessons, I get rid of the chief cause of their sorrows, namely their books. Reading is the curse of childhood, yet it is almost the only occupation you can find for children. Emile, at twelve years old, will hardly know what a book is. "But," you say, "he must, at least, know how to read." When reading is of use to him, I admit he must learn to read, but till then he will only find it a nuisance.
>
> If children are not to be required to do anything as a matter of obedience, it follows that they will only learn what they perceive to be of real and present value, either for use or enjoyment; what other motive could they have for learning? The art of speaking to our absent friends, of hearing their words; the art of letting them know at first hand our feelings, our desires, and our longings, is an art whose usefulness can be made plain at any age. How is it that this art, so useful and pleasant in itself, has become a terror to children? Because the

[6]Jean Jacques Rousseau, *Emile,* trans. Barbara Foxley (New York: Dutton, 1911), p. 81.

child is compelled to acquire it against his will, and to use it for purposes beyond his comprehension. A child has no great wish to perfect himself in the use of an instrument of torture, but make it a means to his pleasure, and soon you will not be able to keep him from it.

People make a great fuss about discovering the best way to teach children to read. They invent "bureaux"* and cards, they turn the nursery into a printer's shop. Locke would have them taught to read by means of dice. What a fine idea! And the pity of it! There is a better way than any of those, and one which is generally overlooked— it consists in the desire to learn. Arouse this desire in your scholar and have done with your "bureaux" and your dice—any method will serve.

Present interest, that is the motive power, the only motive power that takes us far and safely. Sometimes Emile receives notes of invitation from his father or mother, his relations or friends; he is invited to a dinner, a walk, a boating expedition, to see some public entertainment. These notes are short, clear, plain, and well written. Some one must read them to him, and he cannot always find anybody when wanted. . . . Time passes, the chance is lost. The note is read to him at last, but it is too late. Oh! If only he had known how to read! He receives other notes, so short, so interesting, he would like to try to read them. Sometimes he gets help, sometimes none. He does his best, and at last makes out half the note; it is something about going tomorrow to drink cream—Where? With whom? He cannot tell—how hard he tries to make out the rest! I do not think Emile will need a "bureau." Shall I proceed to the teaching of writing? No, I am ashamed to toy with these trifles in a treatise on education.

I will just add a few words which contain a principle of great importance. It is this—What we are in no hurry to get is usually obtained with speed and certainty. I am pretty sure Emile will learn to read and write before he is ten, just because I care very little whether he can do so before he is fifteen; but I would rather he never learnt to read at all, than that this art should be acquired at the price of all that makes reading useful. What is the use of reading to him if he always hates it?

*The "bureau" was a sort of case containing letters to be put together to form words. It was a favourite device for the teaching of reading and gave its name to a special method called the bureau-method, of learning to read. [Translator's note.][7]

In the preceding selection, Rousseau identifies the present interest of the learner as the basic element in his method. In the next selection, Rousseau addresses himself directly to the teacher. He cites undesirable consequences that can result from the overt use of aversive motivation—those situations in which the student knows

[7]Ibid., pp. 80–82.

that the teacher is compelling him or her to do something. Rousseau recommends that the teacher employ a control procedure in which the student thinks that he or she is the master, although the teacher is actually exercising control over the student through access control and positive motivation.

> Young teacher, I am setting before you a difficult task, the art of controlling without precepts, and doing everything without doing anything at all. This art is, I confess, beyond your years, it is not calculated to display your talents nor to make your value known to your scholar's parents; but it is the only road to success. You will never succeed in making wise men if you do not first make little imps of mischief. This was the education of the Spartans; they were not taught to stick to their books, they were set to steal their dinners. Were they any the worse for it in after life? Ever ready for victory, they crushed their foes in every kind of warfare, and the prating Athenians were as much afraid of their words as of their blows.
>
> When education is most carefully attended to, the teacher issues his orders and thinks himself master, but it is the child who is really master. He uses the tasks you set him to obtain what he wants from you, and he can always make you pay for an hour's industry by a week's complaisance. You must always be making bargains with him. These bargains, suggested in your fashion, but carried out in his, always follow the direction of his own fancies, especially when you are foolish enough to make the condition some advantage he is almost sure to obtain, whether he fulfils his part of the bargain or not. The child is usually much quicker to read the master's thoughts than the master to read the child's feelings. And that is as it should be, for all the sagacity which the child would have devoted to self-preservation, had he been left to himself, is now devoted to the rescue of his native freedom from the chains of his tyrant; while the latter, who has no such pressing need to understand the child, sometimes finds that it pays him better to leave him in idleness or vanity.
>
> Take the opposite course with your pupil; let him always think he is master while you are really master. There is no subjection so complete as that which preserves the forms of freedom; it is thus that the will itself is taken captive. Is not this poor child, without knowledge, strength, or wisdom, entirely at your mercy? Are you not master of his whole environment so far as it affects him? Cannot you make of him what you please? His work and play, his pleasure and pain, are they not, unknown to him, under your control? No doubt he ought only to do what he wants, but he ought to want to do nothing but what you want him to do. He should never take a step you have not foreseen, nor utter a word you could not foretell.
>
> Then he can devote himself to the bodily exercises adapted to his age without brutalising his mind; instead of developing his cunning to evade an unwelcome control, you will then find him entirely occupied in getting the best he can out of his environment with a view

to his present welfare, and you will be surprised by the subtlety of the means he devises to get for himself such things as he can obtain, and to really enjoy things without the aid of other people's ideas. You leave him master of his own wishes, but you do not multiply his caprices. When he only does what he wants, he will soon only do what he ought, and although his body is constantly in motion, so far as his sensible and present interests are concerned, you will find him developing all the reason of which he is capable, far better and in a manner much better fitted for him than in purely theoretical studies.

Thus when he does not find you continually thwarting him, when he no longer distrusts you, no longer has anything to conceal from you, he will neither tell you lies nor deceive you; he will show himself fearlessly as he really is, and you can study him at your ease, and surround him with all the lessons you would have him learn, without awaking his suspicions.

Neither will he keep a curious and jealous eye on your own conduct, nor take a secret delight in catching you at fault. It is a great thing to avoid this. One of the child's first objects is, as I have said, to find the weak spots in its rulers. Though this leads to spitefulness, it does not arise from it, but from the desire to evade a disagreeable control. Overburdened by the yoke laid upon him, he tries to shake it off, and the faults he finds in his master give him a good opportunity for this. Still the habit of spying out faults and delighting in them grows upon people. Clearly we have stopped another of the springs of vice in Emile's heart. Having nothing to gain from my faults, he will not be on the watch for them, nor will he be tempted to look out for the faults of others.

All these methods seem difficult because they are new to us, but they ought not to be really difficult. I have a right to assume that you have the knowledge required for the business you have chosen; that you know the usual course of development of the human thought, that you can study mankind and man, that you know beforehand the effect on your pupil's will of the various objects suited to his age which you put before him. You have the tools and the art to use them; are you not master of your trade?[8]

The third selection offers a practical example of how access control and positive motivation may be used to bring about a desired learning outcome (in this selection the student referred to is not Emile):

An idle, lazy child was to be taught to run. He had no liking for this or any other exercise, though he was intended for the army. Somehow or other he had got it into his head that a man of his rank need know nothing and do nothing—that his birth would serve as a substitute for arms and legs, as well as for every kind of virtue. The

[8]Ibid., pp. 84–85.

skill of Chiron himself would have failed to make a fleet-footed Achilles of this young gentleman. The difficulty was increased by my determination to give him no kind of orders. I had renounced all right to direct him by preaching, promises, threats, emulation, or the desire to show off. How should I make him want to run without saying anything? I might run myself, but he might not follow my example, and this plan had other drawbacks. Moreover, I must find some means of teaching him through this exercise, so as to train mind and body to work together. This is how I, or rather how the teacher who supplied me with this illustration, set about it.

When I took him a walk of an afternoon I sometimes put in my pocket a couple of cakes, of a kind he was very fond of; we each ate one while we were out, and we came back well pleased with our outing. One day he noticed I had three cakes; he could have easily eaten six, so he ate his cake quickly and asked for the other. "No," said I, "I could eat it myself, or we might divide it, but I would rather see those two little boys run a race for it." I called them to us, showed them the cake, and suggested that they should race for it. They were delighted. The cake was placed on a large stone which was to be the goal; the course was marked out, we sat down, and at a given signal off flew the children! The victor seized the cake and ate it without pity in the sight of the spectators and of his defeated rival.

The sport was better than the cake; but the lesson did not take effect all at once, and produced no result. I was not discouraged, nor did I hurry; teaching is a trade at which one must be able to lose time and save it. Our walks were continued, sometimes we took three cakes, sometimes four, and from time to time there were one or two cakes for the racers. If the prize was not great, neither was the ambition of the competitors. The winner was praised and petted, and everything was done with much ceremony. To give room to run and to add interest to the race I marked out a longer course and admitted several fresh competitors. Scarcely had they entered the lists than all the passers-by stopped to watch. They were encouraged by shouting, cheering, and clapping. I sometimes saw my little man trembling with excitement, jumping up and shouting when one was about to reach or overtake another—to him these were the Olympian games.

However, the competitors did not always play fair, they got in each other's way, or knocked one another down, or put stones on the track. That led us to separate them and make them start from different places at equal distances from the goal. You will soon see the reason for this, for I must describe this important affair at length.

Tired of seeing his favourite cakes devoured before his eyes, the young lord began to suspect that there was some use in being a quick runner, and seeing that he had two legs of his own, he began to practise running on the quiet. I took care to see nothing, but I knew my stratagem had taken effect. When he thought he was good enough (and I thought so too), he pretended to tease me to give him the other cake. I refused; he persisted, and at last he said angrily, "Well, put it on the stone and mark out the course, and we shall see." "Very good," said I, laughing, "You will get a good appetite, but you will not get the cake." Stung by my mockery, he took heart, won the prize, all the more easily because I had marked out a very short course and taken care that the best runner was out of the way. It will be evident that, after the first step, I had no difficulty in keeping him in training. Soon he took such a fancy for this form of exercise that without any favour he was almost certain to beat the little peasant boys at running, however long the course.[9]

When the Student Interest Method is employed, the student feels that he or she is making the decisions concerning what should be done. If a student wants to learn something, he or she makes the effort; if there is no desire to learn, then no compulsion by someone to do so exists. The teacher may, however, attempt to influence the student through positive motivation and access control. For example, a student may be informed of the rewards that will accrue to him or her as a result of achieving certain learning outcomes; also the student's environment may be structured in such a way that learning experiences of certain kinds are made accessible. The teacher may even use aversive motivation in a nonovert way to induce student effort, but the student still believes that he is not being coerced by anyone. The use of aversive motivation in a nonovert manner is exemplified by the teaching strategy of allowing the student to get into a situation that causes discomfort until he has learned to solve the problem that confronts him. Although the teacher planned for the student to be confronted by the problem, the student is unaware of the teacher's intention and thus believes that there was no compulsion to make the effort required to solve the problem.

In the three traditional methods of teaching, the teacher (as we have already noted) may combine aversive motivation with positive inducements — for example, by asking the student to play an interesting game (through which learning is also supposed to take place), or by providing colorful and pleasing instructional materials to use. The basic character of this approach is nonetheless overtly aversive, since the student knows that he or she is required to play the interesting game or use the attractive instructional materials. In the Student Interest Method, however, the teacher does not overtly use any aversive procedure to foster participaton in the teaching process; the student believes he is free to select the learning activities (if any) in which he desires to engage.

As far as its assumptions about the learning process are con-

[9]Ibid., pp. 105–107.

cerned, the Student Interest Method represents an eclectic approach. It encompasses all of the procedures based on different learning theories of the three traditional teaching methods. For example, an interested student might ask the teacher to tell him about American history, or he might ask the teacher to suggest a model to imitate in order to improve his own writing style; or the teacher might nonovertly cause a malfunction in the student's automobile to induce him to discover both the source of the difficulty and the means to correct it. Any or all of these types of learning experiences would be consistent with the Student Interest Method.

Contemporary Critics of Compulsory Schooling

Although Rousseau's ideas produced a few dedicated followers, the years following his death saw a dramatic increase in compulsory schooling, rather than a reduction in its extent. During the nineteenth century, most modern, industrialized societies enacted compulsory schooling laws, for a variety of reasons: to meet the need for literate workers, to enable every citizen to keep better informed about political events, to instill a sense of patriotism, and to foster religious beliefs.

The first of these laws in the United States was passed in Massachusetts in 1852. Two hundred years earlier in Massachusetts Bay Colony, laws had been enacted which required that instruction be provided to young people and that schools be established, but these laws did not stipulate that the required instruction had to be provided in schools. By 1918 every state in the United States had passed a compulsory schooling law. During the 1960s, however, at least three states (Mississippi, South Carolina and Virginia) repealed or lessened the impact of their compulsory schooling laws — not because of an objection to aversive motivation, but rather as a tactic in their opposition to compulsory racial integration of the schools.

The nature and limits of the state's legal authority with respect to compulsory schooling have been considered in a number of court cases. The general pattern of state court decisions on compulsory schooling is well summarized by Peter De Boer, as follows:

> State courts have decided that the state may not require all children to attend a public school; that the state may require children to attend a public, private, or parochial school; that compulsory atten-

dance laws must be reasonably administered; that parents may use as a legal defense the argument that they had good reason for not sending their child to school; and that a married girl of school age cannot be compelled to attend school. The state courts are in disagreement as to whether parents, in order to meet the requirements of the law, may teach their own children at home or may employ a tutor to teach them; however, the weight of court authority suggests that, in order to do so, parents must be able to show that the children are receiving substantially the same opportunity they would have received in a public school. Some state courts explicity hold that if the statute requires the attendance of a child at a public or private school, education by the parent is not the equivalent of attendance at a private school. As a rule, parents are not permitted to set up the defense that a compulsory school attendance law is in violation of their religious principles.[10]

According to De Boer, the legislative enactments on compulsory schooling in the United States are in fact compulsory participation laws, and not just school attendance laws. "State legislation," he points out, "specifies not only that the children who attend private schools must attend during a period not less than the minimum school year established for public schools, but also that these children must be instructed in the branches of education required to be taught in public schools to children of corresponding age and grade. Some state laws further specify one or more of the following conditions: that private schools include in their curricula courses dealing with state and federal constitutions, good citizenship, and healthful living and that the English language be the medium of instruction."[11]

Several critics of compulsory schooling became prominent in the 1960s. A somewhat earlier proponent of radical change was A. S. Neill, an English educator who established an experimental school named Summerhill in 1922, and who wrote an influential book of the same name. Like Rousseau, contemporary critics object to the use of aversive motivation and favor the adoption of the Student Interest Method of teaching. To be more precise, however, we should say that most contemporary radical critics of compulsory schooling are opposed to compulsory participation in the learning

[10]Peter P. De Boer, "Compulsory Attendance," in *Encyclopedia of Education,* ed. Lee C. Deighton (New York: Macmillan, 1971), 2: 376.
[11]Ibid., p. 378.

experiences provided by schools, although they may implicitly or explicitly accept the notion of compulsory attendance.

A. S. Neill has expressed the following opinion on student interest as an essential element in the teaching process: "We do not consider that teaching in itself matters very much. Whether a school has or has not a special method for teaching long division is of no significance, for long division is of no importance except to those who *want* to learn it. And the child who *wants* to learn long division *will* learn it no matter how it is taught."[12] John Holt has taken the same position. "I think children learn better," he has declared, "when they learn what they want to learn when they want to learn it, and how they want to learn it, learning for their own curiosity and not at somebody else's order."[13] A similar view has been advanced by Paul Goodman: "We can, I believe, educate the young entirely in terms of their free choice, with no processing whatsoever. Nothing can be efficiently learned, or, indeed, learned at all—other than through parroting or brute training, when acquired knowledge is promptly forgotten after the examination—unless it meets need, desire, curiosity, or fantasy."[14] And finally from Herbert Kohl: "The role of the teacher is not to control his pupils but rather to enable them to make choices and pursue what interests them."[15] (Note 7)

SKINNER'S RADICAL PROPOSAL

The second radical criticism of conventional schooling is similar to the proposal to abolish or modify compulsion, in that it stems from a new conception of teaching method. The method involved is that which we shall call the Reinforcement Method. It and the Student Interest Method comprise what we have termed the "modern"

[12]A. S. Neill, *Summerhill* (New York: Hart, 1960), p. 5. (Emphasis in the original.)

[13]John Holt, *The Underachieving School* (New York: Dell, 1970), p. 204.

[14]Paul Goodman, "No Processing Whatever," in *Radical School Reform*, eds. Beatrice Gross and Ronald Gross (New York: Simon and Schuster, 1969), p. 99.

[15]Herbert R. Kohl, *The Open Classroom* (New York: The New York Review, 1969), p. 20.

methods of teaching. These two approaches and the three traditional ones (Telling/Showing Method, Exercise/Imitation Method, and
Discovery/Restructuring Method) constitute the five fundamentally
different conceptions of teaching method thus far developed by mankind.

The Reinforcement Method is based on the reinforcement theory of learning. Edward L. Thorndike (1874–1949), an American educational psychologist, was the first to enunciate clearly the role of
reinforcement in the learning process. Unfortunately, he did not
utilize this idea (which he called the Law of Effect) for the systematic presentation of a new view of teaching method; this was done later by B. F. Skinner. Hence the development of the Reinforcement
Method of teaching may not be attributed to any one person.

Thorndike's Law of Effect

The following selection from Thorndike's *Education: A First
Book* (1912) presents an early statement of his basic principle. "The
Law of Effect," Thorndike writes, "is that, other things being equal,
the greater the satisfyingness of the state of affairs which accompanies or follows a given response to a certain situation, the more likely that response is to be made to that situation in the future. Con-
versely, the greater the discomfort or annoyingness of the state of
affairs which comes with or after a response to a situation, the more
likely that response is not to be made to that situation in the future. . . . This law may be stated more briefly as: Satisfying results
strengthen, and discomfort weakens, the bond between situation
and response." As Thorndike explains, "human nature does not do
something for nothing. The satisfyingness and annoyingness of the
states of affairs which follow the making of the connection [between
situation and response] are the chief forces which remodel man's nature. Education makes changes chiefly by rewarding them. The
prime law in all human control is to get the man to make the desired
response and to be satisfied thereby."[16]

Without providing much detail, Thorndike indicates how the
Law of Effect may be applied. It is, he declares, "the fundamental
law of learning and teaching. By it a crab learns to respond to the

---

[16]Edward L. Thorndike, *Education: A First Book* (New York: Macmillan, 1912), p. 96. (Emphasis removed.)

situation, *two paths,* by taking the one, choice of which has in the past brought food. By it a dog will learn to respond to the situation, *a white box and a black box,* by neglecting the latter if opening it in the past has been promptly followed by an electric shock. By it animals are taught their tricks; by it babies learn to smile at the sight of the bottle or the kind attendant, and to manipulate spoon and fork; by it the player at billiards or golf improves his game; by it the man of science preserves those ideas that satisfy him by their promise, and discards futile fancies. It is the great weapon of all who wish—in industry, trade, government, religion or education—to change men's responses, either by reinforcing old and adding new ones, or by getting rid of those that are undesirable."[17]

In Thorndike's original formulation of the Law of Effect, both "satisfiers" and "annoyers" were considered to have comparable effects on learning outcomes—pleasant consequences would increase the probability that a given response would be repeated, while unpleasant consequences would have an equal but opposite effect. However, Thorndike later modified the Law of Effect; instead of attaching equal importance to satisfiers and annoyers, he considered only satisfying consequences to have a major reinforcing effect.[18]

Skinner's Elaboration of Thorndike's Idea

Burrhus F. Skinner, a contemporary American psychologist who was born in 1904, set forth in his book *The Technology of Teaching* (1968) what is probably the most comprehensive exposition of the Reinforcement Method. Skinner calls attention to the progress made in the use of "contingencies of reinforcement" to bring about desired learning outcomes; he also acknowledges his debt to Thorndike's Law of Effect: "Some promising advances have recently been made in the field of learning. Special techniques have been designed to arrange what are called 'contingencies of reinforcement'—the relations which prevail between behavior on the one hand and the consequences of that behavior on the other—with the result that a much more effective control of behavior has been achieved. . . . The

[17]Ibid., pp. 96–97. (Emphasis in the original.)
[18]See Edward L. Thorndike, *Human Learning* (New York: Century, 1931), p. 46.

Law of Effect has been taken seriously; we have made sure that effects *do* occur and that they occur under conditions which are optimal for producing the changes called learning. Once we have arranged the particular type of consequence called a reinforcement, our techniques permit us to shape the behavior of an organism almost at will. It has become a routine exercise to demonstrate this in classes in elementary psychology by conditioning such an organism as a pigeon. Simply by presenting food to a hungry pigeon at the right time, it is possible to shape three or four well-defined responses in a single demonstration period—such responses as turning around, pacing the floor in the pattern of a figure eight, standing still in a corner of the demonstration apparatus, stretching the neck, or stamping the foot. Extremely complex performances may be reached through successive stages in the shaping process, the contingencies of reinforcement being changed progressively in the direction of the required behavior. The results are often quite dramatic. In such a demonstration one can *see* learning take place. A significant change in behavior is often obvious as the result of a single reinforcement."[19]

Skinner is disappointed, however, by widespread failure to apply the reinforcement theory of learning in the classroom. Taking as his example the teaching of arithmetic, Skinner is critical of the long period of time that elapses between a correct response by the student and the receipt of a reinforcement. Skinner asks, "When is a numerical operation reinforced as 'right'? Eventually, of course, the pupil may be able to check his own answers and achieve some sort of automatic reinforcement, but in the early stages the reinforcement of being right is usually accorded by the teacher. The contingencies she provides are far from optimal. It can easily be demonstrated that, unless explicit mediating behavior has been set up, the lapse of only a few seconds between response and reinforcement destroys most of the effect. In a typical classroom, nevertheless, long periods of time customarily elapse. The teacher may walk up and down the aisle, for example, while the class is working on a sheet of problems, pausing here and there to call an answer right or wrong. Many minutes intervene between the child's response and the teacher's reinforcement. In many cases—for example, when papers are taken

[19]B. F. Skinner, *The Technology of Teaching* (New York: Appleton-Century-Crofts, 1968), pp. 9–10. (Emphasis in the original.)

home to be corrected—as much as 24 hours may intervene. It is surprising that this system has any effect whatsoever."[20]

Even more serious in Skinner's view, however, is the small number of reinforcements provided to the sudent. "Since the pupil," Skinner writes, "is usually dependent upon the teacher for being told that he is right, and since many pupils are usually dependent upon the same teacher, the total number of contingencies which may be arranged during, say, the first four years, is of the order of only a few thousand. But a very rough estimate suggests that efficient mathematical behavior at this level requires something of the order of 25,000 contingencies."[21]

Skinner's attitude, however, is optimistic that the teaching process can be improved by the deliberate utilization of the reinforcement theory of learning. "There would be no point in urging these objections if improvement were impossible," Skinner declares. "The advances which have recently been made in our control of the learning process suggest a thorough revision of classroom practices and, fortunately, they tell us how the revision can be brought about. . . . The whole process of becoming competent in any field must be divided into a very large number of very small steps, and reinforcement must be contingent upon the accomplishment of each step. . . . By making each successive step as small as possible, the frequency of reinforcement can be raised to a maximum."[22]

Characteristics of the Reinforcement Method

The distinguishing feature of the Reinforcement Method is the deliberate provision of reinforcements to the learner *after* a desired response has been made. According to the learning theory on which the Reinforcement Method is based, provision of a reinforcement is necessary to increase the likelihood that desired behavior will be repeated. In other respects, the Reinforcement Method may exhibit characteristics of other teaching methods previously described, with the exception of the Telling/Showing Method. Since the student is expected to make responses, the passive role of the student that is

[20]Ibid., p. 16.
[21]Ibid., p. 17.
[22]Ibid., pp. 19, 21.

postulated in the Telling/Showing Method is not compatible with the Reinforcement Method. But the Reinforcement Method does encompass both the contention that the student learns gradually through practice and the view that the student learns suddenly through attainment of insight. Also, the Reinforcement Method is compatible with the motivational procedures of traditional teaching methods and the Student Interest Method.

For thousands of years, most teachers have, unconsciously, probably made use of reinforcements (for instance, through words of praise after a student responds correctly to a question); but it was not until the formulation of the Reinforcement Method that deliberate utilization of reinforcements to shape learning outcomes became an explicit aspect of teaching method. When used in the schools, the Reinforcement Method is commonly called "behavior modification."[23]

Because rewards are also employed to motivate students (positive motivation), their use in reinforcing learning needs to be clearly differentiated from the use of rewards to elicit student effort. Indeed, one teacher may use a reward (a word of praise, let us say) to elicit student effort, while another teacher may utilize the same reward as a reinforcement. Only the second case, however, would constitute an instance of the Reinforcement Method, since only in that case is the teacher conscious of the reinforcing effect of the word of praise. (Notes 8 and 9)

Skinner's Proposal to Extend the Reinforcement Method

Although he is not usually categorized as such, B. F. Skinner warrants being styled a radical critic of the school system. For one thing, he is against the use of aversive motivation. But more importantly, in his recent book *Beyond Freedom and Dignity* (and previously in *Walden Two* and *Science and Human Behavior*), he proposed that the Reinforcement Method of teaching be adopted both inside and outside the schools. If this were done, it would place student motivational control procedures of the existing school system

[23]For an explanation of this approach, see George A. Fargo, Charlene Behrns and Patricia Nolen, eds., *Behavior Modification* (New York: Pergamon, 1972).

within the context of a planned, society-wide system of reinforcements—in effect transforming the whole society into an educational agency. Hence it would seem appropriate to view Skinner as a radical critic of conventional schooling.

As was pointed out in Chapter 4, whether a particular learned behavior is actually exhibited in a particular situation may depend upon the motivational factors present in the situation in which an individual finds himself, and how these factors are evaluated by the person behaving.[24] According to this interpretation, the environment may be regarded as a structure of rewards and punishments, of which the individual is aware. Before acting a person evaluates the consequences (positive and negative outcomes) that would accrue from various courses of action. He then selects the most satisfactory alternative and acts accordingly. Or the environment may be viewed as providing reinforcements, without concern about the thought processes of the individual in the environmental situation. In the first interpretation, rewards and punishments are seen as encouraging or discouraging performances based on previous learnings; in Skinner's view, reinforcements (or their absences) strengthen or extinguish learned behaviors elicted by the appropriate stimulus.

Of the before-mentioned interpretations, it is relatively unimportant for a consideration of Skinner's proposal which we accept, for the societal incentive structure that would be necessary and the nature of the controlling technique (rewards and punishments, or reinforcements and their absence) would be essentially similar. The basic question Skinner's suggestion poses to society is whether the proposed incentive structure should be established.

In *Beyond Freedom and Dignity* Skinner discusses the role of culture in the control of human behavior. As he defines the term, "culture" encompasses the contingencies of reinforcement that operate in a given society. "A child is born a member of the human species," he explains, "with a genetic endowment showing many idiosyncratic features, and he begins at once to acquire a repertoire of behavior under the contingencies of reinforcement to which he is exposed as an individual. Most of these contingencies are arranged by other people. They are, in fact, what is called a culture, although the term is usually defined in other ways. . . . A culture must be transmitted from generation to generation, and its strength will presum-

---

[24]See section on "Learning Control," Chapter 4.

ably depend on what and how much its new members learn, either through informal instructional contingencies or in educational institutions. A culture needs the support of its members, and it must provide for the pursuit and achievement of happiness if it is to prevent disaffection or defection."[25]

According to Skinner, "the intentional design of a culture and the control of human behavior it implies are essential if the human species is to continue to develop. . . . What is needed is more 'intentional' control, not less, and this is an important engineering problem. The good of a culture cannot function as the source of genuine reinforcers for the individual, and the reinforcers contrived by cultures to induce their members to work for their survival are often in conflict with personal reinforcers. The number of people explicitly engaged in improving the design of automobiles, for example, must greatly exceed the number of those concerned with improving life in city ghettos. It is not that the automobile is more important than a way of life, but rather that the economic contingencies which induce people to improve automobiles are very powerful. They arise from the personal reinforcers of those who manufacture automobiles. No reinforcers of comparable strength encourage the engineering of the pure survival of a culture."

Skinner believes that the control of human behavior is a basic condition of human life. What he desires, therefore, is that this control be exercised on behalf of society. He regards the designers of a culture to be just as much under the control of that culture as other members of the society: "The designer of a culture is not an interloper or meddler. He does not step in to disturb a natural process, he is part of a natural process. The geneticist who changes the characteristics of a species by selective breeding or by changing genes may seem to be meddling in biological evolution, but he does so because his species has evolved to the point at which it has been able to develop a science of genetics and a culture which induces its members to take the future of the species into account. Those who have been induced by their culture to act to further its survival through design must accept the fact that they are altering the conditions under which men live and, hence, engaging in the control of human behavior. Good government is as much a matter of the control of human

---

[25]The quotations in this paragraph and in the two which follow it are from B. F. Skinner, *Beyond Freedom and Dignity* (New York: Knopf, 1971), pp. 127, 152, 175, 177, 180–181.

behavior as bad, good incentive conditions as much as exploitation, good teaching as much as punitive drill. Nothing is to be gained by using a softer word."

RADICAL CRITICISM OF SCHOOL SYSTEM CREDENTIALING

Another target of some of the radical critics is the credentialing function of the conventional school system. By "credentialing" the granting of degrees, diplomas and other certificates is implied. This function of the school system is a major activity—in fact, it has been suggested that credentialing has grown more important than the teaching function of the schools. This in itself would not be sufficient reason to recommend the abolition of school system credentialing, but the critics of credentialing believe it to have a negative effect on the teaching process. This negative effect is attributed to the use of norm-referenced grading as the basis for determining who shall be awarded a credential.[26]

Grading may be either private or public. Private grading refers to the practice of the teacher's giving the student a personal evaluation of his or her performance so that it may be known which areas could be improved. Private grading may also refer to the teacher's practice of making student evaluations to aid in the planning of instructional activities. When students are graded publicly, their grades are reported to other persons (such as parents), entered on official records (such as college transcripts), and have official bearing on whether a student receives a school certificate. Issue 6 is concerned with the public grading of students, because it is public grading which plays a major role in the credentialing process.

The credentialing function of the school system constitutes a major source of student motivational control. Getting a diploma and/or an "A" on a report card represent the basic rewards provided to students by the school system, whereas failing to earn a diploma and/or receiving an "F" on a report card represent the system's basic

---

[26]The term "grading" may be used in two ways: in reference to the evaluation of students, and in reference to the age grouping of students within the school. Unless otherwise indicated, the first meaning of the term shall be the one implied. The expression "nongraded school" refers to one that does not group its students according to age. Therefore, a nongraded school may evaluate its students.

punishments. The credentialing function of the school system also involves access control, since access to other educational opportunities and occupational roles is often contingent upon possession of the appropriate credential from the school system.

School System Credentials

The practice of issuing credentials may be traced to the founding of the first universities in Europe during the Middle Ages (about 1200 A.D.). The Greeks and Romans, although they were responsible for a number of innovations in the operation of schools, did not have school systems that granted degrees. The first universities had their origins in the medieval guild system; in fact, the name "university" comes from the Latin word *universitas*, which meant "guild" or "corporation." Originally, therefore, the term *universitas* would have been applicable to a guild of carpenters as well as to a guild of teachers.

The master's and doctor's degrees meant the same thing in the first universities: they signified that the recipient had been accepted as a fellow teacher by the faculty of the university. The title "master"—a guild term—indicated that the holder of the degree was regarded as a master of his occupation (in this case, the occupation of teacher), while the term "doctor" was a synonym for "teacher." Both "master" and "doctor," therefore, were equivalent to the occupational title "professor" in the first universities. A student became a "bachelor" sometime during the period between his admission to the university and his becoming a master or doctor. When a student became a bachelor he was entitled to carry out certain restricted teaching duties, much like a teaching assistant at a present-day American university.[27]

In the centuries following the establishment of the first European universities, the degree came to mean a standardized award for achievement rather than the title of an occupation. With the founding of Harvard College in 1636, the custom of granting degrees in recognition of achievement was brought from Europe. The

[27]Charles H. Haskins, *The Rise of Universities* (Ithaca: Cornell University Press, 1957), pp. 11, 24; Gordon Leff, *Paris and Oxford Universities in the Thirteenth and Fourteenth Centuries* (New York: Wiley, 1968), pp. 147–160.

bachelor's degree, however, was the only type of earned degree awarded in the United States prior to the Civil War. The first American doctor's degree similar to the contemporary Ph.D. research degree was awarded by Yale University in 1861. It wasn't until the 1870s that the master's became an earned degree.[28]

The right to grant degrees is usually specified in the charters authorizing the establishment of private colleges and universities, or in the legislative enactments governing the founding of public colleges and universities. Princeton University, for example, was given the right to confer "any such degrees as are given in any of the Universities or Colleges in the realm of Great Britain" (1746), and the University of Oregon was authorized to grant "such degrees as are usually conferred by universities, or as they shall deem appropriate" (1872).[29]

Grading

To grade a student is to make a value judgment about him. The process of grading entails using an appropriate standard of evaluation and gathering evidence to determine whether a student has met this standard. It is not enough merely to report that a student has obtained a 78 on a final examination; this raw score is meaningless until it is related to a standard of evaluation. An indication must be made of how the score of 78 compares with the scores of other students who took the same examination, or whether the score is above or below the one established as a prescribed standard.

Before discussing the use of standards any further, however, let us consider briefly how empirical evidence is obtained about the student. Our assumptions are that school system credentials will be awarded with respect to learning outcomes attained by the student, and that the grading of the student will represent an evaluation of his achievement of these outcomes. Since learning as such is unobservable, its existence must be inferred on the basis of student performance.

An essential task of the grader, therefore, is that of collecting empirical evidence concerning the performances of the students be-

[28]Walter C. Eells and Harold A. Haswell, *Academic Degrees* (Washington, D.C.: Government Printing Office, 1960), pp. 22–29.
[29]Quoted ibid., p. 9.

ing evaluated. This evidence may be acquired in various ways: for example, by observing the performance of the students in class; by requesting that students complete specified assignments (such as essays, term papers, and other projects); and by requiring the students to take written examinations or tests.

If valid conclusions are to be drawn from evidence gathered, the evidence obtained on student performance must be valid—that is, the procedure used must actually measure what it is intended to measure. James Thyne has identified four conditions that must hold if an examination is to achieve maximum validity.[30] First, the marking (scoring) of the examination must produce consistent results. As an example, a teacher (who is also a grader) of a 10th-grade history course decides to use a written examination to determine which students in the class have reached a specified standard of performance. Thus the test is being used to assess student achievement in history rather than for some other purpose (such as measuring ability or predicting future success in college). The marking of this examination would be regarded as consistent if the same performances received the same score when marked a second time.

A second condition for validity is what Thyne calls "mark-relevance." When this condition is fulfilled, all performances related to the purpose of the examination are marked, to the exclusion of any others. If, in the example of the history examination, the grader decides that assessment of grammatical usage is not relevant to the purpose of the examination, then marks would neither be deducted for poor grammar, nor given for proper grammar. As Thyne points out, the attainment of this condition is distinct from the fulfillment of the first: "It would be possible to mark consistently, but to mark irrelevant performances or to omit to mark some relevant performances; and it would be possible to mark all the relevant performances, and only relevant performances, but to mark them inconsistently."[31]

Thyne identifies "question-relevance" as a third condition for validity. This requires that all questions irrelevant to the prupose of the examination be excluded (in any case, the answers to such questions would not be marked if the condition of mark-relevance were

[30]James M. Thyne, *Principles of Examining* (New York: Wiley, 1974), pp. 8–19.
[31]Ibid., pp. 14–15.

attained), and that at least a representative sample of all questions relevant to the examination's purpose be asked. Using the history examination again as an illustration, it can be seen that the fulfillment of this condition would require that the questions on the examination deal with every major historical period covered in the course, as well as with each type of skill that was taught.

The fourth condition for validity is "balance." Thyne describes the condition: "the contribution of the various parts of the examination to the final marks must be in accord with the examination's purpose."[32] The problem here is to determine whether all parts of an examination should be given equal importance, or whether some parts should be assigned greater weight than others.

After the grader has marked the examination and obtained the results, either of two different types of standards may be used as the basis for evaluating a given student's examination score. As we have already noted, the raw score obtained on the examination is not a grade. To become meaningful, this score must be compared with an appropriate standard of evaluation.

In *norm-referenced* grading, a student's raw score on the examination is compared with the scores of other students on the same examination. It may be compared with the highest score obtained on the examination, with the mean or median score, or given on a percentile basis (we could report the score to be, say, in the upper 10 per cent of the scores obtained). We might also report the actual rank-order of the score (we could state, for example, that the student ranked fourth in a class of 38). We might also utilize letter grades (such as A, B and C) to represent various percentile rankings, but to do so in the most meaningful way would mean stipulating which percentiles were designated by the letter grades. We would need to indicate that a grade of "A" would mean that the student's score was, say, in the top 5 per cent of all scores obtained, and so forth. Otherwise, the letter grade of "A," for example, would at best imply that there probably were no students who obtained a higher letter grade and that there probably were some other students who obtained a lower letter grade (but we could not know for sure, nor could we know how many).

Norm-referenced grading is appropriate for the selection of a specified number or percentage of students who on some basis outperform other students. However, it also has a serious limitation in

[32]Ibid., pp. 17–18.

evaluating academic achievement: it does not indicate which learning outcomes the student has actually accomplished. A student may be awarded an "A" for attaining nearly all of the desired learning outcomes in a certain course, but it is also possible that he would achieve relatively few of these outcomes and receive the same grade. Thus, under the usual system of norm-referenced grading, we have no way of knowing what a given standing means in terms of learning outcomes actually attained.

There is, however, a way of avoiding this problem, which requires the use of a prescribed score to represent the standard for evaluation. Grading of this type is known as *criterion-referenced*.

Under criterion-referenced grading we can be sure that the successful student has achieved the learning outcomes specified by the standard, because unless he had done so he would not have passed the examination. Furthermore, as Thyne points out, "there is no question of inter-candidate 'competition,' of how one candidate compares with others. In this kind of evaluation a candidate failing to reach the standard would still have 'failed' no matter how many candidates were even worse; a candidate reaching the standard would not suffer even if he were surpassed by everyone else."[33]

The essential difference between norm-referenced and criterion-referenced grading, therefore, is the type of standard used. In the former the standard is the student's *standing* (that is, how he ranks in comparison with other students), while in the latter it is the *performance* of the student (that is, whether or not he has achieved a specified level of performance). The standard may be standing or performance, but not both. If the grader is interested in selecting a certain number or percentage of candidates, norm-referenced grading would be appropriate. If no limit is imposed on the number of candidates, yet the grader wants to be sure that every successful candidate has achieved a specified set of learning outcomes, then criterion-referenced grading would be advisable.

In criterion-referenced evaluation, according to Thyne, "the question of setting a standard is essentially the question of *what* performance is to be specified." This is to be answered on the basis of the purpose of the evaluation; the standard is not to be set arbitrarily. "It has to be the mark," Thyne states, "which is the measure of the criterion. Neither is the criterion set arbitrarily. It has to be a performance (simple or complex) appropriate to the consequences of

[33]Ibid., pp. 102–103.

its being reached or not reached. When a standard is to be set, therefore, the first essential is an explicit statement of what the consequences are, because it is upon the nature of these consequences that the setting of the standard must depend. . . . When entry to a . . . profession depends upon the candidate's possessing skills to be employed in it, the criterion will consist of that body of skills."[34]

It has sometimes been argued that criterion-referenced evaluation does not appropriately recognize the difference between those who barely make the criterion and those who exceed it by a great deal. The response to this criticism is that if such differences are important, their consequences should be identified, and one or more additional criteria should be established to reflect these other consequences. For example, it might be determined that the attainment of a specified level of driving skill warrants awarding a person a driver's license for privately owned passenger cars, but that a higher, specified level of skill is necessary before a license to drive commercial vehicles can be granted. If such differential consequences cannot be or simply are not identified, however, there is no need to indicate how far above the criterion a particular candidate scored.

Certain evaluation procedures exist which may give the impression of being criterion-referenced, but which in reality have norm-referenced characteristics. For example, a teacher may allow students to "contract" for various letter grades: a specified amount of work will earn an "A," a specified lesser amount of work will earn a "B," and so forth. While these different grades require different performances that presumably could be specified in terms of learning outcomes attained, the achievement of these different performance levels has *not* been justified in terms of the consequences that follow from different performance criteria, except to imply that the student who gets an "A" stands higher than the student who gets a "B," and so on. This type of evaluation is norm-referenced rather than criterion-referenced. A similar situation prevails when the grader stipulates in advance of the examination that, say, a score of 90 or above will earn an "A," a score of 80–89 will earn a "B," and so forth. Since these standards are not related to criteria established because of the significance of their consequences, and only serve to rank the students taking the examination, this procedure must be considered norm-referenced rather than criterion-

[34]Ibid., pp. 106–108. (Emphasis in the original.)

referenced. When criterion-referenced grading is used, the grades with respect to each specified standard will be either "pass" or "not pass," or "credit" or "not credit." (Note 10)

Objections to School System Credentialing

To a student, a school system credential and/or a grade of "A" constitute very important rewards. The critics of credentialing recognize this, but they question whether school certificates presently being awarded are adequate indicators of learning, since they are generally based on norm-referenced grading. It is argued that possession of a school certificate or a high grade on a college transcript does not precisely reflect what a person is supposed to have learned. Hence the critics believe that credentialing constitutes an inappropriate reward system for the schools, which should either be eliminated or modified.

School system credentialing is also aversive as well as rewarding, however, because grades are usually awarded at fixed intervals (at the end of each term). Teachers use the threat of a low grade as aversive motivation. As mentioned previously, this is why voluntary attendance of a student at a university eventually acquires an aversive character, even though the initial decision to go to the university may have been based on positive motivation.[35] Moreover, norm-referenced grading is itself aversive, since some students will inevitably be ranked lower than others: there are "winners," but there are also "losers."

As we might expect, therefore, advocates of the Student Interest Method are often opposed to credentialing procedures of the conventional school system. Paul Goodman, for example, asked "why do the teachers grade at all?" and proposed "dispensing with credits, grading, and admissions."[36] John Holt has declared that "we cannot in any true sense be in the education business and at the same time in the grading and labeling business."[37] Ivan Illich has advocated "a law forbidding discrimination in hiring, voting, or admission to centers of learning based on previous attendance at some curriculum."

[35]See section on "Motivational Control," Chapter 4.
[36]Paul Goodman, *Compulsory Mis-education and the Community of Scholars* (New York: Vintage Books, 1964), pp. 255, 323.
[37]John Holt, *Freedom and Beyond* (New York: Dutton, 1972), pp. 250–251.

Illich views school system credentialing as an improper activity "because it does not link relevant qualities or competencies to roles, but rather the process by which such qualities are supposed to be acquired."[38]

SUMMARY

Each of the three radical proposals for change in control of the schools would require a major change in student motivational control features of the conventional school system.

Rousseau's proposal to discontinue the overt use of aversive motivation was offered in 1762 in his book *Emile*. Until that time, a total of three fundamentally different teaching methods had been developed. These methods, which we shall call the *traditional* teaching methods, depend upon the overt use of aversive motivation; they differ from each other with respect to their underlying assumptions about how to control the learning process.

The names that we have applied to the three traditional methods of teaching are the following: Telling/Showing Method, Exercise/Imitation Method, and Discovery/Restructuring Method. In the case of the first of these methods, it is assumed that the student will learn through the presentation of learning experiences by the teacher, with the student in a passive role. The latter two methods require effort on the part of the student. When the Exercise/Imitation Method is used, it is assumed that the student will learn gradually through practice, but when the Discovery/Restructuring Method is used it is assumed that learning will take place relatively suddenly through achievement of an insight on the part of the student.

Emile contains Rousseau's views on a new teaching method, which we have labeled the Student Interest Method. This method depends upon the use of positive motivation or, in some instances, nonovert aversive motivation. Any of the preceding assumptions concerning the control of the learning process are applicable to the Student Interest Method. Although the extent of compulsory schooling has increased considerably since the publication of *Emile*, in recent years a number of educational writers have proposed the adoption of the Student Interest Method. These writers include A. S. Neill, Paul Goodman, and John Holt.

[38]Ivan Illich, *Deschooling Society* (New York: Harper and Row, 1971), pp. 11–12.

The second radical proposal, like the first, is based on a new teaching method. This method (which we have labeled the Reinforcement Method) and the Student Interest Method are the only fundamentally different conceptions of teaching method formulated since the time of the ancient Greeks and Romans. The learning theory which underlies the Reinforcement Method is the assumption that a reinforcement (positive or negative) must be provided after the student makes a response, if the student is to learn. The radical proposal based on the Reinforcement Method would require the establishment of a planned, society-wide system of reinforcements, in effect transforming society into an educational agency. The principal proponent of this suggestion is psychologist B. F. Skinner.

The third radical proposal discussed in this chapter is the one which would eliminate or modify the credentialing function of the school system (the issuance of degrees, diplomas and other school certificates). This proposal would also involve the public, evaluative grading of students by the school system, since at least a minimal amount of grading is necessary when an attempt is made to determine who should receive a school certificate and who should not. Grading requires the use of some standard of evaluation. If the standard involved is the performance of other students on the same examination, then "norm-referenced" grading is being used. If the standard is a specified level of performance, then the procedure is called "criterion-referenced" grading.

The principal objection to the credentialing function of the school system is that school certificates presently are awarded on the basis of norm-referenced grading, and thus constitute inadequate indicators of the achievement of learning outcomes. Another objection of the radical critics is that norm-referenced grading of students has aversive characteristics.

The next chapter shall be devoted to a consideration of the merits of the radical proposals.

GENERAL NOTES AND BIBLIOGRAPHY

1. CLASSIFICATION OF TEACHING METHODS. As noted in the text, an elaboration of the classification of teaching methods in this text is contained in John A. Laska and Stanley L. Goldstein, *Foundations of Instructional Method* (Dubuque, Iowa: Wm. C. Brown, 1973). Many different names have been used

for the designation of teaching methods. Some of these names, such as "lecture method" and "inquiry method," are simply alternative designations for the methods described in this text, or for specific instructional techniques that are part of one of our broader categories. Other terms, such as "phonics method" and "whole-word method," refer to particular characteristics of learning experiences used in connection with one or more of the basic methods we have identified; they do not designate a teaching method in the way we are using the term. The same comment applies to a term such as "contract method," which refers to the motivational procedures used with one or more of the basic teaching methods we have described.

Each of the five teaching methods discussed in this book represents what may be called a "pure" type. Thus each method is described quite abstractly and in terms of its essential characteristics, although in practice many variations and refinements on the basic method might be employed. Further, it should be noted that in practice a teacher might very well combine two or more methods, using one method for a period of time, then changing to another one.

Teaching methods are described and analyzed in other sources such as Charles D. Hardie, *Truth and Fallacy in Educational Theory* (New York: Teachers College Press, 1962) and Ronald T. Hyman, *Ways of Teaching* (Philadelphia: J. B. Lippincott, 1970). Original writings of great educational thinkers also constitute an important avenue for further reading about teaching method. For example, everyone seriously interested in this topic should be acquainted with Rousseau's *Emile*. Several works are available that summarize and interpret the ideas of the great educational thinkers (including their views on teaching method). Among these books are the following: Harry S. Broudy and John R. Palmer, *Exemplars of Teaching Method* (Chicago: Rand McNally, 1965); S. J. Curtis and M. E. A. Boultwood, *A Short History of Educational Ideas* (3rd ed.; London: University Tutorial Press, 1961); Edward J. Power, *Evolution of Educational Doctrine: Major Educational Theorists of the Western World* (New York: Appleton-Century-Crofts, 1969); Robert R. Rusk, *The Doctrines of the Great Educators* (rev. ed.; London: Macmillan, 1965).

2. OVERT USE OF AVERSIVE MOTIVATION. The classical writers on education recognized the overt use of aversive motiva-

tion. Plato (Greece, 427–347 B.C.) wrote in *Protagoras* (trans. Benjamin Jowett):325: "And if he [the child] obeys, well and good; if not, he is straightened by threats and blows, like a piece of bent or warped wood." But the use of positive motivation within the generally aversive context of compulsory schooling was also advocated. Quintilian (Rome, 35–95 A.D.), for example, gave the following specific examples in his *Institutes of Oratory*: "Let the pupil be asked questions and praised for his answers, let him never rejoice in ignorance of anything: . . . let him compete sometimes with others and quite often think himself victorious: let him also be excited by rewards, which at that age are eagerly sought after." Quintilian, *Institutes of Oratory* (trans. William Smail):1, i 20.

3. TELLING/SHOWING METHOD. Documentation referring to the provision of learning experiences in accordance with the assumptions of the Telling/Showing Method is available from several classical writers on education. The writings of Plato, for example, contain a description of teachers and others using verbal stimuli with a passive role for the learner (Telling): "Education and admonition commence in the first years of childhood, and last to the very end of life. Mother and nurse and father and tutor are vying with one another about the improvement of the child as soon as ever he is able to understand what is being said to him: he cannot say or do anything without their setting forth to him that this is just and that is unjust; this is honourable, that is dishonourable; this is holy, that is unholy; do this and abstain from that." Plato, *Protagorus*: 325.

Plato also described the use of nonverbal learning experiences with a passive role for the learner (Showing): "We must . . . supervise craftsmen of every kind and forbid them to leave the stamp of baseness, license, meanness, unseemliness, on painting and sculpture, or building, or any other work of their hands; and anyone who cannot obey shall not practice his art in our commonwealth. We would not have our Guardians grow up among representations of moral deformity, as in some foul pasture where, day after day, feeding on every poisonous weed they would, little by little, gather insensibly a mass of corruption in their very souls. Rather we must seek out those craftsmen whose instinct guides them to whatsoever is lovely and gracious; so that our young men, dwelling in a wholesome climate, may drink in good from every quarter, whence, like a breeze bearing health from happy regions, some influence from noble works constantly falls upon eye and ear from childhood upward, and imperceptibly draws them into sympathy and harmony with the beauty of reason, whose impress they take." Plato, *Republic* (trans. Francis Cornford): 401.

4. EXERCISE/IMITATION METHOD. Statements referring to the provision of learning experiences in accordance with the requirements of the Exercise/Imitation Method are found in the writings of Aristotle (Greece, 384–322 B.C): "The virtues we get by first exercising them, as also happens in the case of the arts as well. For the things we have to learn before we can do them, we learn by doing them, e.g. men become builders by building and lyre players by playing the lyre." The source of this quotation is Aristotle, *Nichomachean Ethics* (trans. W. D. Ross): 1103 a–b. Also: "Imitation is natural to man from childhood, one of his advantages over the lower animals being this, that he is the most imitative creature in the world, and learns at first by imitation." Aristotle, *Poetics* (trans. Ingram Bywater): 1448b.

Plato also described the use of exercise in the form of games, so as to provide both learning experiences and positive motivation (although as noted previously, positive motivation would be provided within the generally aversive context of obligatory school attendance): "In that country [Egypt] arithmetical games have been invented for the use of mere children, which they learn as a pleasure and amusement." Plato, *Laws* (trans. Benjamin Jowett): 819.

5. MENTAL DISCIPLINE. An excellent statement of the mental discipline view is found in the writings of Isocrates (Greece, 436–338 B.C.): "Most men see in such studies [as astronomy and geometry] nothing but empty talk and hairsplitting; for none of these disciplines has any useful application either to private or to public affairs; nay, they are not even remembered for any length of time after they are learned. . . . These disciplines are different in their nature from the other studies which make up our education. . . . For while we are occupied with the subtlety and exactness of astronomy and geometry and are forced to apply our minds to difficult problems . . . we gain the power, after being exercised and sharpened on these disci-

plines, of grasping and learning more easily and more quickly those subjects which are of more importance and of greater value. . . . I would call it a gymnastic of the mind." Isocrates, *Antidosis* (trans. George Norlin): 261–267. Plato made a similar comment about the advantages of arithmetic: "Even the dull, if they have had an arithmetical training, although they may derive no other advantage from it, always become much quicker than they would otherwise have been." Plato, *Republic*: 526.

6. DISCOVERY/RESTRUCTURING METHOD. The best classical illustration of the provision of learning experiences in a manner characteristic of the Discovery/Restructuring Method is in the teaching procedure we usually refer to as the "Socratic Method," and which is attributed to the famous Greek philosopher Socrates (469–399 B.C.). The teaching method of Socrates, however, generally did not make overt use of aversive motivation, because his "students" came to him voluntarily to engage in discussions. Hence, although learning experiences offered by Socrates are characteristic of the Discovery/Restructuring Method, technically the "Socratic Method" as practiced by him would be regarded as the unconscious utilization of the teaching method later advocated by Rousseau, since Socrates does not appear to have realized that his reliance on positive motivation also constituted a teaching innovation. It seems appropriate, therefore, to consider the "Socratic Method" as an illustration of the Discovery/Restructuring Method, especially since Socrates was quite aware that his use of learning experiences represented an important innovation.

The various dialogues of Plato depict Socrates using his method; in the *Meno* there is an explicit discussion of Socrates' teaching method.

7. ADVOCATES OF NONCOMPULSORY EDUCATION. For additional informaton on the views of Rousseau, see: William Boyd, *The Educational Theory of Jean Jacques Rousseau* (London: Longmans, Green, 1911); C. H. Dobinson, *Jean-Jacques Rousseau,* (London: Menthuen, 1969); Jean Guehénno, *Jean-Jacques Rousseau,* trans. John Weightman and Doreen Weightman (2 vols.; New York: Columbia University Press, 1966).

A representative collection of writings by the contemporary radical critics of education is provided in Beatrice Gross and

Ronald Gross, eds., *Radical School Reform* (New York: Simon and Schuster, 1969). See also: John Holt, *Freedom and Beyond* (New York: Dutton, 1972); Ray Hemmings, *Children's Freedom: A. S. Neill and the Evolution of the Summerhill Idea* (New York: Schocken, 1973).

8. REINFORCEMENT METHOD. For additional information on the views of Thorndike and Skinner, see: Richard I. Evans, *B.F. Skinner: The Man and His Ideas* (New York: Dutton, 1968); Geraldine Joncich, *The Sane Positivist: A Biography of Edward L. Thorndike* (Middletown, Conn.: Wesleyan University Press, 1968); Leo Postman, "The History and Present Status of the Law of Effect," *Psychological Bulletin* 44 (1947): 489–563.

9. PESTALOZZI, MONTESSORI, AND DEWEY. These three eminent writers on education are frequently mentioned as having made important contributions to our conceptions of teaching method. However, an analysis of their writings shows that the teaching approaches they advocated conform to one or more of the methods discussed in this chapter.

Johann Heinrich Pestalozzi (1746–1827), born in Zurich, Switzerland, wrote extensively on education. He also tried to put his ideas about teaching method into practice, attracting international attention for the school he operated in Yverdon from 1805 to 1825. Pestalozzi's view of teaching method is generally consonant with the Exercise/Imitation Method, or the Discovery/Restructuring Method. Since a given educational writer may have expressed different views on teaching method at different times, the classification accorded the writer should be considered an identification of his basic position. Also, because a given writer's statements about method often can be interpreted in more than one way, the identification should be regarded as a tentative one. Pestalozzi read Rousseau's *Emile* and apparently tried some of Rousseau's techniques in educating his own son. But Pestalozzi was unwilling to dispense with the overt use of aversive motivation, as various selections from his diary make clear. Although in his later educational writings he emphasized the need for a teacher to love his students, this love was to be provided within the context of the students' being required to participate in educational experiences provided by the teacher (aversive motivation).

Maria Montessori (1870–1952), born in Chiravalle, Italy,

was a medical doctor who initially became involved with the education of retarded children. She then applied her method to the education of normal children living in a slum district of Rome (the school was called a Children's House). As in the case of Socrates, Montessori's name is also associated with a teaching method. But after examining her views on teaching, it is evident that her approach is representative of the Exercise/ Imitation or Discovery/Restructuring methods (including the mental discipline view). She developed special didactic materials to facilitate the acquisition of sensory discriminations by the child, and believed that teachers should make overt use of aversive motivational procedures.

John Dewey (1859–1952), born in Burlington, Vermont, was a professional philosopher, but he also had a strong interest in education and teaching method. During the early part of his career he was associated with the operation of an experimental school at the University of Chicago. Dewey's basic view of teaching method exemplifies either the Discovery/Restructuring or the Exercise/Imitation Method, or possibly the Student Interest Method (although this does not seem very likely). He believed the student would learn as the result of inquiry or problem-solving. His views were popularized during the 1920's and 1930's under the general name "progressive education." Dewey seemed to assume that children will be required to attend school. Also, though his statements are quite vague, he apparently believed that something more than just informing the student of the beneficial consequences of engaging in certain educational experiences would be required, in order to induce effort from the student (for example, he writes of "directing the child's activities" and refers to overt "guidance given by the teacher to the exercise of the pupil's intelligence"). Hence it is very unlikely that Dewey's view of teaching is consonant with the Student Interest Method. For additional information, see Laska and Goldstein, *Foundations of Teaching Method.*

10. EXAMINATIONS. The problems entailed in constructing valid examinations are outlined in most educational psychology textbooks and numerous specialized works on the topic of measurement and evaluation. Included among these specialized sources is: James M. Thyne, *Principles of Examining* (New York: Wiley, 1974). Another basic source is Benjamin S.

Bloom, J. Thomas Hastings and George F. Madaus, *Handbook on Formative and Summative Evaluation of Student Learning* (New York: McGraw-Hill, 1971). See also, for example, Victor H. Noll and Dale P. Scannell, *Introduction to Educational Measurement* (3rd ed.; Boston: Houghton Mifflin, 1972) and David A. Payne, *The Assessment of Learning* (Lexington, Mass.: D. C. Heath, 1974). A comprehensive survey on the use of examinations in school systems is provided in Joseph A. Lauwerys and David G. Scanlon, eds., *Examinations* (New York: Harcourt, Brace and World, 1969).

MERITS OF THE RADICAL PROPOSALS

CHAPTER 6

Until a few years ago, most people had an abiding faith in the school system. Parents encouraged their children to work hard in school; they themselves saved money so their children would have an opportunity to attend college. And if society encountered a difficult social problem, more often than not the long-range solution adopted was to add something new to the curriculum of the schools (for example, the addition of such programs as "drug education," "sex education," "black studies," and so forth).

This belief in the efficacy of our schools had been shared by most of the nation's educational policy makers. Despite the attention that radical critics had begun to attract in the early 1960s, it was not until a year or two after the publication in 1966 of a U.S. Government-sponsored research report prepared by James Coleman that considerable concern began to be expressed by policy makers about the effectiveness of the school system.[1]

The concept "effectiveness of schooling" refers to the extent to which intended outcomes of the school system are actually being achieved. Therefore, to ascertain the effectiveness of the school system, some measurement of its outcomes must ordinarily be obtained. Once this has been done, the question, "How effective is the school system?" can be answered by comparing the measured outcomes with some standard. If these outcomes come close to the standard, it can then be said that the schools are very effective; if

[1]James S. Coleman, *Equality of Educational Opportunity* (Washington, D.C.: Government Printing Office, 1966).

the outcomes do not, however, approach the standard, then it would be said that the schools are relatively ineffective.

In Coleman's investigation, a sample survey was utilized as the basis for collecting data on the students, teachers and facilities of the public primary and secondary schools. Test scores and other data were obtained in 1965 for approximately 600,000 students in about 4,000 schools located throughout the United States. Using a test of verbal achievement as the measure of student school success, Coleman attempted to determine the contribution that differences among schools make to an explanation of variations in academic achievement, taking non-school factors into account.

Coleman's basic finding was a startling one to believers in the relatively high effectiveness of schools. He reached the conclusion "that schools bring little influence to bear on a child's achievement that is independent of his background and general social context; and that this very lack of an independent [school] effect means that the inequalities imposed on children by their homes, neighborhood, and peer environment are carried along to become the inequalities with which they confront adult life at the end of school." This conclusion, he states, "is the implication that stems from the following results taken together: 1. The great importance of family background for achievement; 2. The fact that the relation of family background to achievement does not diminish over the years of school; 3. The relatively small amount of school-to-school variation that is not accounted for by differences in family background, indicating the small independent effect of variations in school facilities, curriculum, and staff upon achievement; 4. The small amount of variance in achievement explicitly accounted for by variations in facilities and curriculum; 5. Given the fact that no school factors account for much variation in achievement, teachers' characteristics account for more than any other—taken together with the results . . . which show that teachers tend to be socially and racially similar to the students they teach; 6. The fact that the social composition of the student body is more highly related to achievement, independently of the student's own social background, than is any school factor; 7. The fact that attitudes such as a sense of control of the environment, or a belief in the responsiveness of the environment, are extremely highly related to achievement, but appear to be little influenced by variations in school characteristics."[2]

[2]Ibid., p. 325.

It should be emphasized that the Coleman findings do not mean that the schools have no effect on student achievement. What they do indicate, however, is that observed differences among schools (with respect to such variables as teacher experience and science laboratory facilities) had very little association with observed differences in student verbal ability test scores, if social factors are also taken into account. It is quite possible, therefore, that schools are all so similar in what they do that they are of approximately equal effectiveness; this is certainly as plausible as saying that "schools do not make any difference."

The Coleman report findings pose a problem for educators in that they do not allow us to say which school factors could be changed to increase the effectiveness of the schools. Whereas highway safety engineers, for example, are able to utilize research data to identify those factors in the highway system that could be improved to reduce the number of traffic accidents (if the requisite funds were made available), educational policy makers cannot cite comparable research evidence for their recommendations. As Marshall Smith has pointed out, "with regard to the differences among schools in resources that we conventionally measure and consider in making policy, there are few that give us leverage over students' achievement. Within the fairly broad boundaries of existing variations, the simple manipulation of per-pupil expenditure or the hiring of more experienced teachers or the instituting of a new curriculum does not lead to dramatic changes in students' verbal achievement."[3] It is this implication of the Coleman report which caused such a stir among educational policy makers. Instead of being able to request additional financial resources to "improve" the schools, policy makers find themselves unable to rely on a common-sense justification for their request.

Moreover, some of the researchers who have most carefully studied the effectiveness of the conventional school system have recently expressed a willingness to consider the possibility of introducing radical change. Harvey Averch and his colleagues, for example, after completing a review of the available research on the effectiveness of schools, refer to the "suggestion that substantial im-

[3]Marshall S. Smith, *"Equality of Educational Opportunity:* The Basic Findings Reconsidered," in *On Equality of Educational Opportunity,* eds. Frederick Mosteller and Daniel P. Moynihan (New York: Vintage Books, 1972), p. 315.

provement in educational outcomes can be obtained only through a vastly different form of education." They acknowledge "that there is little research dealing with the effectiveness of these forms of education. And there is certainly a possibility that they may be less effective than the current system. At this point we can only say that the research has not identified any way of obtaining significant improvements in educational outcomes throughout the current system."[4] In a similar vein, Marshall Smith concludes his reassessment of data from the Coleman report with a suggestion that we consider radically different approaches to education: "the available evidence strongly suggests that our present thinking about the problems of education is inadequate. . . . We may need to think about ways to restructure radically the educational institution rather than ways to reallocate ineffective resources."[5] Finally, from Mosteller and Moynihan we have the following recommendation: "Revolutionary ideas can be most valuable. The caveat as always is not to get locked into an idea. We are not searching for *the* one good way to educate people, only for better ways and for a variety of ways that will serve the individual and the nation well."[6] (Note 1)

In Chapter 5 we examined the three proposals that constitute the radical criticism of conventional schooling—those proposals which, if adopted, would have a major impact on the exercise of student motivational control. One proposal is to abolish or modify compulsory schooling. This proposal is based on the Student Interest Method of teaching. A second proposal of the radical critics is to institute a planned, society-wide system of reinforcements. The principal advocate of this suggested change is B. F. Skinner. Still a third proposal involves the elimination or modificaton of school system credentialing, with its present reliance on the practice of norm-referenced grading. We shall try in this chapter to assess the arguments for and against the student motivational control features of conventional schooling and arrive at some conclusions—tentative as they might be—about the desirability of retaining the conventional school system.

[4]Harvey A. Averch et al., *How Effective Is Schooling? A Critical Review and Synthesis of Research Findings* (Santa Monica, Calif.: Rand Corporation, 1972), p. xii.

[5]Smith, "The Basic Findings Reconsidered," p. 316.

[6]Frederick Mosteller and Daniel P. Moynihan, "A Pathbreaking Report," in *On Equality of Educational Opportunity*, eds. Mosteller and Moynihan, p. 56. (Emphasis in the original.)

Should Compulsory Schooling
Be Eliminated or Modified?
Issue 4 :⎯⎯⎯⎯⎯⎯⎯⎯⎯⎯⎯⎯⎯⎯⎯⎯⎯⎯⎯⎯⎯⎯⎯⎯⎯⎯⎯⎯⎯⎯⎯⎯⎯|

Basic Arguments

Rather than argue that noncompulsory schooling would always be more effective than compulsory schooling, radical critics such as John Holt contend that the costs (particularly psychological costs) of using aversive motivation to get students to learn outweigh the possible benefits. They believe that a reliance on aversive motivation (even as a last resort) represents an inhumane procedure, which is detrimental to the teaching process. In the following excerpt from *How Children Fail*, Holt describes the atmosphere of fear that pervades the school system when it is aversively controlled, and calls attention to the negative results produced by this situation.

Children see school almost entirely in terms of the day-to-day and hour-to-hour tasks that we impose on them. This is not at all the way the teacher thinks of it. The conscientious teacher thinks of himself as taking his students (at least part way) on a journey to some glorious destination, well worth the pains of the trip. If he teaches history, he thinks how interesting, how exciting, how useful it is to know history, and how fortunate his students will be when they begin to share his knowledge. If he teaches French, he thinks of the glories of French literature, or the beauty of spoken French, or the delights of French cooking, and how he is helping to make these joys available to his students. And so for all subjects. . . . Maybe *I* thought the students were in my class because they were eager to learn what I was trying to teach, but they knew better. They were in school because they had to be, and in my class either because they had to be, or because otherwise they would have had to be in another class, which might be even worse. . . .

So the valiant and resolute band of travelers I thought I was leading toward a much-hoped-for destination turned out instead to be more like convicts in a chain gang, forced under threat of punishment to move along a rough path leading nobody knew where and down which they could see hardly more than a few steps ahead. School feels like this to children: it is a place where *they* make you go and where *they* tell you to do things and where *they* try to make your life unpleasant if you don't do them or don't do them right.

For children, the central business of school is not learning, whatever this vague word means; it is getting these daily tasks done, or at least out of the way, with a minimum of effort and unpleasantness. Each task is an end in itself. The children don't care how they dispose of it. If they can get it out of the way by doing it, they will do it; if experience has taught them that this does not work very well, they will turn to other means, illegitimate means, that wholly defeat whatever purpose the task-giver may have had in mind.[7]

The principal argument of the supporters of compulsory schooling is that even aversive motivation may sometimes be necessary to induce a child to learn those things which are important to the welfare of the child and that of society. The child cannot always be expected to know what is good for him; adults are responsible for getting him to learn things he might otherwise ignore. As a last resort, therefore, the supporters of compulsion believe that if a child refuses to learn something a teacher judges to be good for him, then aversive means should be employed to induce him to make the effort to learn.

Education is thus viewed as a duty imposed on the child for his own good as well as for that of the public, rather than as a right, guaranteed to the individual, which he may exercise at his own discretion. Different variations of this basic argument that were advanced by the early proponents of compulsory schooling in the United States have been summarized by De Boer: "Invoking the precedents of states' rights, they argued that if a state has the right to tax property to maintain public schools, it has the right to compel the youth to use the facilities provided. Or, that if a state has the right to compel the vaccination of pupils against the threat of disease, it has the right to compel 'moral vaccination.' Or, that if the state has the right to prevent parents from starving their children, it has the right to prevent 'mental starvation.' Or, that if the state has the right to compel military service, it has the right to compel school attendance. Proponents also argued that the right of the state to compel the universal education of its eligible citizens would serve as security against crime, misery, loss of property, and disregard for law and order."[8]

A similar society-oriented justification for compulsory schooling has been made in recent years, and derives from a belief that the school system has an important role in promoting economic and so-

[7]John Holt, *How Children Fail* (New York: Dell, 1970), pp. 45–47. (Emphasis in the original.)

[8]Peter P. De Boer, "Compulsory Attendance," in *Encyclopedia of Education,* ed. Lee C. Deighton (New York: Macmillan, 1971), 2: 377.

cial development. Educational decision makers in the less-developed countries of the world have noted that advanced countries have school systems that are attended by all school-age children; in less developed countries, school enrollments consist of a much smaller proportion of the eligible population. They have concluded that compulsory schooling is necessary for less developed countries to achieve the levels of economic and social development already reached in Western societies.

Furthermore, compulsory schooling may produce learning outcomes which are advantageous for society and which are not reflected in the explicit goals of the school system. Under compulsory schooling, Reagan observes, "students are likely to learn 'factory virtues' such as punctuality, toleration of boredom, acceptance of authority."[9] Compulsory schooling also performs other useful non-educational functions for society—the schools serve as a "babysitter," for example, and as a means for keeping young persons off the labor market.

Compulsory schooling is also viewed as serving the best interest of the individual (as well as that of society) by providing each person with an awareness of his total cultural heritage. Each school-age child should be given access to this heritage, it is argued, whether he or she recognizes its value or not, and in spite of any particularistic religious or ethnic identification acquired from his or her parents. Some persons maintain that combining compulsory school attendance with a mandatory program of study for all schools—with the curricular emphasis on common societal values— would allow the schools to contribute to national cohesion by fostering a sense of community.

Still other arguments have been advanced for compulsory schooling. The abolition of compulsory schooling, it is contended, would be detrimental to those students whose parents do not insist that they attend school, and/or who do not provide alternative educational opportunities. Gerald Reagan has pointed out that the "abolition of compulsory schooling would minimize the number who attain advanced schooling and would maximize the 'distance' between those who have advanced schooling and the rest of the population."[10]

[9]Gerald M. Reagan, "Compulsion, Schooling, and Education," *Educational Studies* 4 (1973): 2.
[10]Ibid., p. 5.

Radical critics agree that forcing a student to learn might cause him or her to engage in learning activities that might otherwise be avoided; but they suggest that truly important learning outcomes would be achieved more effectively by waiting until the student wanted to learn and did not feel coerced. All children, they maintain, will learn if they have an interest. If it is impossible to convince a child that achieving a particular learning outcome would be for the child's own benefit, then the outcome is not sufficiently important for compulsion to be used. Later the child might change his mind about the desirability of this learning outcome, in which case that would be the appropriate time for him to try to attain the outcome, because he would then be personally interested in achieving it.

According to proponents of the Student Interest Method, anything important that the student has missed can be made up later, when he becomes aware of the value of attaining the learning outcome in question. If, however, the student never comes to appreciate the need for achieving a given learning outcome, then this would be good evidence that the particular outcome was not, in fact, very important, because if it were the student would make an effort to attain it. (Note 2)

Discussion of the Arguments

One of the difficulties that may be encountered in attempting to resolve the issues raised by the radical critics is the fact that very little relevant empirical knowledge is available about the consequences that could be expected to follow the adoption of their proposals. Therefore, personal convictions must, very often, be considered as to what seems reasonable. These convictions are based on extrapolations from personal experience and results of limited empirical research, sometimes bolstered by historical analogy. It would seem that definitive conclusions cannot be reached.

As far as the proposal to abolish or modify compulsory schooling is concerned, there are three factors that must be given further consideration: the meaning we give to the concept of compulsory schooling, the age of the student, and the learning outcomes desired.

The term "compulsory schooling" may refer to at least three different things. What is meant by the concept, therefore, may determine to a large extent whether the idea is accepted or rejected.

Compulsory schooling can simply mean that a student is obliged to attend school, but within the school aversive motivation is not used. It can also mean that the student is compelled both to attend school and to participate in prescribed learning experiences within it (this is how compulsion is used in the conventional school system). Finally, the concept can mean that aversive motivation is used to induce the student to attend school and to attain prescribed learning outcomes.

Some radical critics are willing to accept the first definition of compulsory schooling. They believe that mandatory attendance is in the best interest of young persons, since they would presumably be subject to parental control if they were not in school, and not all parents are able or willing to provide appropriate educational experiences for their children. However, radical critics who accept compulsory attendance favor use of the Student Interest Method within the school. Using the Student Interest Method within a school means that teachers inform their students that no compulsion to learn exists: the student is free, if he wishes, to play games all day, read comic books, or even to sleep. However, various opportunities to learn, for those children who wish to do so, are provided by the teachers. Displays of learning materials (often called "interest centers"), established at different places within the classroom, allow the student to utilize these materials in accordance with his or her interests. Teachers, who are available to assist students with their learning problems, also make recommendations about the desirability of particular learning activities.

The best examples of this approach are A.S. Neill's Summerhill school and some schools that use the so-called "open classroom" approach. It should be pointed out, however, that the term "open classroom" is often applied to classrooms that are physically open (in the sense of not being enclosed within four permanent walls) and which provide individualized instruction, but which still depend on aversive motivation to induce students to learn. Sometimes the aversive technique consists of requiring the student to enter into contracts that he or she is obliged to fulfill; other times coercion is supplied by "loving" teachers who become less so when students do not do what they are told to. (Note 3)

A consideration of compulsory schooling in relation to the age of the student represents another way that some agreement on the compulsory schooling issue may be attempted. The age group presently subject to compulsory schooling legislation in the United

States generally consists of persons between six and sixteen years of age. Why are persons at the age of thirty not subject to compulsory schooling legislation? It would seem that a belief exists to the effect that young persons do not necessarily know what is good for them, whereas adults do. Another approach to the compulsory schooling issue, therefore, is to attempt to determine at what age a person acquires the ability to decide for himself the kinds of learning experiences he should have.

Finally, it may be possible to obtain a solution to the compulsory schooling issue by inquiring which learning experiences and/or learning outcomes, if any, are of such importance to the individual and/or society that they warrant the use of aversive motivation. For example, if other motivational procedures fail, should everyone be compelled to learn to read, any more than everyone should be compelled to learn to play tennis? Since compulsory schooling continues to exist, it is possible that certain learning outcomes are expected to be attained by the student. It would thus seem incumbent upon anyone advocating compulsory schooling that he or she identify as precisely as possible those learning outcomes personally judged to be worth the cost of aversive motivation. It should also be demonstrable that these outcomes cannot be achieved through the use of positive motivation; for it might be possible to avoid the use of aversive motivation, if sufficiently attractive rewards for the attainment of the prescribed learning outcomes were provided. Let us suppose that every young person was promised $1,000 upon achievement of a prescribed set of learning outcomes, equivalent to what we now expect of secondary school graduates. This sum of money would probably induce most students to complete their studies. It might even encourage them to finish a year or two earlier, thereby affording a net saving in economic resources.

Should positive motivation not be regarded as effective or economically feasible for all students, the advocates of compulsory schooling might wish to consider aversive motivation on a ratio reinforcement basis as an alternative to a fixed-interval reinforcement basis. Termination of compulsory schooling constitutes a major negative reinforcement for the student, but in the existing school system this reinforcement does not occur until the student has remained in school for a prescribed number of years or has fulfilled the sequence of courses prescribed for the secondary school diploma. The present procedure represents the use of fixed-interval reinforcement, which, as was indicated in Chapter 4, is a less effective technique than ratio reinforcement. It would be quite simple, however, to utilize ratio reinforcement. All that would be necessary would be to announce that all compulsory schooling obligations would be fulfilled as soon as the student had attained a set of pre-scribed learning outcomes (and, for those learning outcomes that cannot be adequately measured, that the student had participated in prescribed learning experiences). Provisions would then need to be made to permit each student to achieve the desired learning out-comes at his own pace, so that the attainment of these learning out-comes would be contingent upon the amount of effort exerted by the student.

The use of either positive motivation or aversive motivation with ratio reinforcement (as described above) would facilitate the achievement of a set of desired learning outcomes. Under the pres-ent procedure of using aversive motivation on a fixed-interval rein-forcement basis, it has not been necessary to stipulate precisely what it is that all secondary school graduates are expected to have learned.

In conclusion, it seems clear that the advocates of aversive mo-tivation in the schools need to specify the kind of compulsory schooling envisioned (compulsory attendance, compulsory participa-tion in a prescribed educational program, or the mandatory attain-ment of specified learning outcomes), the age group to which it should apply, and the learning experiences to be made obligatory (and/or the learning outcomes to be attained, if any). Once this is done, it is probable that the issue of compulsory school will have been greatly clarified, if not resolved.

Should a Planned, Society – Wide System of Reinforcements Be Established?

Issue 5:

In advancing his proposal for the establishment of a planned, society-wide system of reinforcements, B. F. Skinner gives principal emphasis to the argument of greater effectiveness. While recogniz-ing that some forms of control (such as aversive motivation) are ob-jectionable, he maintains that "human behavior is wholly deter-mined by genetic and environmental forces." Therefore, undesirable and out-moded methods of control must be dispensed with, and procedures that will be most effective in producing the kind of society we want must be followed. "Man is largely responsible for the environment in which he lives," Skinner points out. "He has changed the physical world to minimize aversive properties and maximize positive reinforcements, and he has constructed governmental, religious, educational, economic, and psychotherapeutic systems which promote satisfying personal contacts and make him more skillful, informed, productive, and happy. He is engaged in a gigantic exercise in self-control, as the result of which he has come to realize more and more of his genetic potential. . . . By accepting the fact that human behavior is controlled—by things if not by men—we take a big step forward, for we can then stop trying to avoid control and begin to look for the most effective kinds."[11]

A description of a community that has instituted a planned structure of incentives is offered in Skinner's novel, *Walden Two*. In this book, Skinner (by means of the character Frazier) discusses the community's conception of the "Good Life." According to Frazier, good health is one of the necessities for the Good Life. The Good Life also entails "an absolute minimum of unpleasant labor" and a "chance to exercise talents and abilities" through sports, hobbies, arts and crafts, and various scientific pursuits. Frazier declares that "intimate and satisfying personal contacts" are also necessary: "We must have the best possible chance of finding congenial spirits. . . . We discourage attitudes of domination and criticism. Our goal is general tolerance and affection." Finally, Frazier points out, "the Good Life means relaxation and rest. We get that in Walden Two almost as a matter of course, but not merely because we have reduced our hours of work. In the world at large the leisure class is perhaps the least relaxed. The important thing is to satisfy our needs. Then we can give up the blind struggle to 'have a good time' or 'get what we want.' We have achieved a true leisure."[12]

Carl Rogers, a leading critic of Skinner's ideas, has challenged Skinner's conception of the Good Life. Rogers argues that "if we choose some particular goal or series of goals for human beings and then set out on a large scale to control human behavior to the end of achieving those goals, we are locked in the rigidity of our initial choice."[13] Instead, Rogers prefers to view man as a "process of be-

[11]B. F. Skinner, *Contingencies of Reinforcement: A Theoretical Analysis* (New York: Appleton-Century-Crofts, 1969), pp. 45–46.

[12]B. F. Skinner, *Walden Two* (New York: Macmillan Paperbacks, 1962), pp. 159–161.

[13]Carl Rogers, "Some Issues Concerning the Control of Human Behavior," *Science*, November 30, 1956, p. 1062.

coming." The Good Life, for Rogers, "is the process of movement in a direction which the human organism selects when it is inwardly free to move in any direction. . . . The general qualities of this selected direction appear to have a certain universality. . . . The person who is psychologically free moves in the direction of becoming a more fully functioning person. . . . It involves the stretching and growing of becoming more and more of one's potentialities."[14]

There is nothing, however, in Skinner's advocacy of a society-wide, planned system of reinforcements that precludes adoption of the Rogerian conception of the Good Life in place of the *Walden Two* version—or any other conception of the Good Life, for that matter. It is very important for our consideration of Skinner's proposal that his views on educational *means* (the subject of Issue 5) be separated from his views on the penultimate/ultimate *end* of education.

Another problem that has been raised in connection with the Skinner proposal is the question of *who* would serve as the designers of the culture. A response that Skinner has given to this question is contained in the following excerpt, in which it is suggested that behavioral scientists will have an important role to play.

> Although science may provide the basis for a more effective cultural design, the question of who is to engage in such design remains unanswered. "Who *should* control?" is a spurious question—at least until we have specified the consequences with respect to which it may be answered. If we look to the long-term effect upon the group the question becomes, "Who should control if the culture is to survive?". . . Since a science of behavior is concerned with demonstrating the consequences of cultural practices, we have some reason for believing that such a science will be an essential mark of the culture or cultures which survive. The current culture which, on this score alone, is most likely to survive is, therefore, that in which the methods of science are most effectively applied to the problems of human behavior.
>
> This does not mean, however, that scientists are becoming self-appointed governors. It does not mean that anyone in possession of the methods and results of science can step outside the stream of history and take the evolution of government into his own hands. Science is not free, either. It cannot interfere with the course of events; it is simply part of that course.[15]

In *Walden Two* Skinner provides the reader with some details

---

[14]Carl Rogers, *On Becoming a Person* (Boston: Houghton Mifflin, 1961), pp. 187, 191, 196, 395.

[15]Skinner, *Science and Human Behavior* (New York: Macmillan, 1953), pp. 445–446. (Emphasis in the original.)

about the form of government he considers most desirable. The community of Walden Two is governed by a Board of Planners, which consists of six members. The Planners are not elected; replacements are selected by the Board itself. Skinner regards this arrangement as a limited despotism, because "the despot must wield his power for the good of others. If he takes any step which reduces the sum total of human happiness, his power is reduced by a like amount. . . . Insofar as the Planners rule at all, they do so through positive reinforcement. They don't use or threaten to use force. They have no machinery for that. In order to extend their power they would have to provide more and more satisfying conditions. A curious sort of despotism." Skinner explicitly rejects a democratic form of government for Walden Two, arguing that "it fails to take account of the fact that in the long run *man is determined by the state.* A *laissez-faire* philosophy which trusts to the inherent goodness and wisdom of the common man is incompatible with the observed fact that men are made good or bad and wise or foolish by the environment in which they grow." Skinner is also critical of the governmental system of the Soviet Union: "The Russians are still a long way from a culture in which people behave as they *want* to behave, for their mutual good. In order to get its people to act as the communist pattern demands, the Russian government has had to use the techniques of capitalism. On the one hand it resorts to extravagant and uneven rewards. But an unequal distribution of wealth destroys more incentives than it creates. It obviously can't operate for the *common* good. On the other hand, the government also uses punishment or the threat of it. What kind of behavioral engineering do you call that?"[16]

In his more recent book, *Beyond Freedom and Dignity,* Skinner indicates that a democratic form of government may be the type necessary to undertake a deliberate design of a culture: "The principle of making the controller a member of the group he controls should apply to the designer of a culture. A person who designs a piece of equipment for his own use presumably takes the interests of the user into account, and the person who designs a social environment in which he is to live will presumably do the same. He will select goods or values which are important to him and arrange the kind of contingencies to which he can adapt. In a democracy the controller is found among the controlled, although he behaves in

[16]Skinner, *Walden Two,* pp. 54–55, 264, 272, 273, 276. (Emphasis in the original.)

different ways in the two roles." Skinner also observes that so-called controllers of a society are not free to do as they please; they are themselves subject to contingencies of reinforcement: "The misuse of a technology of behavior is a serious matter, but we can guard against it best by looking not at putative controllers but at the contingencies under which they control. It is not the benevolence of a controller but the contingencies under which he controls benevolently which must be examined. All control is reciprocal, and an interchange between control and countercontrol is essential to the evolution of a culture."[17] In a properly designed culture, therefore, the culture design itself would reinforce the "controller" as well as the "controllee" for the kinds of behavior desired of both within the culture.

Critics of Skinner's proposal very likely would contend that he has failed to provide an adequate answer to the question, "Who should control education?" It is difficult to imagine how controllers can themselves be controlled, especially if they are able to establish and/or alter their own contingencies of reinforcement. How can we be certain that a controller would not find the accumulation of personal property more reinforcing than service to society? How can we be certain that a controller would not try to obtain the reinforcements that come from giving special benefits and privileges to the members of his family? And how can we be certain that a controller would be willing to relinquish the personal satisfaction that comes from the exercise of power to another person chosen to replace him as controller? These are all questions that many persons would like to have answered before making a decision to adopt Skinner's proposal.

The proposal that Skinner set forth for a deliberately designed culture has also been criticized by some writers precisely because it might be too effective. Negley and Patrick, for example, refer to the "shocking horror" of the utopian society described in Skinner's *Walden Two*. "Of all the dictatorships espoused by utopists," they regard Skinner's as "the most profound, and incipient dictators might well find in this utopia a guide book of political practice."[18]

Is the criticism of Negley and Patrick acceptable? Their con-

[17]B. F. Skinner, *Beyond Freedom and Dignity* (New York: Knopf, 1971), pp. 172, 182–183.

[18]Glenn Negley and J. M. Patrick, *The Quest for Utopia* (New York: Schuman, 1952), p. 590.

tention would seem to be that the more effective the educative process is, the more it should and would be abhorred. But since the educative process produces *desired* learning outcomes, how can we condemn it for being very effective, unless we are willing to condemn any sort of education? Either the educative process produces valued outcomes or it doesn't; if it does, then it would seem that higher value should be placed on effective educational activities than on less effective ones, provided that the costs do not outweigh the benefits.

Another objection to Skinner's proposal is that a planned, society-wide system of reinforcements would abridge men's freedom. Skinner (speaking through his character, Frazier) maintains that Walden Two "is the freest place on earth. And it is free precisely because we make no use of force or the threat of force. . . . By skillful planning, by a wise choice of techniques we *increase* the feeling of freedom." The reason the members of the Walden Two community feel free is that they are controlled through positive reinforcement (positive motivation), which means that they can always reject the wishes of the controller without suffering any decrease in their state of well being. Frazier points out that in Walden Two "we can achieve a sort of control under which the controlled . . . nevertheless *feel free*. They are doing what they want to do, not what they are forced to do. That's the source of the tremendous power of positive reinforcement."[19] (Note 4)

Skinner has made an important contribution to educational studies by calling attention to the need to consider education in relation to the incentive structure of society. As obvious as this relationship may seem, statements are repeatedly made urging us to accept certain goals for education, without ever making reference to the establishment of an incentive structure to elicit the behaviors represented by these goals. The present reluctance to structure a planned, society-wide system of reinforcements, without first having made a careful examination of the costs and benefits involved, is understandable. However, we may be condemning our schools to relative ineffectiveness if we refuse to do any systematic planning of the societal incentive structure.

We shall return to the question of whether a planned, society-wide system of reinforcements should be established when we consider in Chapter 10 the proposal to establish an educative society.

---

[19]Skinner, *Walden Two*, pp. 262–263. (Emphasis in the original.)

Should School System Credentialing
Be Eliminated or Modified?
Issue 6:_____|

The radical critics opposed to the issuance of credentials by the school system argue that such certificates do not constitute adequate measures of academic achievement. In the medieval university—when the award of a degree meant that the recipient was qualified to join the faculty as a teacher—the school certificate was a meaningful indicator of accomplishment. It would have been somewhat equivalent to a football coach today telling a young man who had trained diligently that he "made the team." But what significance does a contemporary high school diploma or bachelor's degree have?

At best only a very general notion usually exists of what may be expected from a high school or college graduate. If the student's school record is consulted, there is little specific information beyond a listing of course titles to suggest the learning outcomes the student has attained. The school certificate may, in fact, simply mean that the student was adept at pleasing his instructors and/or that he was faithful in attending class. Even if the student had acquired some important learning outcomes, because of the transient nature of learning a person who received a school certificate ten years or even six months ago may have forgotten a considerable amount of the learning required to earn the credential. Or, in the case of course credits accumulated simply to obtain a credential, substantial forgetting may even occur before the certificate is acquired. Yet once issued, a school certificate is rarely, if ever, rescinded.

Since meeting the learning requirements for a school certificate could involve considerable effort, some students seek an easier solution. In the American school system individual instructors are usually responsible for developing and administering examinations, as well as eventually assessing the results of them. Because of this, some students seek to be placed in the classes of those instructors who are "easiest." Incompetent instructors, to avoid criticism by students and others, frequently resort to practices of leniently grading and/or providing a less demanding curriculum, hoping thereby to insure their popularity and preserve their employment. Often when instructors do try to maintain "standards," an adversary relationship between teacher and student is created which can be detrimental to the teaching process and its effectiveness.

Consequently, the critics of credentialing argue, success in obtaining a school certificate does not always mean that successful learning has occurred. Before expansion of the school system in the nineteenth century, perhaps this situation could have been tolerated, especially since relatively few persons would have been affected. But in the present-day school system expensive resources are wasted, and large numbers of persons are not, in fact, learning what they are presumed to be learning. Moreover, the students themselves are dissatisfied; they have become aware of the hypocrisy in what they are doing. As Edgar Friedenberg has observed, the credentialing function of the schools "creates cynicism and despair among students and educators who perceive that . . . the credential is awarded in recognition of qualities quite different from the competencies it is supposed to certify."[20]

Another major criticism of present credentialing practices is of their aversive character. As was pointed out in Chapter 5, teachers use the threat of a low grade as aversive motivation. Even the voluntary attendance of students at universities entails an aversive, task-stimulator role on the part of university instructors, because reinforcements are provided on a fixed-interval basis.

On the other hand, the proponents of school system credentialing argue that degrees and other school certificates are very helpful to prospective employers and school admissions officers. Their utility is demonstrated by the fact that employers make extensive use of school certificates in selecting employees. School credentials are thus regarded as good indicators of student capabilities, although the most important competency they signify is probably quickness to learn rather than the attainment of specified learning outcomes. Moreover, the students who obtain certification under the present credentialing system have probably had to demonstrate perseverance and conformity to the dominant values of society, which prospective employers and school admissions officers may also regard as desirable characteristics.

Credentials and grades also serve to motivate the student. The student knows that access to certain occupations and higher schools is dependent upon or facilitated by the possession of a school certificate and/or good grades (for example, access to the occupations of

[20]Edgar Z. Friedenberg, "Status and Role Identity in Education," in *Education and Social Policy,* eds. C. A. Bowers, Ian Housego and Doris Dyke (New York: Random House, 1970), pp. 151–152.

medical doctor, lawyer, university professor, and admission to universities). Also, once a person acquires a school certificate he gains a status that can never be taken away from him, even if he later forgets everything he was required to learn to get the certificate.

The right to issue degrees and other certificates, furthermore, is enormously important to the school system because of the monopolistic control over access to certain occupations that this right confers upon the school system. Having such monopolistic control means that teachers and school administrators need not be overly concerned with how effective they are, since students have no real alternative to school attendance if they wish to enter most professional occupations. Thus school administrators and teachers can have a self-serving interest in granting school credentials. (Note 5)

Possible Solutions to the Credentialing Issue

In raising their objections to the credentialing practices of the conventional school system, radical critics have exposed what appears to be a fundamental paradox in the operation of our schools. The declared reason for the existence of schools is to facilitate the attainment of desired learning outcomes. Yet instead of utilizing criterion-referenced testing—which would be consonant with the goal of accomplishing specified learning outcomes—the school system employs norm-referenced evaluation. The latter procedure is consonant with the function of selecting and sorting students, but it is not appropriate if teaching is to be the principal function of the schools.

One solution to this problem is to redefine the basic purpose of the school system and to declare it primarily an instrument for selecting and sorting, thus making its purpose conform to its actual function. But if we permit the school system to function mainly as an elaborate mechanism for the identification of those individuals who are quick to learn and who have the personal qualities (perseverance, ambition, and so forth) that are desired, say in new employees, then the costs of schooling may not be warranted on economic grounds. Is it necessary to subject students to twelve or sixteen years in the school system simply to find out who the quickest learners are, when aptitude tests that would serve this purpose (and with considerably much less cost to the students and society) are available?

It is interesting to note in this connection that school system credentialing may not be absolutely indispensable to prospective employers. Once a job applicant is hired, for example, his promotions and salary increases are dependent upon an evaluation of his on-the-job performance. Employers are thus capable of making their own evaluations of employees after they have been hired; it would seem, therefore, that employers should also be capable of evaluating job applicants—perhaps by giving their own examinations or even by instituting a trial period of employment. Some employers in fields in which school credentials are not relevant (the owners of professional football teams, for example) have developed elaborate procedures for the identification of suitable employees and their subsequent evaluation, thus showing that employers can discover effective ways for the selection of new personnel without the aid of school credentials.

Another solution to the credentialing dilemma is to reaffirm that the primary purpose of the school system is to foster the attainment of desired learning outcomes and then to make the actual functioning of the school system correspond with its purpose. The defenders and the critics of school system credentialing could resolve their differences if they were to agree that the schools should primarily be concerned with the attainment of specified learning outcomes. The radical critics acknowledge the motivational value of school certificates; on the other hand, even the strongest defender of credentialing would probably concede that, as indicators of the attainment of specified learning outcomes, school certificates are at least to some extent inadequate. Therefore, if the adequacy of school certificates as indicators of the accomplishment of specified learning outcomes were to be significantly improved, and if the aversive effects of grading were to be curtailed, then both the critics and the supporters of credentialing would probably agree that school certificates need not be abolished. This would require the adoption of criterion-referenced grading in place of norm-referenced evaluation. We suggest that this "credentialing compromise" be accepted to resolve the credentialing issue.

Performance Objectives

The use of criterion-referenced evaluation will entail a specification of the standards of performance that students are expected to achieve. Such prescribed outcomes are known as *performance objectives* or *behavioral objectives;* their use in the teaching process is generally referred to as *competency-based instruction.* (Note 6)

When combined with criterion-referenced grading, performance objectives allow the school system to give adequate meaning to its certificates. Instead of issuing high school diplomas, for example, that do not specifically state what the student has learned, there is no reason in principle that a diploma could not be accompanied by a statement of all the significant learning outcomes successfully achieved by the student.

It should be recognized, however, that a great deal of effort would be required to develop the performance objectives to be subsumed under the various certificates issued by the school system. Since certificates would signify the attainment of specified learning outcomes, the school system would have to be involved in an ongoing attempt to ascertain and evaluate the relevance of these outcomes. Furthermore, examinations given to determine whether a student has attained the prescribed learning outcomes would have to be prepared with great care to insure that rote memorization will not suffice when meaningful learning is expected.

The fact that a person may later forget what he knew at the time he passed a credentialing examination, and the fact that human knowledge is constantly expanding, could also be taken into account if school certificates were based on performance objectives. Each certificate could be given an expiration date. A person would then be required to pass an updating examination if he wished to maintain his credential beyond a specified period of time. The updating examination would give the certificate holder an opportunity to demonstrate that the learning outcomes required for the particular certificate involved were not forgotten. Also, if new learning outcomes had been established as requirements for the certificate, a person would be able to demonstrate that he or she was keeping abreast of these new developments. (Note 7)

Elimination of Fixed Time Limits for Learning

The adoption of criterion-referenced testing will also require that students be provided with a flexible time period for the accomplishment of stipulated learning outcomes, instead of the fixed time limits which prevail under norm-referenced testing. If we have criterion-referenced evaluation and want every student to attain the performance standard, it makes no sense to permit only one examination at a fixed time. Instead, the student must be allowed to take the examination when he wishes, and as many times as he wishes. If the student does poorly on a particular examination, the teacher can diagnose the student's learning difficulties and prescribe individualized remedial learning experiences, so that the student will have an increased probability of passing the examination the next time he takes it.

As a result of utilizing a flexible rather than a fixed time period, virtually every motivated student will be able to achieve a given learning objective.[21] Imagine what it would be like if a hospital gave its patients a stipulated period of time in which to get well. Some patients would obviously perform better than others, and this would be quite acceptable if we merely wished to rank the patients on the basis of which ones were the quickest to regain their health. But if we want the maximum number of patients to get well (as we do, of course), then we need to have a flexible time period for each patient's recovery.

Two important consequences will follow the elimination of fixed time limits for learning. One consequence is that students will be reinforced on a ratio rather than a fixed-interval basis. The student will receive a reinforcement whenever he makes a sufficient effort to achieve a prescribed learning outcome. As was previously pointed out, ratio reinforcement is a more effective motivational procedure than fixed-interval reinforcement.

The second consequence of the elimination of fixed time limits for learning is related to the use of ratio reinforcement. Teachers will not have to coerce students into making an effort to learn, since the task-stimulator role required when fixed-interval reinforcement is used would no longer be appropriate. Therefore, teachers will have no need to be aversive (even if students are compelled by society to attend school); they can devote their full attention to helping students to learn. (Teachers would have more difficulty in being aversive in any case, since the threat of giving low grades will no longer be possible when norm-referenced evaluation is eliminated.)

[21]See John B. Carroll, "A Model of School Learning," *Teachers College Record* 64 (1963): 722–733.

Can All Learning Outcomes Be Measured?

The objection has been raised that a credentialing system based on the attainment of prescribed competencies would be inadequate, since for some learning outcomes (for example, music appreciation) it is extremely difficult or impossible to specify which behaviors a student would be expected to exhibit. The critics argue that if schools utilize performance objectives and criterion-referenced grading, teachers would ignore learning outcomes that cannot be measured and concentrate their efforts on inducing the attainment of measurable outcomes, some of which might be quite trivial.

It is obvious that there are learning outcomes which are very difficult or impossible to measure. But if some learning outcomes cannot be measured, we should not expect them to be considered for the purpose of student evaluation, in any case. Thyne has the following observation on this point: "If the marking is to be relevant and consistent, [the grader] must set out criteria by which all candidates' answers are to be judged. Admittedly, this may be very difficult, but if the examiner does not *have* criteria by which to assess originality, creativity, organisation, expressiveness, and so forth, how can he claim any validity for his marks? And one would seem to have cause to be suspicious of an examiner who assures us that he does have criteria, but cannot say, even to someone expert in the topic, what the criteria are. . . . One sometimes hears reference to 'imponderables,' and assertions that in such cases the rules of examining, which may be good enough for mundane issues, cannot possibly apply. We can but reply that if something is believed to be 'imponderable,' then one should have the courage of one's convictions and stop trying to weigh it."[22]

If students were not graded for unmeasurable performances, would this mean that the schools would have to stop trying to foster learning outcomes such as music appreciation? Not at all: the schools might certainly continue to provide the learning experiences believed to produce unmeasurable learning outcomes; they would simply not try to evaluate students for the attainment or nonattainment of unmeasurable outcomes. Schools could issue certificates of attendance rather than ones of competency in cases of un-

[22]James M. Thyne, *Principles of Examining* (New York: Wiley, 1974), p. 250. (Emphasis in the original.)

measurable learning outcomes. (A certificate of attendance would state that its holder had attended a specified number of classes which provided specified types of learning experiences.) But since many learning outcomes probably can be reduced to specific performances, it is probable that the schools can issue competency certificates in most instances; if not, the issuance of certificates of attendance will have to suffice.

Is It Necessary to Know Who Has Learned the Most?

It is argued sometimes that the present norm-referenced grading system (which ordinarily utilizes A-B-C-D-F letter grades) does, in fact, tell whether a minimum set of desired learning outcomes has been achieved: if a person receives an "F," he has not attained the required standard; if he earns a "D" or above, he has met the standard. In addition, it is contended, the present system also tells how far above the minimum standard a given student ranks—that is, it indicates who has learned the most.

This argument may be answered by recalling a basic point from the previous chapter. In the discussion of characteristics of criterion-referenced evaluation, it is indicated that the performance which constitutes the standard must be meaningful, with respect to the consequences of its being met or not; the standard cannot be an arbitrary one. Therefore, it is difficult to imagine that a single course of study offered by the school system would require more than one standard—or that a single course would even need a standard of its own. To take mathematical skills as an example, the school system would be expected to set a general standard of performance appropriate for the average citizen, and a number of specialized standards pertaining to the requirements of certain occupational groups (such as teachers, electricians, and highway engineers). It is doubtful, however, that a single course of study would be sufficient to prepare a person for the relevant examination; it is much more likely that several courses would be required.

In any case, with respect to grading, once an appropriate standard has been established it would only be necessary to indicate whether a person has passed or failed a particular competency examination. If passing the examination meant, for example, that a person has acquired all of the mathematical skills deemed appropriate for the average citizen, then it need only be stated whether or not the person has passed. It would make no sense to give the person who scores the highest an "A" and the one who barely passes a "D." If another level of mathematical competency is required, say, for a highway engineer, a separate examination to measure performance would have to be provided—but, then again, the only grade necessary on such an examination would be a "pass."

Relationship of Licenses to School Credentials

Our proposal to increase the meaningfulness of school credentials would, in effect, give school credentials some of the characteristics of *licenses*. The idea behind a licensing system is to enable society to protect itself from certain types of incompetent behavior. For example, before being permitted to drive an automobile a person must pass a state-administered test to become a licensed driver, because driving a car is a potentially dangerous activity, not only to the driver, but to society. Similarly, in the case of medical doctors, lawyers, dentists, and certain other professional practitioners, society requires that they be licensed by the state, thereby protecting the layman who does not have the capability of judging for himself the competence of these practitioners. In those occupations in which employers can make the necessary judgments about competence, licensing is generally not required, as in the case of secretaries.

A state licensing system ordinarily is operated independently of the school system. However, in some instances members of various professional groups desiring to limit the number of persons having access to their professions have convinced state officials that a prescribed period of schooling and/or a prescribed school credential are necessary before license applications can be made. Let us assume, however, the existence of a licensing system without school system prerequisites for professional licenses. A person who wished to obtain a license would be expected to demonstrate through a state-administered examination the achievement of prescribed skills and other kinds of learning. Acquisition of the requisite skills would be the responsibility of the individual, who could: work as an apprentice to someone already in possession of the appropriate skills; use libraries; have private tutors; or study in a school.

If a person desiring a license studied in a school, it would be the result of a decision that this was the best way to prepare for the license examination. Only those courses believed to be relevant to his or her goal would be taken. Hence, since the student would be the one to suffer for not learning, the primary concern in each class attended would be with learning—not just with "getting through the course"—because the school would have no jurisdiction over whether the student received a license. The role of the school would be only to facilitate attainment of the learning outcomes required for the license, not to provide the certificate itself. It would be up to the student to judge whether a given course were relevant or not. Therefore, if a course were very helpful, the instructor could expect a large number of students to register for it.

It may be contended that licenses are not reliable guides to competence. It is pointed out, for example, that although teachers in the public primary and secondary schools are certified (licensed) by the state, it does not necessarily follow that they are competent. One response to this contention is that the principle of licensing is not at fault, but rather the way this principle has been implemented is. Licenses can be granted without sufficient evidence of competence, or they may be given only after a lengthy period of various forms of testing of the applicant, including a practical phase. Moreover, a license may be granted for only a limited time, in which case the license holder wishing to renew his license must submit to a reexamination.

Broader Implications of the Credentialing Proposal

The compromise proposal for the resolution of the school credentialing issue would seem to have some very important implications for the entire question of the control of education. The compromise proposal is clearly relevant to the issue of compulsory schooling. If a meaningful school credentialing system were established, teachers would no longer be able to use the aversive control procedure so frequently relied upon (the threat of low grades). However, because the student would then have an important and concrete goal to work for (the school certificate defined in terms of performance objectives), a strong reaction to this positive inducement might be expected—especially in secondary schools and universities. Many students would wish to attain the learning outcomes signified by a school certificate, because they would know that such certificates would be valuable, and that no alternative would exist to achieving the specified learning outcomes in order to obtain the credential. Thus, use of meaningful credentials as a motivator of student effort would mean that teachers could operate in accordance with the Student Interest Method.

Making school credentials sufficiently attractive would facilitate utilizing students' desires to earn certificates to induce attainment of learning outcomes that might otherwise be rejected. The various subjects which comprise the so-called "liberal arts" are an example of what students might be induced to learn through their desire to obtain school credentials. University students might be reluctant to study history, literature and natural sciences, but when these subjects are included as requirements for a credential, students study them. Later on in life a student might be glad to have studied liberal arts subjects; if asked to make his or her own selection of subjects, however, the importance of liberal arts might not be appreciated. In this way students can be positively motivated to attain learning outcomes that will later prove to be both for their own good and for the good of society. The use of credentialing to induce students to learn often carries with it the assumption or view that older and more experienced members of society know better than students which learning outcomes should be acquired. But because this procedure involves positive rather than aversive motivation, the radical critics of compulsory schooling should have no objection to the control technique utilized.

Establishment of a meaningful school credentialing system would also facilitate creation of the planned, society-wide system of reinforcements advocated by B. F. Skinner. The need to specify performance objectives as they relate to various school certificates could be one of the principal factors in this development, since reaching agreement on the nature of the learning outcomes represented by credentials would entail societal effort to determine which outcomes are desirable and need to be encouraged.

Another important effect that the new credentialing system would have is on the role of the teacher. Simply, the teacher would be given an opportunity to become truly professional. As we discussed in Issue 2, the role of the teacher could change from that of disciplinarian and student adversary to that of student helper and instructional manager. If students were to view the teacher as someone assisting them in preparing for prescribed examinations, then the problem of motivating recalcitrant students would no longer face teachers. But competency in assisting students to learn would be a must—otherwise there would be no call for his or her services. This would put the teacher in a situation similar to that of a medical doctor, who does not have to coerce patients to visit or to undergo the treatment prescribed. If a patient feels sufficiently unwell to require the doctor's help, he will visit the doctor; if a patient values the outcome of improved health more than the unpleasantness of the treatment, then he will follow the doctor's advice.[23]

Like the doctor, the teacher will need to have professional competence. The professional expertise of the teacher would consist primarily of the ability to diagnose learning difficulties of students and to prescribe the appropriate types and sequences of learning experiences necessary for students to attain the learning outcomes desired, in the most efficient manner. This means that the teacher would need to have access to a body of professional knowledge that would enable him or her to assess the learning difficulties of students. Similarly, access to a body of professional knowledge that would facilitate the determination of which teaching strategies are most efficient in reaching a given learning outcome would be required. Because his or her activities would consist mainly of diagnosis and prescription, the teacher would have relatively little time to act as the provider of learning experiences. Instead, extensive use of instructional materials (such as specially prepared textbooks, films, multi-media programs, and so forth) would have to be made. Even if the teacher had the competence to present personally the most appropriate types and distributions of learning experiences for each student (which is very doubtful), it is obvious that the time to do so would not be found, without serious interference with the roles of diagnostician and prescriber. Therefore, materials that can accomplish instructional tasks better than the teacher could must be utilized, leaving those tasks to the teacher which are uniquely his or hers to perform, and which will demand the highest level of professional skill.

If the teacher is to become an instructional manager, the first step must be to eliminate time-consuming activities of disciplining students and being the personal provider of learning experiences. This can be done if the new credentialing system based upon criter-

[23]See Chapter 3 for a discussion of transforming teaching into a true profession. On the role of performance objectives in the emergence of the "teacher-manager," see Ivor K. Davies, *Competency Based Learning: Technology, Management, and Design* (New York: McGraw-Hill, 1973), pp. 19–31.

ion-referenced examinations is adopted. A considerable effort will be required, of course, to prepare necessary instructional materials and to train teachers in the skills of diagnosis and prescription. Under the present credentialing system (in which student evaluation is based on norm-referenced grading), there has been little incentive to develop instructional materials and thereby increase the professional expertise of teachers. It may be expected that educational researchers will have a major role to play in developing these instructional materials and in gathering and imparting knowledge about the educative process that will be an essential part of the teacher's professional expertise. (Note 8)

In the following selection, radical critic Holt presents his conception of what the new role for the teacher as student helper, rather than student adversary, would be like. Whereas in the description above we resorted to an analogy with the medical doctor, Holt compares the teacher to an expert guide and, in another simile, to a well-qualified travel agent:

> We talk a lot about teachers "guiding" in schools. Most of the time we just mean doing what teachers have done all along—telling children what to do and trying to make them do it. There is, I suppose, a sense in which the word "guide" can mean that. If I guide a blind man down a rough path, I lead him, I decide where he is to go, give him no choice. But "guide" can mean something else. When friends and I go on a wilderness canoe trip in Canada, we plan our trip with a guide who knows the region. We know what we are looking for— fishing good enough to give us a chance to catch our food, a chance of good campsites, trails not too rough to portage and not too obscure to follow, not too many people, no airplanes dropping in, no loggers. We discuss this or that lake, this or that alternative route, how long it would take to get from this place to that. Eventually, using the guide's answers to our questions, we plan our trip. He, knowing the landings, the places—often hard to spot—where the trails meet the lake's edge, comes with us, to help us get where *we* have decided we want to go.
>
> Or, as a friend of mine put it, we teachers can see ourselves as travel agents. When we go to a travel agent, he does not tell us where to go. He finds out first what we are looking for. Do we care most about climate or scenery, or about seeing new cultures, or about museums and entertainment? Do we want to travel alone or with others? Do we like crowds or want to stay away from them? How much time and money do we want to spend? And so on. Given some idea of what we are looking for, he makes some suggestions. Here is this trip, which will take so long and cost so much; here is this one, here is that. Eventually, *we* choose, not he. Then, he helps us with our travel and hotel arrangements, gets us what tickets and information we need, and we

are ready to start. His job is done. He does not have to take the trip with us. Least of all does he have to give us a little quiz when we get back to make sure we went where we said we would go or got out of the trip what we hoped to get. If anything went wrong he will want to hear about it, to help us and other clients plan better in the future. Otherwise, what we got out of the trip and how much we enjoyed it is our business.[24]

CONCLUDING COMMENTS

In light of our discussion of the Coleman report and the three radical proposals, do schools "make a difference"? The answer that we shall give is in the affirmative. This positive response is not, however, based on examination of additional evidence; rather, it is derived from a consideration of the role of learning experiences in the control of behavior.

School systems provide motivated students with learning situations not as readily available elsewhere: at least to that extent they must make a difference. The schools apparently do succeed in imparting to most students a minimum set of skills (for example, in reading and writing). If the education of each student were left to the initiative of the student or to that of his parents, it is very likely that these uniform outcomes would not be achieved. As Mosteller and Moynihan have noted, "schools make a very great difference to children. Children don't think up algebra on their own." [25]

There is, in fact, some research evidence to support the contention that schools do make a difference, if they provide learning experiences that cannot be readily obtained elsewhere. The following selection by Jencks reviews this evidence:

Schools are . . . usually closed during the summer months. Both the folklore among teachers and the available evidence suggest that children's test scores increase more slowly over the summer than during the school year. In some cases children's scores actually drop over the summer. A study of New York City, for example, found that the average child's reading scores improved almost three times as fast during the school year as during the summer. The average black child's scores improved nearly as fast as the average white child's scores while school was in session, but they hardly improved at all

[24]John Holt, *What Do I Do Monday?* (New York: Delta, 1970), pp. 70–71. (Emphasis in the original.)

[25] Mosteller and Moynihan, "A Pathbreaking Report," p. 21.

over the summer. This particular study concluded that only half the achievement gap between black and white children in New York City was attributable to differential growth during the school year. The other half was explained by differential growth over the summer. This highly suggestive study has not yet been replicated.

These findings imply that if all elementary schools were closed down, so that growing up became an endless summer, white middle-class children might still learn much of what they now learn. Some of these children are taught to read before they enter school anyway, and some of them read a great deal at home, developing their skills without any help from school. But most poor black children would probably not learn to read without schools. The cognitive gap between rich and poor and between black and white would thus be far greater than it is now. [26]

Another study that tends to show that schools do make a difference is one that was conducted by the International Association for the Evaluation of Educational Achievement. As the following summary notes, this study indicates that the variable "opportunity to learn" (which presumably represents the amount of time the student was in contact with relevant learning experiences) is associated with student achievement:

[A] study of the factors influencing academic achievement offers tentative evidence that in some areas, at least, the schools do make a difference. Undertaken by the International Association for the Evaluation of Educational Achievement (IEA), the study attempted to identify those factors that determine students' success in the schools of twenty-two countries, including the United States. Six subject areas (science, reading comprehension, literature, English, French, and civic education) were surveyed at three age levels (ten, fourteen, and eighteen) over a period of nine years. Analysis of the enormous volume of data collected will doubtless continue for years, but initial findings were reported [November, 1973] at an international conference at the Harvard Graduate School of Education.

It is hardly surprising that the IEA study strongly supports the conclusions of the Coleman Report concerning the powerful influence of home background on success in the classroom. This influence was found to be particularly important at the earlier age levels (ten and fourteen years) and in the areas of reading comprehension, literature, and civic education. The public factors that appear to be most closely related to student achievement are the father's occupation (economic and social class), the father's and mother's level of education, and the number of books in the home. The data do not document any cause-and-effect relationship—the phrase "related to" is as far as the re-

[26]Christopher Jencks, *Inequality: A Reassessment of the Effect of Family and Schooling in America* (New York: Basic Books, 1972), pp. 87–88.

search scholars will go—but the clear implication is that these areas of academic competence are "home oriented" and reflect the attitudes and values of the home environment. But an important element that the IEA data add to our awareness of the problem is documentation for the fact that throughout the world, in many different cultures, children develop the basis for future verbal ability, the most vital capacity for academic success in contemporary school, before they ever enter school.

On the other hand, the evidence produced by the IEA study indicates that schooling is strongly related to academic achievement in science and in the study of foreign languages. One of the strongest variables in accounting for differences in achievement among national systems of education, for instance, is the "opportunity to learn," the degree of student exposure to given areas of a subject. There is some evidence, too, that teacher competence, both in subject matter and teaching technique, varies greatly among nations and is related to student performance. A third factor that appears to bear a significant relationship to the level of student achievement, both in comparisons among nations and among schools within single nations, is the time a student devotes to a subject. [27]

If the difference that schools make has not always been detected in available research, one explanation is that the research may have been inadequately conducted. For example, J. E. Morsch and E. W. Wilder declared in 1954 that "no single, specific, observable teacher act has yet been found whose frequency or percent of occurrence is invariably [and] significantly correlated with student achievement."[28] A decade later Norman E. Wallen and Robert M. W. Travers reviewed the available research on teaching methods and agreed that "teaching methods do not seem to make much difference, or to phrase it more appropriately, there is hardly any direct evidence to favor one method over another."[29] But it can be asked whether the research studies these authors reviewed were conducted with sufficient precision, particularly with respect to (1) the definition and observation of important method variables, and (2) the measurement of learning outcomes.

With respect to the first point, most published studies in which different teaching methods have been compared apparently were

[27]James Cass, "Do Schools Make a Difference?" *Saturday Review/World,* January 12, 1974, p. 59.

[28]Quoted in Ned A. Flanders and Anita Simon, "Teacher Effectiveness," in *Encyclopedia of Educational Research,* ed. Robert L. Ebel (4th ed.; New York: Macmillan, 1969), p. 1423.

[29]"Analysis and Investigation of Teaching Methods," in *Handbook of Research on Teaching,* ed. N. L. Gage (Chicago: Rand McNally, 1963), p. 484.

carried out without explicit definitions of important method variables, and without careful observation throughout the experiment of whether the teaching methods being studied actually were used. Thus a teacher who declared he was lecturing might in fact have done something other than just lecture, and similarly with a teacher who declared he was using the discusssion approach. Where the second point is concerned, present measures of learning outcomes are quite crude. How, for example, should we measure the acquisition of the "ability to think"? It is quite possible, therefore, that differences between teaching methods may not have been revealed in previous experimental and correlational research, simply because it has not been possible to measure relevant changes in the dependent variable (the learning outcome).

Learning experiences are not only essential for the attainment of learning outcomes, but some types of learning situations are probably more effective than others for the achievement of certain learning outcomes. Regardless of what the available research has yet been able to demonstrate, most teachers seem to learn through experience which types of learning situations are more conducive to the attainment of given learning outcomes. For example, an experienced teacher invariably utilizes learning experiences characteristic of the Exercise/Imitation Method if his goal is the teaching of skills. If specific, factual knowledge is to be taught, then the types of learning experiences that correspond to the Telling/Showing Method would generally be used. And if the student is expected to acquire basic understandings, the teacher often resorts to those types of learning experiences characteristic of the Discovery/Restructuring Method. Selection of these different types of learning experiences for the indicated goals applies to all kinds of students— young and old, bright and not so bright.

In addition to their intrinsic nature, the distributive characteristics of learning experiences (such as their patterning and relative intensity, as well as the number of times a particular experience is repeated) seem to affect the ease with which a desired learning outcome is attained. For example, a set of learning experiences presented in one sequence may result in highly efficient learning, while the same set in another sequence may be inefficient. Bruner, a contemporary advocate of the Discovery/Restructuring Method, has recognized the importance of this factor. He emphasizes the need for the teacher to choose an appropriate sequence of learning experiences: "Instruction consists of leading the learner through a sequence of statements and restatements of a problem or body of knowledge that increase the learner's ability to grasp, transform, and transfer what he is learning. In short, the sequence in which a learner encounters materials within a domain of knowledge affects the difficulty he will have in achieving mastery. There are usually various sequences that are equivalent in their ease and difficulty for learners. There is no unique sequence for all learners, and the optimum in any particular case will depend upon a variety of factors, including past learning, stage of development, nature of the material, and individual differences."[30]

In conclusion, learning experiences provided by school systems are important. The reason that studies of school effectiveness (such as the Coleman report) have failed to demonstrate unambiguously the significance of schooling is very likely the fact that students with the same backgrounds probably are motivated to a comparable extent, regardless of the primary or secondary school they attend. And, since these schools have similar curricula through which relevant learning experiences are provided, students have relatively the same opportunity to acquire desired learning outcomes. Given the similarity of school curricula (and the additional opportunities available to motivated students to obtain relevant learning experiences, should a particular school or teacher be deficient), it is hardly surprising that student background factors seem to account for the major differences in student achievement. Relevant learning experiences are nevertheless essential to the attainment of desired learning outcomes.

Furthermore, adoption of the three radical proposals in modified form might increase the effectiveness of the school system. As far as the first proposal is concerned, compulsory school attendance without compulsory participation and/or achievement may be sufficient for the accomplishment of those learning outcomes perceived as essential by both students and society. If students and society disagree about the importance of certain learning outcomes, then use of positive motivation would probably bring about their accomplishment. If all else failed, compulsory achievement of specified learning outcomes could be imposed. All of these measures seem superior to the present practice of compulsory participation in learning experiences provided by the school. If this radical proposal were adopt-

---

[30]Jerome S. Bruner, *Toward a Theory of Instruction* (Cambridge, Mass.: Harvard University Press, 1966), p. 49.

ed, students would also probably achieve specified learning outcomes much sooner than they presently would, thereby making the schools more efficient, as well as more effective.

The adoption of the second and third proposals would also increase school effectiveness. Establishment of a society-wide system of reinforcements that is planned to some extent would certainly have a beneficial effect on the acquisition and utilization of desired learning outcomes. Similarly, if criterion-referenced grading without fixed time limits were instituted, the school system would inevitably become more effective in the achievement of stipulated learning outcomes. In fact, if this reform were adopted, it probably would have the effect of bringing about or facilitating adoption of the first and second radical proposals. More will be said about the importance of criterion-referenced examinations in Chapter 10.

SUMMARY

The purpose of this chapter is to try to reach some tentative conclusions about whether the radical proposals for control change should be adopted.

The critics of compulsory schooling argue that using aversive motivation to induce students to learn is an inhumane procedure that produces negative outcomes, such as making students hostile and afraid. These critics believe that if something is important enough for the student to learn, then upon realizing this, the student will make the effort to learn. Supporters of compulsory schooling contend that the child may not always know what is good for him or her; hence learning must be compelled, if it is not voluntary. It is further argued that a child must sometimes be compelled to learn for the benefit of society.

While the compulsory schooling controversy does not have a definitive answer, some useful clarifications can be provided. Compulsory schooling may mean one of three things: (1) compulsory school attendance; (2) compulsory participation in specified learning experiences; and (3) the compulsory attainment of prescribed learning outcomes. Compulsory schooling may apply to any age group, and to wide ranges of learning experiences and outcomes. It would seem incumbent on any proponent of compulsory schooling, therefore, that he or she should be able to specify the type of compulsory schooling desired, as well as the age group and learning experiences/learning outcomes (if any) to which the overt use of aversive motivation should apply.

Skinner maintains, in support of his proposal, that all behavior is controlled, systematically or otherwise. Therefore, he believes that a planned, society-wide system of reinforcements should be established to induce the behaviors desired by society. Critics of this proposal question the advisability of giving so much power to the "controllers."

The critics of school system credentialing argue that school certificates are inadequate indicators of the attainment of learning outcomes. While not denying this, the supporters of school certificates point out that the certificates serve to motivate students, and are useful to prospective employers.

To resolve the credentialing controversy, it is proposed that the school system retain its credentialing role, with the following changes: (1) that criterion-referenced grading and performance objectives be employed; (2) that students be given unlimited time. This "credentialing compromise" would require reaffirmation that the achievement of desired learning outcomes is the central purpose of the school system, rather than selecting and sorting of students on the basis of quickness to learn.

Acceptance of the compromise proposal for resolving the credentialing controversy would have broad implications for the school system. Also, by placing the teacher in the role of the student's helper rather than his adversary, and by specifying exactly what the student is expected to learn, considerable incentive will exist for the development of a body of professional knowledge for teachers.

GENERAL NOTES AND BIBLIOGRAPHY

1. EFFECTIVENESS OF SCHOOLS. Because of the significance of its findings, the Coleman report has been critically reviewed by a number of scholars. See, for example, Samuel Bowles and Henry M. Levin, "The Determinants of Scholastic Achievement—An Appraisal of Some Recent Evidence," *Journal of Human Resources* 3 (1968): 3–24; *Do Teachers Make a Difference?* (Washington, D.C.: U.S. Government Printing Office, 1970); and Frederick Mosteller and Daniel P. Moynihan, eds., *On Equality of Educational Opportunity* (New York: Vintage Books, 1972). As far as Coleman's application of his research

methodology is concerned, most authorities would probably concur with the view reached by Marshall Smith after an intensive re-analysis of the Coleman data: "In general, the results of the re-examination affirm and strengthen the overall conclusion of the Report." Smith, *"Equality of Educational Opportunity:* The Basic Findings Reconsidered," in *On Equality of Educational Opportunity,* eds. Mosteller and Moynihan, p. 311.

In a broader sense, the findings of the Coleman report are subject to question: as a correlational (not experimental) study, it suffers from the weaknesses inherent in this type of research procedure. Moreover, since its data were collected in a single year, and yet it purports to deal with long-term effects of schooling, its results are difficult to interpret. This report also suffers from a common problem in teaching studies—that of finding suitable measures for independent and dependent variables. Do the number of books in the school library, the average salary of teachers, and the number and size of science laboratories adequately represent differences in the quality of schools? Or are other independent variables, such as use made of school facilities and the teaching abilities of teachers, more important? The former variables are the ones usually used in studies of school effectiveness (because data on them are easy to collect), while the latter ones are seldom employed (because these variables are difficult or even impossible to measure). The same difficulty exists with respect to dependent variables. Do scores on a paper and pencil test of a limited range of cognitive learning outcomes really measure the effects of schooling? Some persons would contend that affective learning outcomes are also important, as well as such outcomes as creativity— which outcomes, of course, are difficult or impossible to measure satisfactorily.

2. COMPULSORY SCHOOLING ARGUMENTS. For a survey of arguments both for and against compulsory schooling, see: *Summerhill: For and Against* (New York: Hart, 1970); Daniel U. Levine and Robert J. Havighurst, eds., *Farewell to Schools?* (Worthington, Ohio: Charles A. Jones, 1971). Arguments against compulsory schooling are provided in William F. Rickenbacker, ed., *The Twelve-Year Sentence* (LaSalle, Ill.: Open Court, 1974) and Carl Bereiter, *Must We Educate?* (Englewood Cliffs, N. J.: Prentice-Hall, 1973). Basic arguments for compulsory schooling are presented in Cornelius J. Troost, ed., *Radi-*

cal School Reform: Critique and Alternatives (Boston: Little, Brown, 1973).

Compulsory schooling laws are discussed in the following sources: Stephen Arons, "Compulsory Education: The Plain People Resist," *Saturday Review,* January 15, 1972, pp. 52–57; Hillary Rodham, "Children Under the Law," *Harvard Educational Review* 43 (1973): 487–514; Stephen Arons, "Compulsory Education: America in Mississippi," *Saturday Review/World,* November 6, 1973, pp. 54–57; Howard M. Johnson, "Are Compulsory Attendance Laws Outdated?" *Phi Delta Kappan* 55 (1973): 226–232; Albert N. Keim, ed., *Compulsory Education and the Amish* (Boston: Beacon, 1975).

3. STUDENT INTEREST METHOD COMBINED WITH COMPULSORY ATTENDANCE. Several authors have advocated use of the Student Interest Method in conjunction with compulsory school attendance. One of them is Herbert Kohl, who utilizes the term "open classroom" to designate the approach. See Herbert R. Kohl, *The Open Classroom* (New York: The New York Review, 1969). G. Louis Heath shares Kohl's interpretation of the open classroom concept in *The New Teacher* (New York: Harper and Row, 1973), pp. 83–84: "The child is free to choose his own learning experiences in the open classroom. . . . The teacher . . . serves as a catalyst and guide for each child's learning experiences." Barbara Blitz states in *The Open Classroom: Making It Work* (Boston: Allyn and Bacon, 1973), pp. 60–61, that "teachers of open classrooms usually . . . allow students to select their own activities and areas of learning." But, she points out, this does not mean that the teacher forsakes all forms of control. "The total organization of the class and the materials available within it gives control over how children spend their time and what they learn. If you have a magnificently equipped woodworking table in your classroom but only a few math materials, it will not be surprising if more of your students excel in woodworking than in math. Therefore, even giving great freedom to students to choose what they will learn and when, we still maintain controls inherent in the school situation." A. S. Neill describes the restrictions on individual freedom that prevail at Summerhill school on p. 348 of *Summerhill* (New York: Hart, 1960): "In Summerhill, a child is *not* allowed to do as he pleases. . . . He is allowed to do as he pleases only in things that affect *him*—

and only him. He can play all day if he wants to, because work and study are matters that concern him alone. But he is not allowed to play a cornet in the schoolroom because his playing would interfere with others." (Emphasis in the original.)

For a general treatment of the open classroom concept, see Bernard Spodek and Herbert J. Walberg, eds., *Studies in Open Education* (New York: Agathon, 1975).

4. SKINNER'S PROPOSAL. An excellent survey of the major arguments for and against the proposal of B. F. Skinner is provided in Anne E. Freedman, *The Planned Society: An Analysis of Skinner's Proposals* (Kalamazoo, Mich.: Behaviordelia, 1972). See also: Richard I. Evans, *B. F. Skinner: The Man and His Ideas* (New York: Dutton, 1968); Frank Milhollan and Bill E. Forisha, *From Skinner to Rogers: Contrasting Approaches to Education* (Lincoln, Nebr.: Professional Educators Publications, 1972); Arthur Koestler, *The Ghost in the Machine* (New York: Macmillan, 1967); Joseph Wood Krutch, *The Measure of Man* (New York: Grosset and Dunlap, 1954); Noam Chomsky, "The Case Against B. F. Skinner," *New York Review of Books,* December 30, 1971, pp. 18–24; Harvey Wheeler, ed., *Beyond the Punitive Society* (San Francisco: W. H. Freeman, 1973).

5. ARGUMENTS CONCERNING CREDENTIALING. While published arguments in favor of school system credentialing are rare, several authors have questioned its efficacy. See, for example: Paul Goodman, *Compulsory Mis-education and the Community of Scholars* (New York: Vintage Books, 1964); David Hapgood, *Diplomaism* (New York: Scribners's, 1971); Ivan Illich, *Deschooling Society* (New York: Harper and Row, 1971); and John Holt, *Freedom and Beyond* (New York: Dutton, 1972).

Arguments for and against the grading of students are presented in Howard Kirschenbaum, Rodney Napier and Sidney B. Simon, *Wad-ja-get? The Grading Game in American Education* (New York: Hart, 1971). Criticisms of present grading practices are found in Howard Becker, Blanche Geer and Everett C. Hughes, *Making the Grade: The Academic Side of College Life* (New York: Wiley, 1968) and Richard C. Anderson et al., eds., *Current Research on Instruction* (Englewood Cliffs, N.J.: Prentice-Hall, 1969). Arguments in favor of grading are given in Arthur Thomas Tees, "In Defense of Grades," *School and Community*, October, 1968, pp. 12–13, and R. A. Feldmesser, "The Positive Functions of Grades," *Educational Record* 53 (1972): 66–72.

6. PERFORMANCE OBJECTIVES. The preparation of these is discussed in the following: Eva L. Baker and W. James Popham, *Expanding Dimensions of Instructional Objectives* (Englewood Cliffs, N. J.: Prentice-Hall, 1973); H. H. McAshan, *The Goals Approach to Performance Objectives* (Philadelphia: W. B. Saunders, 1974). See also W. Robert Houston, ed., *Exploring Competency Based Education* (Berkeley, Calif.: McCutchan, 1974). For a critique of behavioral objectives, see Herbert D. Simons, "Behavioral Objectives: A False Hope for Education," *Elementary School Journal* 73 (1973): 173–181.

7. CREDENTIALING RE-EXAMINATIONS. An example of a credentialing system that required periodic re-assessments of holders of credentials to determine their competency is the traditional Chinese examination system. A brief description of the system has been provided by Wolfgang Franke, who points out that all *sheng-yuan* (holders of a first degree) who did not pass a higher examination ("by far the majority") had to take regular examinations (*sui-k'ao*) "to keep status as members of the literati." These examinations, while called "annual," were actually given triennially. See Wolfgang Franke, *The Reform and Abolition of the Traditional Chinese Examination System* (Cambridge, Mass.: Center for East Asian Studies, Harvard University, 1960), p. 10.

8. TEACHER AS INSTRUCTIONAL MANAGER. The role of the teacher as instructional manager has been described by the advocates of the teaching approach known as "mastery learning." One of the basic features of mastery learning is the use of criterion-referenced evaluation without fixed time limits. See William G. Spady, "The Sociological Implications of Mastery Learning," in *Schools, Society, and Mastery Learning*, ed. James H. Block (New York: Holt, Rinehart and Winston, 1974), pp. 91–116.

WHAT SHOULD BE THE GOALS OF EDUCATION?

PART THREE

EDUCATIONAL GOALS AND THE FUNCTIONS OF SCHOOLING

CHAPTER 7

Each time the educative process is used, the person employing it must have some goal in mind, since education is an intentional process. For this reason, the question "What should be the goals of education?" is one of the two fundamental educational policy questions chosen for examination.

GOALS OF EDUCATION

The term "goal" is equivalent to the terms "purpose," "aim," and "objective." A *goal* is a factor that guides a person's behavior in an activity that is directed toward the accomplishment of an end. In other words, a goal is a projected end or projected outcome.

Does Education Necessarily Imply Goals?

It has been suggested by some educational writers that objectives such as "the self-realization of the individual," "wisdom," and "citizenship" do not constitute educational goals. R. S. Peters, for example, has stated that "going to school is not a *means* to these [educational aims] in the way in which getting on a bus is a means to getting to work. . . . These very general aims are neither goals nor are they end-products. Like 'happiness' they are high-sounding ways of talking about doing some things rather than others and doing them in a certain manner."[1]

[1]R. S. Peters, *Authority, Responsibility and Education* (3rd ed.; London: George Allen and Unwin, 1973), p. 124.

Many educational ends—perhaps nearly all of the most basic goals—can be characterized as being general or vague. But this fact should not prevent them from being considered as aims. In the same way that an operational definition[2] derives its meaning from a less precise term, a concrete educational objective can only be justified in terms of some more distant goal. Therefore, general goals must be tolerated, even though personal preferences for discussing the more specific aims of education may exist.

As William Frankena has suggested, the controversy over whether education implies goals appears to be mainly a semantic one: "Those who deny that education has ends or that educators must have aims seem always to end up talking about much the same thing in a slightly different idiom."[3]

Goals "of" or "for" Education?

Although we shall continue to use the expression "goals of education" in this book, it probably would be more accurate to say "goals for education." The educative process does not have goals, of course: it is human beings who have goals which they apply to education.

The learner may set his own educational goals, or someone else may establish them on his behalf. In the latter case it is often necessary to use motivational control to induce the learner to act in accordance with the educational goals set for him. As we shall see (particularly in Chapter 10), this factor (of motivational control) is extremely important in discussing the goals of education.

Learning: The Principal Declared Purpose of Schools

How can we determine what the educational goals of a given society are? Since a goal can never be seen, the alternatives for us are to analyze what people say about goals and to try to infer their

---

[2]See section on "Confirmation of Empirical Statements," Chapter 2.
[3]William K. Frankena, "Educational Values and Goals: Some Dispositions to Be Fostered," in *Theories of Value and Problems of Education,* ed. Philip G. Smith (Urbana: University of Illinois Press, 1970), p. 99.

existence from what people do. It should be obvious, therefore, that to describe the present goals of education in the United States would be a formidable, if not impossible, task. We would have to know what every educational policy maker intended to accomplish through his efforts. What every parent wanted with respect to the education of his or her children would have to be known. And we would have to know the plans of every student in the school system. Added to this complex problem of data collection would be the problem of understanding or interpreting statements a person might make about his or her educational goals and the problem of how to infer goals from behavior.

Are there not in existence any official statements of national educational goals that we could consult? In view of what has just been said about the problems of obtaining data on goals, even in the most totalitarian society a document describing the goals of its school system would be of only limited utility. An official statement of national educational goals can tell us something about the thinking of the person or persons who wrote it (although the statement may be a political document and thus not express the genuine views of its authors), but it may reveal relatively little about the personal goals of the teachers and the students to whom it applies.

With these limitations in mind, we note that official statements of national educational goals invariably stipulate that learning is the principal purpose of the school system. A collection of official statements describing educational goals of various nations is provided in the *World Survey of Education*. According to the U.S. Office of Education, which prepared the statement on the goals of education in the United States, the "broad aims of education are the preservation, further expansion, and transmission of knowledge and the development of attitudes, skills, and techniques which will serve to promote and improve the welfare of all while recognizing and protecting the integrity of each individual human being."[4] All of these broad aims pertain to the accomplishment of learning outcomes. Furthermore, there is no reference in this statement to any other types of educational objectives.

The statement in the UNESCO survey on the educational goals of the United Kingdom was prepared by the United Kingdom

[4]*World Survey of Education* (Paris: UNESCO, 1969), 5:1307. The statements on educational goals in the two paragraphs which follow this one are, respectively, from pages 1187 and 1165 in this source.

National Commission for UNESCO. It emphasizes the attainment of learning outcomes as the basic purpose of education and refers to the educational (school) system as a means for achieving these goals. The "broad aim" of education, the Commission writes, "is to ensure that every child of school age receives education suitable to his age, ability and aptitude, and that general, professional and vocational courses are available for all those who have left school and can profit from them. The function of the educational system is conceived as contributing towards the spiritual, moral, mental and physical development of the community by providing all citizens with the means of developing the various talents with which they are endowed, and so enriching the inheritance of the country."

In the Soviet Union, the basic goals of education are described as having a similar focus on the accomplishment of desired learning outcomes. The statement prepared by the National Commission of the U.S.S.R. for UNESCO indicates that the broad national aim of education is to enable the young "to develop to the full their spiritual and physical capacities, creative abilities and gifts and to train them for adult life and for work as active builders of communist society. The full development of the personality is regarded as a continuous process, beginning before school age, continuing in an organized form through school and higher education and carrying on throughout adult life in socially useful work and various forms of creative activity. Particularly important in the development of the young is general and polytechnical education, to provide a firm grasp of the fundamentals of science, inculcate a communist world outlook, prepare them for working life in accordance with the increasing demands of science, technology and society, and with their own wishes and abilities, and to provide a moral, aesthetic and physical education. The all-round development of the personality which is the aim of communist education can be achieved only by tackling all these tasks together." (Note 1)

Widespread agreement thus exists that the broad purpose of education is to bring about the attainment of desired learning outcomes. This purpose is also applied to the school system, the principal instrumentality for the achievement of society's educational objectives. As mentioned in Chapter 1, however, the schools perform several other functions besides that of teaching. One of these is that of credentialing, which is part of the selecting and sorting function of the schools. As pointed out in Chapter 6, when the credentialing function entails norm-referenced evaluation, there is a contradiction between this function and the teaching function of the school system, and society must choose which of them should have priority.

It is essential to the consideration of the goals of education to give explicit attention to the functions of the school system. There may be other functions of schooling that are inimical to the accomplishment of its principal declared purpose, or which at least warrant explicit recognition by educational policy makers in their decision making. In any event, it would seem that educational policy making can benefit from a knowledge of which functions the school system is performing and how well they are being carried out. For these reasons, therefore, the functions of schooling need to be examined.

FUNCTIONS OF THE SCHOOL SYSTEM

The term "functions" of schooling pertains to the actual outcomes of the school system. A "goal," on the other hand, refers to a projected outcome. The goals and the functions of the school system, therefore, may correspond, or they may differ.

The term "function" may also be used to designate the role or activities of the school system, as well as its consequences. In Chapter 6, for example, we discussed the credentialing and teaching functions of the school system, by which were meant the school system's activities in the issuance of school certificates and the role of the school system in the production of desired learning outcomes. Thus the term "function" has the dual significance of the symbol E (M) in our representation of the means-ends chain (from one point of view something may be considered as an end; from another point of view it may be regarded a means to something else). We shall use the term "effects" to refer unambiguously to the ends, results, consequences, or outcomes of schooling.

The functions of schooling may be differentiated on the basis of whether they constitute *manifest* or *latent* functions. Manifest functions, according to Robert Merton, "are those objective consequences . . . of the system which are intended and recognized by participants in the system." Latent functions are "those which are neither intended nor recognized."[5] The definition of a latent func-

[5]Robert K. Merton, *Social Theory and Social Structure* (rev. ed.; Glencoe, Ill.: Free Press, 1957), p. 51.

tion shall be expanded to include those functions which are recognized but not intended or sanctioned.

Despite the obvious importance of having a precise knowledge of the functions of schooling, relatively little systematic research is available. This may seem incredible, in view of the fact that most business firms keep careful records of the sales of their products and often try to find out about the extent of customer satisfaction with these products (audience surveys for television programs would be a case in point). Yet as far as the results of schooling are concerned, there appears to be little concern on the part of those in control of the American school system (as well as on the part of those who control the school systems of other countries) for undertaking systematic research to find out about these effects. Of course, it is not ethically feasible to conduct an experiment in which a randomly selected group of students is provided with schooling and a comparable group is denied schooling. To ascertain the effects of having attended school, therefore, correlational studies or other less rigorous types of research (such as case studies) must be resorted to. Even these research studies, however, have been relatively infrequently accomplished.

Most of the research on school functions that exists is concerned with the manifest functions of schooling. For example, there are studies which deal with the role of the schools in the transmission of culture from one generation to the next, thereby preserving the cultural heritage; other studies document the effects of schools in changing culture, through the development of new knowledge and the inculcation of new attitudes.

The effects of the school system in preparing members of society for their social roles have been investigated in research on the process of socialization. Some research has also been conducted in recent years on the economic effects of the school system (studies of the relationship between schooling and individual income and between schooling and economic growth). But much less attention has been given to the latent functions of schooling. (Note 2)

Teaching Function

The school system deliberately produces learning outcomes (its teaching function). Because it is recognized by system participants, and since the declared purpose of schooling is to foster the attainment of learning outcomes, teaching constitutes a manifest function.

The deliberate transmission of culture from one generation to the next is an important part of the manifest teaching function of the schools. The term "culture" is used here in its general anthropological sense, not in the more limited sense of an appreciation of, say, fine paintings and good music. One of the first anthropological definitions of "culture" was given by Edward Tylor. Culture, he said, is "that complex whole which includes knowledge, belief, art, morals, law, custom, and any other capabilities and habits acquired by man as a member of society."[6] A representative contemporary definition of the term is that offered by Johnson: "Culture consists of abstract patterns of and for living and dying. Such abstract patterns are cultural to the extent that they are learned directly or indirectly in social interaction and to the extent that they are part of the common orientation of two or more people."[7] Both of these definitions indicate culture to be something learned within a society, and that culture is what accounts for the patterns of behavior that characterize the members of a given society.

It is mainly within the curriculum that the deliberate cultural transmission activities of the school take place. Although the term "curriculum" has already been used several times, it may be helpful to offer a formal definition at this point. As we use the term, a curriculum is identical to an instructional program: the organized, goal-directed provision of learning experiences within a school or the school system. A curriculum is not a document that describes what the instructional activities of the school or school system are expected to involve; it is the actual instructional program itself.

In the United States a project known as the National Assessment of Educational Progress represents a systematic attempt to obtain data on the effectiveness of the school curriculum in transmitting culture. The National Assessment project is administered by the Education Commission of the States. A total of ten learning areas (science, citizenship, writing, art, career and occupational development, literature, mathematics, music, reading, and social studies) and four age groups (9-year olds, 13-year olds, 17-year olds in and

---

[6]Edward Tylor, *Primitive Culture* (7th ed.; New York: Brentano's, 1924), p. 1.

[7]Harry M. Johnson, *Sociology: A Systematic Introduction* (New York: Harcourt, Brace, 1960), p. 82.

out of school, and young adults aged 26–35) were originally stipulated for coverage in the assessment. During 1969 the first assessments were made in three learning areas (science, citizenship, and writing), utilizing a carefully selected sample of 100,000 persons to represent the entire country. A variety of exercises were administered to determine the extent of learning of those included in the sample. The learning areas of science, reading and mathematics were to be assessed every three years; other learning areas were to be assessed every six years. The results of National Assessment are similar to those of a census. These results reveal the percentages of persons in the four age levels of the sample who are acceptably able to answer a question or perform a task.

Although some National Assessment exercises provided to the four age groups are to be different, some of them are to be identical, thereby permitting a direct comparison of the amount of learning acquired or retained by the four groups. An analysis of the results of the 1969 science assessment for young adults in comparison with 17-year olds has revealed, for example, that there was a decrease in the percentage of correct responses "in nearly all exercises associated with classroom experiences or textbook study." However, where general experience might have contributed to a person's knowledge, the young adults usually gave a higher percentage of correct responses than the 17-year olds.[8]

The preceding discussion of the school system as an agency for the intentional transmission of culture might suggest an essentially passive, conservative role for the schools. And in some societies this might indeed be the case. In other societies, however, the universities function as producers and transmitters of *new* culture. The principal way in which universities perform this innovative function is through research and other creative activities. Scholars in the university often carry out research projects that are intended to produce new knowledge. Scientists, for example, attempt to develop new theories, and historians try to obtain a clearer understanding of our past. Painters and musicians may also serve as university faculty members, devoting part of their time to creative activities.

[8]National Assessment of Educational Progress, *Summary of Report 1: Science, National Results* (Washington, D.C.: Government Printing Office, 1970), p. 12.

Selecting and Sorting Function

The second important manifest function of the schools that needs to be discussed is that of *selecting and sorting*. The school system accomplishes the selecting and sorting of students in the following ways: (1) It selects some students for admission to certain schools and instructional programs and denies access to other students. (2) It sorts (grades) students relative to one another by means of norm-referenced grading. (3) It sorts out those students who will be awarded school certificates and denies these certificates to other students. The second and third of these three activities were considered in Chapters 5 and 6, in connection with the school system's credentialing function. The contradiction that exists between the teaching function of the school system and its credentialing role—at least when credentialing is based on the practice of norm-referenced grading—was also described.

The process of selecting and sorting is a manifest function of the schools, because it is both intended and recognized. Although this function is rarely, if ever, included among the stated goals for the school system, it is of great significance to students, parents, and teachers. A major consequence of possession of school system credentials (or of having none at all) is the difference in income associated with different types of credentials.

One explanation for the correlation between schooling and income is that those with the greatest amounts of schooling have been the most successful in achieving the learning outcomes intended by the school system and they are being rewarded accordingly. A second explanation holds that the persons who are successful in school are those who are able to learn more quickly than others, those who are more persistent, and those who are more highly motivated. Since by and large the schools do not explicitly teach these qualities, the award of school certificates merely serves to screen out those students who have certain innate abilities or who have acquired latent learning outcomes such as conformity to rules and regulations, punctuality, and deference to superiors. If these natural abilities and latent learning outcomes are valued by employers, then employers would be expected to hire persons who have been successful in school rather than those who have not.

Mark Blaug has argued that the second of the above explanations is the simplest one. "The better educated are generally more flexible and more motivated," he writes, "adapt themselves more easily to changing circumstances, benefit more from work experience and training, act with greater initiative in problem-solving situations, assume supervisory responsibility more quickly and, in short, are more productive than the less educated even when their education has taught them no specific skills. . . . Employers may regard a paper qualification as a reliable indication of personal ability, achievement drive and perhaps docility, reasoning that, say, a graduate must make a better salesman than a man who has never met the challenge of higher education; the graduate gets the job and the better pay, not because higher education has improved his skills, but simply because the degree identifies him as the better man. . . . Putting the same case more circumspectly, suppose that among all applicants otherwise the same, graduates would make better workers than non-graduates six times out of ten; an employer lacking other information and unwilling to incur screening costs or a high rate of labour turnover would nevertheless hire the graduate ten times out of ten; as a result, the non-graduate would experience longer periods of unemployment and would tend to earn less while working."[9]

Christopher Jencks has expressed a view very similar to Blaug's. Jencks believes that the differences in income that are related to varied amounts of schooling derive largely from the role of school credentials in controlling "access to highly paid occupations, not from the fact that it enables men in a given occupation to earn more." Jencks found, after a review of the available research, that IQ and school grades have only a modest correlation with occupational success: "If two men in the same occupation have IQ scores that differ by 15 points, their incomes will differ by an average of 5 or 10 percent. If we compare men with the same amount of education but different grades, income differences are again trivial. Men who receive high grades in college and in professional schools earn no more in business than men who receive poor grades in the same institutions. The same is true in engineering. Most studies of the relationship between high school grades and economic success have also found negligible correlations, even when occupation was not held constant. . . . All the evidence we have reviewed points in the same direction. Most jobs require a wide variety of skills. Standard-

[9]Mark Blaug, *An Introduction to the Economics of Education* (London: Allen Lane The Penguin Press, 1970), pp. 30–31.

ized tests measure only a very limited number of these skills. If an individual with low scores has the necessary noncognitive skills, and if he can get into an occupation, his performance on the job will not usually be appreciably below the norm for the occupation. Entering many high-status occupations does, however, depend on having met formal or informal educational requirements, and meeting these requirements is extremely difficult for people with low test scores. Thus, an individual with low scores has considerably less chance of getting into a high-status occupation than if he had high scores."[10]

Some researchers have tried to assess the impact of the selecting and sorting function of the school system on the social structure. To what extent do the schools facilitate social mobility (the movement of more talented persons into higher social strata and less talented ones into lower social strata)? To what extent does the school system serve to maintain the existing social structure, by permitting children from upper class families to have better educational opportunities than children from lower class families? Unfortunately, we can provide no firm answers to these questions. The available evidence indicates that the American school system performs both functions—it is a means for social mobility, and it also permits parents from upper class families to confer advantages upon their children. Different studies have reported somewhat different results, but it may be suggested that the two functions are of approximately equal significance. We must add that this interpretation is complicated by the fact that children with high measured ability tend to come from high socio-economic status families. (Note 3)

Latent Learning Function

In addition to its manifest teaching function, the school system performs an extremely significant latent learning function. This function is called latent because it is generally unintended and unrecognized.

A good illustration of this latent function is the learning of sex roles in schools. This effect is primarily the result of interaction among students; the interaction between students and teachers, in

[10]Jencks, *Inequality: A Reassessment of the Effect of Family and Schooling in America* (New York: Basic Books, 1972), pp. 186–187.

which teachers may praise certain behaviors and condemn others; the portrayal of the roles of men and women in textbooks; and the procedures entailed in the operation of the schools—its rules and rituals. The stories presented in primary school reading textbooks, for instance, usually convey a stereotyped view of boys doing things and playing an active role in society, while girls are depicted as being relatively passive (although as noted in Chapter 1, this situation is now being changed). Whereas boys may be encouraged or even required to take industrial arts courses in secondary school, girls are often prohibited from taking them. Girls generally do not participate in interscholastic sports. Meanwhile, teachers reinforce these conceptions of appropriate behavior by insisting that girls be "ladylike" and by being more tolerant of aggressive behavior on the part of boys.

The acquisition of conformist and competitive behaviors by students is another aspect of the latent learning function of the schools that has now been identified by several observers. To cope with the rules and regulations imposed upon them by the school, students develop those behaviors which permit them to survive. They learn to be punctual for their classes, tolerate boredom, and obey the wishes of persons in authority. The schools also offer rewards (high grades, certificates, teacher praise) to those students who outperform their classmates in completing school tasks. Hence students acquire a variety of behaviors that allow them to cope with this competitive environment: they learn to work hard, to be especially alert for clues as to what is expected of them, to be "nice" to teachers, and even to cheat if the opportunity presents itself.

Another extremely important latent learning outcome is attributable to the selecting and sorting activities of the school system. When norm-referenced grading is utilized, some students inevitably will be ranked lower than others. As Martin Carnoy points out, "the tests which screen the fast learners from the slow end up screening the children of the relatively well-off and educated from the children of the poor and unacculturated. Since poor children generally do badly in school, they are branded as 'failures' early in life, destined for jobs which require little skill and originality, simply because they were unable to succeed at these school tests and exercises. Worse, perhaps, is the self-concept of these dropouts. The society reinforces, through schooling and other institutions, the self-image of incompetence and ignorance for those who do not succeed in school." Schooling, Carnoy concludes, thus "helps to preserve stability in the [socio-economic] system by indirectly acting to make this group believe that they have *no right* to the fruits of development because they are not sufficiently *prepared.*"[11]

The means by which the schools accomplish these and other latent learning outcomes has been termed the "hidden curriculum." The hidden curriculum consists of the generally unintended and unrecognized learning experiences which students are exposed to in school. Actually, the term "hidden curriculum" is something of a misnomer. "Curriculum" was previously defined as a planned set of learning experiences; hence, according to this definition, a hidden curriculum would be a planned set of learning experiences that is deliberately kept hidden. However, most users of the term consider the hidden curriculum to be a set of unrecognized, inadvertent learning experiences; it is not deliberately hidden, only unnoticed. Therefore, we shall continue to employ the term in this way. It is certainly a very vivid expression, and one worth retaining.

It seems clear that the existence of the latent learning function of the school system should be made known to educational policy makers, who can then decide, for example, which aspects of the hidden curriculum to retain and which to eliminate (if that is possible). They might even want to enhance the desirable aspects of the hidden curriculum, so that its beneficial consequences might be increased. If some features of the hidden curriculum have a countervailing relationship to the regular curriculum but cannot be readily eliminated, the policy makers should be aware of this, so that appropriate remedial steps can be taken, such as strengthening the regular curriculum.

Latent Nonlearning Functions

Several other latent functions of the school system that do not involve learning may be identified. While they are probably not unrecognized, these activities are nevertheless classifiable as latent functions because they are not explicitly intended or sanctioned. One of the most significant of these is the custodial or "baby-sitting" function of the schools. In the words of David Goslin, "the school also serves as a place to send the children to get them out of the

[11]Martin Carnoy, *Education as Cultural Imperialism* (New York: McKay, 1974), p. 12. (Emphasis in the original.)

home. Temporary relief from the task of taking care of the children is thereby provided for the mother. The most notable effect of this aspect of the educational process has been to increase the number of roles available to women, including women with children. No longer must a young woman contemplate spending the major part of her life taking care of her children. Instead she may look forward to contributing to the society and the community, as well as to her family, in a number of different ways, while at the same time creating new and meaningful identities for herself in addition to her role as a mother. The effect on the labor force has been to increase the number of females who are holding full- or part-time jobs and in general to facilitate the acceptance of women into many occupations formerly closed to them. To the extent that women have become increasingly involved in community affairs, the rise of the club woman and the community service organization run by women volunteers can be attributed in part to this function of the school."[12]

The school system also has an important latent role in bringing together prospective marriage partners. "The school," Goslin observes, "also plays an important part in the courtship process by providing a setting in which boys and girls can interact informally and participate in a variety of social activities under the supervision of adults. In this respect the school contributes to the maintenance of the social structure of the community and society by exerting a localizing influence on mate selection. At the college level the institution has a similar conservative effect on social structure because colleges tend to attract students having similar social backgrounds or coming from common geographical areas."[13] (Note 4)

CONCLUDING COMMENTS

With the perspective afforded by the discussion in this chapter, we may now consider our fundamental educational policy question: What should be the goals of education?

For convenience, we shall divide this basic question into two important subquestions. The first of these derives from the fact that a society is composed of many different individuals. Therefore, in at-

[12]David A. Goslin, *The School in Contemporary Society* (Glenview, Ill.: Scott, Foresman, 1965), pp. 11–12.
[13]Ibid., p. 13.

tempting to formulate the goals of education, it is necessary to decide how to allocate or distribute learning experiences to the various members of society. Should each person receive equal education, or should there be differences? In other words, how should we divide the limited resources available for education? Although this question is obviously of immense importance to each individual, it is also of vital significance to the society, for the type of society achieved depends upon how the available learning experiences are distributed.

The second problem that must be considered when addressing our basic question about the goals of education is that of deciding which learning outcomes should be sought through education. Whereas the first subquestion focuses on the problem of *who* should be educated, the second is concerned with *what* should be learned. The reason for engaging in an educational activity is to produce a desired learning outcome, which may lead directly to an ultimate end, or which may constitute an intermediate end in a complex means-ends chain. In either case, the formulation of an educational goal entails the specification of a learning outcome.

The means-ends procedure is particularly useful in the justification of policy statements about the learning outcomes that should be achieved. We can try to identify the penultimate or ultimate end of education and, having accomplished this, attempt to determine which means (learning outcomes and curriculum) will lead to our end. Alternatively, we can try to demonstrate that a proposed learning outcome is desirable with respect to the intermediate and remote ends that it serves. We can also try to show that a proposed means (such as a new curriculum) will lead to desirable learning outcomes and more distant ends. In considering which learning outcomes should be accomplished, we may focus, therefore, on the curricular means, examine policy statements about desirable learning outcomes, or start with the remote ends of education.

In contemplating the use of the school system for the achievement of our basic educational objectives, we cannot proceed very far in the formulation of educational goals without requiring data about the functions of schooling. Which means lead to which ends must be known, and the best information about these means-ends relationships comes from an analysis of the present school system. If an end is projected for the schools without taking account of their actual functions, then it may be found that the desired end is not attainable; or if it is achieved, it may be discovered that other valued outcomes have been lost. In deciding which learning outcomes should be sought, and how they should be distributed among the members of society, the multiple functions of the school system must be kept in mind. Some functions of schooling should be regarded as important side effects of utilizing the school system as our means of education. As mentioned earlier, no policy statement can be fully justified unless the side effects of the means-ends chain that has been proposed are considered.

SUMMARY

The question "What should be the goals of education?" is one of the two fundamental educational policy questions we are considering. A *goal* is a projected end or outcome; this term is equivalent to "purpose," "aim," and "objective."

Educational goals cannot be seen, although their existence can be inferred from statements that people make about their purposes and from actions that seem to be directed toward the attainment of an end.

A review of official statements about the goals of education reveals that learning is the principal declared purpose of the school system. Yet as noted previously, the schools perform several functions besides that of teaching. One of these—the selecting and sorting function—detracts from the teaching function if norm-referenced evaluation is used. Society must, therefore, decide which of these functions should have priority in the school system.

The *functions* of schooling are its actual outcomes (as distinguished from goals, which are projected outcomes). The term "function" is also used to designate the role or activities of the school system, such as teaching and selecting and sorting.

An important distinction needs to be made between manifest and latent functions of schooling. A *manifest* function is one that is both intended and recognized; a *latent* function is one that is not intended or sanctioned (it may or may not be recognized).

The teaching function of the school system is, of course, a manifest function. Through its teaching activities, the schools deliberately transmit culture from one generation to the next. Although cultural transmission is essentially a conservative function, some parts of the school system (for example, the universities) may be engaged in creating and disseminating new culture.

Another important manifest function of the school system is the selecting and sorting of students. This is accomplished through: (1) restricting access to certain instructional programs; (2) using norm-referenced grading; and (3) awarding school certificates to some students, while denying them to others. A major consequence of this function is the difference in income that is associated with the achievement and possession of different types of school certificates.

In addition to manifest functions, the schools perform latent learning functions of importance. Examples of learning outcomes that are generally unintended and unrecognized are: the learning of traditional sex roles, the fostering of conformist and competitive behaviors, and the acquisition of a negative self-concept by students who have done poorly in school. The situations responsible for the latent learning function of the schools have been termed the "hidden curriculum."

The schools also accomplish several latent non-learning functions. Included in this category are the custodial ("baby-sitting") function and the bringing-together of prospective marriage partners.

GENERAL NOTES AND BIBLIOGRAPHY

1. EDUCATIONAL GOALS: CONCEPTUAL AND DESCRIPTIVE. Relatively few sources are available on the conceptual and descriptive aspects of educational goals, in contrast with the plentitude of sources in which normative considerations are discussed. See L. M. Brown, ed., *Aims of Education* (New York: Teachers College Press, 1970); Richard L. Derr, *A Taxonomy of Social Purposes of Public Schools* (New York: McKay, 1973); and Adrian Dupuis, ed., *Nature, Aims, and Policy* (Urbana: University of Illinois Press, 1970).

2. FUNCTIONS OF SCHOOLING. There is no book which provides a comprehensive survey of the functions of the school system. Among the best sources for a general treatment of this topic are: Orvile G. Brim, *Sociology and the Field of Education* (New York: Russell Sage Foundation, 1958)—Chapter 8, "The Functions of Education"; David A. Goslin, *The School in Contemporary Society* (Glenview, Ill.: Scott, Foresman, 1965)—Chapters

1, 4, 5, and 6; James B. McKee, *Introduction to Sociology* (New York: Holt, Rinehart and Winston, 1969)—Chapter 14; and Burton R. Clark, *Educating the Expert Society* (San Francisco: Chandler, 1962)—Chapters 1 and 2. Robert Dreeben's *On What Is Learned in School* (Reading, Mass.: Addison-Wesley, 1968) is much less comprehensive than its title suggests, focusing primarily on the learning of cultural norms and the political effects of schooling. Herbert Hyman, Charles R. Wright and John S. Reed, *The Enduring Effects of Education* (Chicago: University of Chicago Press, 1975) also has a relatively limited scope.

Among the important functions of the school system not discussed in this chapter is the provision of activities which foster the physical development of the student. Schools may also offer health services and free lunches to students. Another significant non-learning outcome is illustrated by the case of a student's making friends or joining a certain fraternity in college. After leaving college, friends and fraternity connections may be helpful in furthering his career. Schools often serve a recreational or entertainment function (through such things as sports contests, student dramatic productions, student bands, and so forth) for the communities in which they are located.

3. MANIFEST FUNCTIONS OF SCHOOLING. The general sources mentioned in Note 2 are also useful for this topic. Many studies have been produced which deal with specific aspects of the manifest cultural transmission effects of the schools. See, for example, Allen H. Barton, *Studying the Effects of College Education* (New Haven, Conn.: Edward W. Hazen Foundation, 1959); Rebecca S. Vreeland and Charles E. Bidwell, "Classifying University Departments: An Approach to the Analysis of Their Effects Upon Undergraduates' Values and Attitudes," *Sociology of Education* 39 (1966): 237–254; Norval D. Glenn, "The Trend in Differences in Attitudes and Behavior by Educational Level," *Sociology of Education* 39 (1966): 255–275.

The relationship between schooling and individual incomes is discussed in several sources, including: Mark Blaug, *An Introduction to the Economics of Education* (London: Allen Lane The Penguin Press, 1970); John Vaizey, *The Political Economy of Education* (New York: Wiley, 1972); Richard S. Ekhaus, *Estimating the Returns to Education* (Berkeley, Calif.: Carnegie Commission on Higher Education, 1973); Ivar Berg, *Education and Jobs: The Great Training Robbery* (Boston: Beacon, 1971); Margaret S. Gordon, ed., *Higher Education and the Labor Market* (New York: McGraw-Hill, 1974); Paul Taubman and Terence Wales, *Higher Education and Earnings* (New York: McGraw-Hill, 1974).

A considerable body of research is also available on the relationships between schooling and economic growth. Several studies have attempted to measure the correlation between the amount of schooling in a country and its level of economic development. For an illustration of this approach, see Frederick Harbison and Charles A. Myers, *Education, Manpower, and Economic Growth* (New York: McGraw-Hill, 1964). However, although it is evident that the most economically advanced nations are those which also have the greatest extent of schooling, it is not so obvious whether it is because of prosperity that some countries have been able to afford more schooling than others, or whether some countries are wealthier than others because they have invested more resources in the expansion of their school systems.

For a general treatment of the selecting and sorting function of the school system, see Robert J. Havighurst and Bernice L. Neugarten, *Society and Education* (4th ed.; Boston: Allyn and Bacon, 1975), pp. 14–111. Contrasting views on the topic of social mobility are provided in the following sources: R. J. Herrnstein, *I.Q. in the Meritocracy* (Boston: Atlantic-Little, Brown, 1973); Maurice Levitas, *Marxist Perspectives in the Sociology of Education* (London: Routledge and Kegan Paul, 1974). Also see the essays by Marcus Raskin and Samuel Bowles in Martin Carnoy, ed., *Schooling in a Corporate Society* (2nd ed.; New York: McKay, 1975). The credentialing effects of the school system are discussed in the works by Berg, Gordon, and Taubman and Wales, cited above. For a satirical treatment of the selecting and sorting function of the school system, see Michael Young, *The Rise of the Meritocracy, 1870–2033* (Baltimore, Md.: Penguin Books, 1961).

4. LATENT FUNCTIONS OF SCHOOLING. Many radical critics have discussed the latent functions of the school system. See, for example, John Holt, *How Children Fail* (New York: Dell, 1970); Ivan Illich, *Deschooling Society* (New York: Harper and Row, 1971). See also Martin Carnoy, *Education as Cultural*

Imperialism (New York: McKay, 1974); Everett Reimer, *School Is Dead* (Garden City, N.Y.: Doubleday, 1971); Joel H. Spring, *Education and the Rise of the Corporate State* (Boston: Beacon, 1972); Nancy Frazier and Myra Sadker, *Sexism in School and Society* (New York: Harper and Row, 1973).

For a discussion of the hidden curriculum, see the following: Benson R. Snyder, *The Hidden Curriculum* (Cambridge, Mass.: MIT Press, 1973); Philip Jackson, *Life in Classrooms* (New York: Holt, Rinehart and Winston, 1968); and Frazier and Sadker, *Sexism in School and Society,* cited above. Although the term is not explicitly applied, the hidden curriculum is also treated in Willard Waller, *The Sociology of Teaching* (New York: Wiley, 1965) and Holt, *How Children Fail,* cited above.

SHOULD WE HAVE
EQUAL EDUCATION?

CHAPTER 8

There are at least two different ways that the term "equal education" may be interpreted. One interpretation holds that equal education means the equalization of educational *opportunity*. The advocates of the goal of equal educational opportunity believe that any advantage in gaining access to schools that some persons might have as a result of parental status should be eliminated; instead, a fair chance should be provided within the school system for all talented students. The equalization of educational opportunity "has a strong appeal because it puts selection on a more efficient basis than in a hereditary system, it provides a safety value for talented malcontents and it preserves personal liberty. But this in no way means that the distribution of income or wealth at any particular time will necessarily be more equal than in a system of hereditary privilege."[1] In other words, equal educational opportunity means that everyone will have an equal chance to become unequal. (Note 1)

The second interpretation of equal education is based on the view that education should foster a more equal society—that educational outcomes should be equal. The outcomes referred to consist of learning *outcomes* and certificates that are direct consequences of attending school, plus the other effects (such as income and status) that are attributable to these outcomes.

This chapter's purpose is to examine the major arguments that have been advanced in relation to these two different concepts.

[1]Paul Moorman, "The Great Obstacle to Equal Opportunity Is Inherited Wealth," *Times Higher Educational Supplement,* January 24, 1975, p. 9.

Should We Have Equal
Educational Opportunity?
Issue 7: _____

The view that educational opportunity should be equalized
may be further divided into two differing approaches. One approach
is concerned with equalizing access to schools, while the other is
concerned with equalizing educational programs.

Equal Access to the School System

If the system provided equal access to schools, all students
would have an equivalent opportunity to attend the school or educational program of their choice. Although various schools and curricula comprising the school system might be of different types and
quality, personal characteristics of prospective students (such as
race, sex, age, religious affiliation) would not be used as the basis for
denying admission to any school. Equal access would also require:
(1) that academic requirements for admission to educational programs be eliminated, and (2) that any financial obstacles in the way
of the student's attending a particular school or educational program be removed (through the use of grants or loans, as necessary).

During the classical period of ancient Greece and Rome, access
to schooling was limited, with the principal recipients being male
children whose parents belonged to the most affluent segment of society. This limitation on access to schooling was achieved by making
formal education primarily a parental responsibility (rather than a
public one), and by requiring that fees be paid. Around the middle of
the nineteenth century a major change in societal policy regarding
access to schooling took place. Instead of restricting access to the
school system to those whose parents could afford school fees, a new
policy of universal, free, compulsory schooling was instituted in
many countries of Western Europe and in the United States.

In Western Europe during the 1950–60 decade, the situation
regarding access to schooling and the distribution of school credentials was generally as follows. All children of compulsory school age
had the opportunity to attend free public primary schools (although
the parents of some of these children elected to send them to private
schools). This phase of schooling lasted from four to six years, after
which school system authorities (often by means of an examination)

determined which future scholastic opportunities were available to each student. Those who were selected—about 20 per cent of the students—were granted access to the public secondary school program that prepared students for admission to the university; the remaining 80 per cent (except for those students whose parents could afford private university-preparatory secondary schooling) were shunted into a variety of other programs that did not prepare students for university admission. Completion of the university-preparatory secondary school program (both public and private) was marked by another examination. The number who passed this examination represented approximately 5 per cent of the total number of persons in the society in the relevant age cohort; the number completing the program for the first university degree was about half this number (2–3 per cent of the total number of persons of the relevant age).

By contrast, in the United States during the 1950–60 decade, there was generally no formal determination by school system authorities of which students could enter the university-preparatory secondary school program (of course, not all students who entered this program would necessarily finish). In any case the university-preparatory secondary program was not acutely different from the non-university-oriented program; in fact, a student who completed secondary school in either program undoubtedly could find some university-level institution that would admit him to the bachelor's degree program. Approximately two-thirds of the Americans who were of the relevant age were actually graduating from secondary school in 1960; of this number perhaps one-quarter went on to obtain a bachelor's degree (15–20 per cent of the total number of persons of the relevant age).

In recent years countries of Western Europe have attempted to modify or eliminate the selection procedures governing access to the university-preparatory secondary school program, thereby doubling or tripling the number of persons eligible for university admission. The number of persons completing secondary school in the United States has also increased; the figure now represents about 75 per cent of the total number of persons of relevant age.

The point of the preceding discussion is to show that, in Western Europe, only a relatively small percentage of persons is able to complete the higher levels of the school system. Western Europeans sometimes criticize the American system for its supposed "lack of quality." However, a highly selective school system would be expected to have a higher average level of ability in its graduates than an open system such as the American. For a more valid comparison one should compare the average level of ability of all of the Western European university graduates with the average level of ability of the top 10–15 per cent of American university graduates.

The United States, which probably has a higher proportion of school-age population completing the secondary school and university levels than any other nation, has a significant percentage who do not finish secondary school. Thus the school system unquestionably acts as an important mechanism for selecting and sorting. In industrialized societies virtually every person must submit to this form of processing by the school system.

One of the major barriers preventing the achievement of equal access to schooling in the United States was eliminated in 1954, with the Supreme Court decision in *Brown* v. *Board of Education*. The Court held that "in the field of public education" the provision of racially segregated school facilities is "inherently unequal," thereby rendering unconstitutional any state or local regulation which utilized race as a criterion for school admission. Thus the two most important factors that still seem to be preventing the attainment of equal access in the United States are: (1) academic requirements for admission to some universities and some university programs, and (2) economic costs entailed in providing and attending secondary schools and universities. (Note 2)

Academic Requirements for University Entrance

Many universities in the United States refuse access to students who fail to meet stipulated academic requirements for admission, such as the attainment of minimum scores on aptitude tests, the prior completion of prescribed programs of study in lower schools, and the possession of favorable letters of recommendation. The justification offered by universities for policies of selective admission includes the arguments that "standards" must be maintained, and that more buildings and teachers would be needed to accommodate increased numbers of students.

The first of these arguments does not seem very well founded: the number of students enrolled in the university should have no effect on "standards," since only those who achieve specified learning outcomes should receive degrees. The argument that more facilities and teachers will be required if university enrollments are expanded has much more validity. In fact, if academic requirements for admission were abolished, it would probably be necessary to establish many new universities, as well as special programs not now part of the traditional university curriculum (such as remedial programs), to accommodate the increased demand for university educational opportunities. But if the necessary additional university teachers, programs and facilities could be made available, then there would seem to be no good reason for the school system to wish to restrict access to the university. (It is assumed, of course, that instructional programs would be appropriately individualized, so that the rate of progress of one student would not handicap another student.)

One of the most significant recent developments for eliminating academic requirements for university access in the American school system was the adoption of an "open admissions" policy by the City University of New York. Under this policy, everyone who graduated from a New York City high school since June, 1970, is eligible for admission to one of the two- or four-year colleges comprising the City University of New York system. The only academic requirement for university access is a high school diploma; neither the type of program pursued by the student in high school, nor his record of academic achievement (grades), affects his eligibility for admission.

Access to Schooling: Economic Costs

The problem of what should be done about the economic costs of schooling (the costs of providing teachers and school facilities and those of student maintenance) is undoubtedly the central one in the question of whether equal access to the school system should be instituted. This problem brings us to a direct consideration of what, if anything, society wishes to do about providing equal access. There would seem to be three courses of action open to any society: (1) the provision of schools and the support of students can be declared by society to be a private matter; (2) society can make loans available to some or all students; and (3) the schooling of some or all students can be subsidized by society.

Until the middle of the nineteenth century the first course of action was the one generally followed in the United States. Then it was decided as a matter of societal (state) policy that all young persons should be required to attend schools. Concomitantly, a decision was also made to subsidize the period of compulsory schooling, through the provision of free public schools, although the provision of food, lodging and clothing for students was considered to be a private matter. Later the principle of free public schooling for all was applied to secondary and, in some cases, to post-secondary levels. However, many public universities expect the student to pay for a certain proportion of the costs of tuition.

The major issues today are whether there should be public subsidies for maintenance of students at the secondary and post-secondary levels or whether, at the very least, loans should be made available to some or all students at the post-secondary level.

Many countries have recognized that some students are deterred from seeking admission to the university or even from completing their studies in secondary school because of the economic costs entailed. As a result, programs of financial support have been inaugurated for the purpose of providing maintenance subsidies to needy students. Once these programs are begun, the tendency is for them to expand, which could possibly result in a situation of all students' being paid salaries. As Frank Bowles has noted, "equalization schemes almost invariably become steadily larger and larger in their scope. This process is seemingly inevitable unless there is a radical change in official policy, as once equality of opportunity— rather than manpower needs or the interests of the intellectually outstanding—is established as the basis of an aid scheme, there is constant pressure by students, by educationists and even by politicians to include yet another section of the student body. In time, almost all students are assisted, and the sums they receive cover most of their educational and maintenance costs. Eventually, therefore, it is realized that there is little point in withholding aid from the remaining students, and that the money saved through applying a means test to determine how great a student's financial need is, and thus how much he should receive, is comparatively small in relation to the total cost of the aid programme, and is largely counterbalanced by the extra administrative costs. A campaign is then started to abolish the means test, and aid becomes in effect a salary paid by the state to all students. This salary type of aid scheme is, however, still only a logical conclusion towards which all equalization programmes appear to be tending. It has not as yet been established in any country, though the United Kingdom is very near it."[2]

Richard Nixon, former President of the United States, stated that he would like to have the economic factor eliminated as a reason for unequal access to the university. In a message to Congress on March 19, 1970, he expressed the view that "no qualified student who wants to go to college should be barred by lack of money. That has long been a great American goal; I propose that we achieve it now. Something is basically unequal about opportunity for higher education when a young person whose family earns more than $15,000 a year is nine times more likely to attend college than a young person whose family earns less than $3,000. Something is basically wrong with federal policy toward higher education when it has failed to correct this inequity."[3]

There is some doubt, however, that financial aid would significantly increase the number of high school students who decide to enter the university. After reviewing the available research, George Nash found that "although money emerges as an important factor, it has come to be generally accepted that grant aid alone, offered at the end of the senior year of high school, will have relatively little effect on increasing the number and proportion of students who will attend college."[4] A similar conclusion was reached by the staff of the Commission on Human Resources and Advanced Education. They contend that "to assume that simply by increasing financial support and opening up new educational opportunities, we will automatically enable all bright but poor youth to attend college, is naive. . . . Although loan and scholarship programs to assist in financing the post high school education of disadvantaged youth are necessary, they are not sufficient. If we are to solve the problem of filling society's needs for talented persons in high-level positions, we must intervene much earlier in the developmental history of the individual."[5]

[2]Frank Bowles, *Access to Higher Education* (Paris: UNESCO, 1963), p. 187.

[3]Quoted in Murray Milner, *The Illusion of Equality* (San Francisco: Jossey-Bass, 1972), p. 33.

[4]George Nash, "Student Financial Aid, College and University," in *Encyclopedia of Educational Research,* ed. Robert L. Ebel (4th ed.; New York: Macmillan, 1969), p. 1347.

[5]J. K. Folger, H. S. Astin and A. E. Bayer, *Human Resources and Higher Education* (New York: Russell Sage Foundation, 1970), pp. 322–323.

Mark Blaug has argued that we should provide financial aid to students in secondary school, if we wish to overcome the economic handicaps of students from working class families. Although university students in England (where Blaug lives) generally receive fairly sizable grants to help cover their expenses, a working class student who attends the last three years of secondary school must forgo the income he might otherwise earn during this period, since during these last three years he is legally old enough to work, if he so desires. Yet grants are not provided to secondary-school students in England, with the result that large numbers of working-class students in the secondary-school-age group elect to withdraw from school. "Unwilling to face up to the costs of true equality," Blaug writes, "we have instead created a system in which education between fifteen and eighteen is effectively distributed in accordance with the purchasing power of parents—the absence of fees still leaves parents paying indirectly for two-thirds of the total costs of secondary education—after which we award those who have survived the race with [a grant] equivalent to 60 per cent of what they could earn at that age in productive employment."[6]

Discussion of Equal Access Arguments

The arguments surrounding the issue of whether we should have equal access to schooling are relatively easy to identify and assess. The denial of access to schooling on the basis of students' personal characteristics has been largely eliminated in the United States. While most universities and colleges still impose academic requirements for admission, some schools have been attempting to reduce or eliminate this barrier to admission. Except for the argument that increased university enrollments require increased provision of university facilities and, hence, economic costs, there does not seem to be a good argument that can be advanced for a limitation of access to schools based on academic requirements. As long as learning outcomes are specified by school certificates (the compromise proposal discussed in Chapter 6) and the speed of learning of one student is not allowed to affect the pace of another, it cannot be maintained that increased enrollments will result in "lower stand-

[6]Mark Blaug, *An Introduction to the Economics of Education* (London: Allen Lane The Penguin Press, 1970), p. 295.

ards." The school certificate will mean no more or less than the learning outcomes that are stipulated for its attainment.

The principal argument against equal access to schools must rest on the grounds of economic cost. The provision of school facilities costs money, as does the provision of food, housing and clothing to students. But if the money is not made available, then only those students whose parents could afford the costs of schooling would, for example, be able to enter medical school or law school. To have equal access to education, there must be no financial barriers to school attendance. The real question, therefore, is whether society is willing to transfer funds from the more affluent families to the less affluent in order to enable students without sufficient financial resources to participate in the instructional programs of their choice.

This transfer of funds would certainly entail economic costs (manifested through higher taxes) for some segments of society. But if such financial assistance is not provided, then each person's educational opportunities will be largely dependent upon the wealth of his or her parents. A transfer of funds for educational purposes from the affluent to the less affluent will in effect give the entire society the responsibility of providing educational opportunities for its children.

A basic argument against equal access is the contention that financial support of poor students combined with elimination of academic admissions requirements would be wasteful—that "too many" doctors and lawyers, for example, might be produced. However, if we accept the free market as the basic principle for the organization of the economy, we would expect that the supply of medical doctors and lawyers will adjust to the demand for medical and legal services. As supply increases in relation to demand, the incomes of medical doctors and lawyers will fall, thus reducing the incentive for students to enter these professions and thereby bringing about an appropriate supply of medical doctors and lawyers. If a planned economy is favored, the economic planners could in a similar fashion control the numbers of medical doctors and lawyers by reducing the salaries paid to them.

It is possible, of course, that a person might enter a medical school simply to learn about medicine, but without the intention of ever working as a medical doctor. Would not such studies be wasteful? The individual in this example presumably derives considerable personal benefit from learning about medicine, otherwise he or she would not spend time studying the subject. For the time that a student of working age spends in school represents an important economic cost—the loss of the income he or she could have earned if gainfully employed. It would be expected, therefore, that the factor of income forgone would deter most students from mere dilettantism. If, however, dilettantism were still perceived as a problem, students could be given loans instead of grants (or some combination of loans and grants) to cover the costs of their schooling and maintenance. To encourage a student to work in the occupation for which he or she had been trained, part or all of these loans could be forgiven after a specified number of years are spent in that occupation. On the other hand, society might consider schooling to be so worthwhile that it would welcome any person into the school system for as long as he or she wished to attend.

If such a compelling case can be made for equal access to education, then why has it not been instituted in the United States? One reason would seem to be that the incomes of certain professional groups (such as medical doctors, lawyers, dentists and veterinarians) are benefited by a situation in which there is restricted access to the schools that prepare students for these occupations. This is not to say that all members of these professional groups favor selective access, but the majority probably do, or at least the majority of the most influential members of these professions probably do.

Another reason is found in the vested interests of colleges and universities, particularly those which have "elite" status in the present school system or which aspire to such status. Some colleges and universities presently are regarded as being of better quality than others; if truly equal access were instituted, however, any student who wanted it would be allowed admission to, say, Harvard University.

If the number of students who applied exceeded the capacity of a university, either some additional campuses would need to be established, or the students admitted would have to be selected on a random basis. It seems clear that if this were done the status of a university such as Harvard would decline, since the present reputation of this type of university no doubt derives from the fact that only select students are admitted. Also, under the present norm-referenced credentialing system, such students will inevitably appear to do well, almost irrespective of the professional teaching abilities of the faculty. Thus it is in the interest of such universities to maintain selective admissions and norm-referenced student evaluation.

But why do we not have equal access to schooling at the primary and secondary levels? One explanation is that it is presently unconstitutional for public funds to be used for the support of private primary and secondary schools; hence it has not been possible to provide equal access to these schools. As far as public schools are concerned, presumably it has been administratively more convenient (and in some cases legally necessary pursuant to desegregation rulings) to require student attendance at designated schools, rather than to permit freedom of choice and provide compensation to students for transportation expenses. Therefore, those who might wish to equalize educational opportunity in the public primary and secondary schools have given more attention to the concept of equal programs than to that of equal access.

Equal Educational Programs

One of the most important contemporary educational policy controversies in the United States is the question of whether equivalent programs for public primary and secondary schools should be provided. All public primary and secondary schools are not now equivalent, since some have more financial resources available to them, and some have student body compositions that are believed to foster the attainment of desired learning outcomes to a greater extent than student body compositions of other schools. However, since students are ordinarily required by school system authorities to attend designated schools, it has been possible for wealthier parents to choose to live in those school districts (or in those areas of a given school district) that provide what are generally regarded as the "better" public schools. For those who believe in hereditary privilege, this situation is quite acceptable. Those who favor a meritocratic approach to compulsory primary and secondary schooling have sought to equalize the chances for social mobility of every student in our public primary and secondary schools by equalizing these schools.

The concept of equal programs—despite the present controversy surrounding it—would seem to have a very limited place in the school system. If school system authorities were to abolish the policy of requiring attendance at designated public primary and secondary schools, this would permit students and/or their parents to select the schools the students would attend (equal access). Differences in the quality of the schools would then be less cause for preoccupation. If our concern is with educational outcomes (equal or unequal), then the provision of equal programs is also irrelevant. For if we favor equal outcomes and believe that the school system is a factor in their attainment, then we will probably want compensatory (different) educational programs, rather than equal ones. Likewise, if unequal outcomes are favored, differentiated programs will probably be desired.

Nevertheless, because of the importance of the controversy over equal programs in the contemporary American school system, this problem warrants examination. There are two questions related to this problem which have become particularly controversial: (1) Should equivalent financial resources be provided to all publicly supported primary and secondary schools? (2) Should the student composition of public primary and secondary schools be ethnically balanced? (Note 3)

Financial Inequalities in the School System

There are significant financial inequalities in the American public school system that may be assumed to bring about differences in the quality of educational programs available. According to David Cohen, "it is hardly news that some schools are rich and others poor; nor is it a surprise that the rich ones are likely to be found in well-to-do communities, and the poor ones in less affluent places. . . . In Arkansas (the state with the lowest average expenditure for public schooling), the highest-spending 10 per cent of the districts in 1961 devoted $160 or more per pupil to the education of their charges, and the lowest 10 per cent spent $99 or less per pupil; in New York (the state with the highest average outlay for schooling), the top 10 per cent of the districts spent $465 or more, and the lowest 10 per cent spent $333 or less on each student. Studies in individual states since then show that such disparities persist."[7]

There are, Cohen suggests, two main reasons for the unequal financial resources available to the public primary and secondary schools: "First, the central cities usually experience more than aver-

[7]The quotations in this paragraph and in the two which follow it are from David K. Cohen, "The Economics of Inequality," *Saturday Review,* April 19, 1969, p. 64.

age competition for tax dollars; they have more problems which local taxation is supposed to alleviate (poverty, aging, ill health), and they provide services for people who work there, but live elsewhere (fire and police protection, sanitation). . . . [Second,] even if municipal overburden did not exist, the same tax rates would not raise the same amount of money in all communities. Those with more rundown and unproductive land tend to have lower assessed valuations than communities with more well-kept and productive property. Many communities of the first sort are rural (with depleted farmland and underpopulated hamlets), but many others are urban, replete with slums, decaying business districts, and industrial wastelands. . . . When communities with different assessed valuations are taxed at the same rate, the per capita revenue yield varies; communities with the lower valuations raise less even though they make the same tax effort. . . . The average affluent homeowner in a well-to-do community is required to sacrifice a smaller proportion of his income to pay his share of an $800 annual per pupil outlay, than would a less well-off homeowner in a central city or depressed rural area. Affluent communities can raise more money for schools at lower tax rates than poor communities can at higher rates."

Cohen believes that "programs of state foundation and equalization aid could eliminate these local differences, but generally they do not. The reasons vary from state to state, but a few basic ones are similar. In many states, the aid formulas were designed decades ago to help finance the nonurban districts, which at the time were disadvantaged. Over the years, many of the rural areas became affluent suburbs, and many of the cities grew relatively poor. The state aid formulas, however, have not always been updated. In many metropolitan areas, state school aid programs deliver more dollars per pupil to suburban than to central-city schools. In 1964, for example, Detroit received $189 per pupil from Michigan, while the average suburban receipt per pupil was $240. But even in those states where efforts have been made to reverse these trends the remedies are only partly effective, because state education departments are reluctant to equalize completely the tax burden among rich and poor districts. . . . The reluctance to correct this situation, of course, is political. State education departments are answerable to legislatures, which in turn must account to constituents. Parents and schoolmen who are relatively well-off may pay lip service to the idea of equal educational opportunity, but they also will use the political process to protect their advantage and that of their children."

The question of whether the financing of public primary and secondary schools should be equalized (at least within each state) has been the subject of several court cases in recent years. Many state legislatures have also begun to re-examine the existing arrangements in their respective states for the collection and distribution of public school funds, with a view toward creating a more equitable system of public-school financing.

Achievement of financial equality would permit the schools to become equivalent with respect to teacher salaries, instructional materials, and school buildings. However, one variable which cannot be equalized through the attainment of financial equality is the student composition of the schools. As discussed in Chapter 6, there is evidence that, for a given student, the racial/socio-economic background of those who attend school with him is a factor which affects that student's learning outcomes. To have truly equivalent educational programs, it would seem necessary to equalize the student composition of our schools, especially with respect to ethnic backgrounds of students (since ethnic characteristics are strongly correlated with socio-economic characteristics). Therefore, the school integration controversy needs to be examined.

Controversy Over School Integration

In 1954 the Supreme Court ruled in *Brown* v. *Board of Education* that racially segregated public primary and secondary schools are unconstitutional. This decision of the Supreme Court prevents the schools from using access control to restrict admission of students on the grounds of race. As a result of subsequent decisions of the courts, those parts of the United States which formerly maintained a system of legally segregated schools (*de jure* segregation) have been required to do more than just eliminate racial restrictions on access to schooling. They have been requested by the courts to take affirmative steps to bring about a situation in which racially integrated schooling prevails. But areas in which racially segregated schools exist because of nondeliberate factors such as housing patterns (*de facto* segregation) have not been required to eliminate segregated schooling.

To bring about school integration, school districts have usually resorted to aversive rather than positive motivation. It is important to recognize the distinction between desegregation and integration and the control techniques necessary to achieve both conditions. Whereas school desegregation has been relatively easy to implement (all that is required is that racial restrictions on access be dropped), the use of aversive motivation to effect school integration has engendered considerable hostility.

Much of the present controversy in the United States over integrated schooling is focused on the question of whether students should be compulsorily bused as part of the effort to achieve ethnically balanced schools. There seems to be considerable reluctance by white parents to permit the busing of their children to schools in other ethnic neighborhoods. A recent sample survey conducted by the U. S. Commission on Civil Rights provides some relevant data. As reported by Marvin Wall, "the Commission survey asked whether parents would send their children to a new and better school in a neighborhood predominantly occupied by residents of another race. Forty-nine percent of the nonwhite respondents said they would choose such a school, while 34 percent would stick with their neighborhood school. Seventy-five percent of the whites, however, would cling to the neighborhood school, and only 17 percent would send their children into a new and better school in a predominantly black neighborhood."[8]

An explanation for the unwillingness of many white parents to accept compulsory busing has been suggested by John and Lois Scott. "The special difficulty in programs for school integration," they write, "is that they affect members of the dominant white group in a most sensitive part of their lives; that is, they affect the family, especially in its universal function of defining the social position of children. In Western societies all members of a family are commonly judged to occupy the same social class, regardless of age or sex. Parents desire to pass on to their children a status at least as good as their own. This makes the family the most conservative of all social institutions, the slowest to change in an otherwise rapidly changing society. In America today we may have parents who are liberals, yet a 'liberal parent' is almost a contradiction in terms. . . . Families concentrate on providing their offspring with training that will give them an advantage in the otherwise relatively open competition for valued positions in society. . . . As competition for valued positions becomes more and more open, the selection

[8]Marvin Wall, "What the Public Doesn't Know Hurts," *Civil Rights Digest*, Summer, 1973, p. 27.

of environments and schools that will aid in establishing status becomes more and more important. The middle-class white parent's fear of the impact of inter-racial contacts on his children's training does not depend simply on an unlettered racist belief that black children are 'inherently' stupid or immoral, although this may play some part. He is fearful mainly because society is stratified, because parents are anxious to pass on their stratified status, and because most black children are poor."[9]

Because they are very concerned with the social status of their children, and because racial integration of schools would mean socio-economic integration of them as well, upper-class and middle-class parents will resort to a variety of tactics to defeat plans for school integration. The Scotts point out that "most arguments for large-scale school integration presume that white parents can be outmaneuvered by paired schools, 'educational parks' and squadrons of school buses. But this presumption is unrealistic for it is the parents rather than the schools that have the greater strategic flexibility. . . . The whites' main defense against integration is to move, and the general movement is to the suburbs. . . . Families can move across school-district and municipal boundaries far faster than integration plans can. Fathers can commute longer distances than school children can be bused."

The Scotts reach a pessimistic conclusion about prospects for achieving ethnically balanced schools in the immediate future: "The advocates of integration often appeal to impending crisis. We are told that the damage done to black children through segregation is so terrible and costly that any means of eliminating it is justified, and that rapid integration alone affords relief. But there has always been much in social life that is terrible and tragic. Rational social action must derive not simply from moral outrage but also from possible means of redress. One might claim with equal fervor that the damage done to the minds and souls of middle-aged women because they have grown sexually unattractive to men is so terrible and costly that any means of eliminating it is justified; and that a redefinition by Federal fiat of nubile appeal alone affords relief. After all, notions of sexual attractiveness, like notions of racism, are mere

[9]The quotations in this paragraph and in the two which follow it are from John Finely Scott and Lois Heyman Scott, "They Are Not So Much Anti-Negro as Pro-Middle Class," *New York Times Magazine,* March 24, 1968, pp. 107, 110, 117, 120.

cultural artifacts. The facts are that short of truly dictatorial authority over the education of white children, we lack the means to produce widespread school integration so long as white parents do not favor it."

An alternative course of action to the busing of school children for purposes of racial balance is the proposal to change the residential patterns of the suburbs by making available adequate housing in them for lower-income families. This suggestion has been presented in an article by Linda and Paul Davidoff and Neil Gold. They call attention to the fact that "the suburbs contain the largest share of America's population. In 1970, 36 per cent of the people lived in suburban parts of metropolitan regions, 30 per cent in the central cities and 34 per cent in rural areas." But, they point out, "many suburban communities have maintained controls over the kinds of families who can live in them." These controls are the result of zoning laws and housing construction codes, the effect of which "is to prohibit all but the most costly forms of housing development."

From an economic standpoint, the Davidoffs and Gold contend it would be far less expensive if low income housing were built in the suburbs instead of the central cities. They note that "the 19th-century English garden-city movement laid down the principle that the cheapest—and most wholesome—form of housing for working-class families was the attached cottage, or row house, built so that each unit would have access to common open space. But in America, housing built for low-income and moderate-income families has generally been 'projects' in the central cities: massive apartment towers built on the sites of destroyed ghettos, on land that is close to the city's hub and therefore so expensive that building at lower densities is not possible."

Another fact about the suburbs that has received very little attention is their importance as places of employment. According to the Davidoffs and Gold, "the service sectors of the job market—the shopping centers and colleges, for instance—have followed the roads and the population. . . . The demand for cheaper land . . . has brought more companies—and jobs—to the suburbs."

The principal conclusion in the school integration controversy thus seems quite clear. The more affluent families will resist send-

[10]The quotations in this paragraph and in the two which follow it are from Linda Davidoff, Paul Davidoff and Neil W. Gold, "The Suburbs Have to Open Their Gates," *New York Times Magazine*, November 7, 1971, pp. 40, 42–44.

ing their children to those schools which they believe would reduce the advantage their children might otherwise gain from schooling. A possible solution is to require the suburbs to eliminate zoning practices which have prevented the emergence of ethnically integrated residential patterns.

Discussion of Equal Programs Arguments

The proponents of equivalent schooling for everyone contend that if certain educational programs are made obligatory by society, then in fairness to each student they should be of the same quality. It is this view which constitutes a major argument in favor of equal programs.

Another argument advanced by persons who hold the equal programs conception of equal educational opportunity is that equal access to schooling—the other conception of equal educational opportunity—is not feasible (perhaps because of discriminatory practices within the local community which might inhibit a student from exercising free choice). They also maintain that it is undesirable to have as much diversity of educational programs as would probably exist in a situation of equal access to schools (either because they do not consider appropriate the diversity of outcomes to which these diverse programs might lead, or because they do not trust the students to make the right choices about programs and outcomes).

A major opposing view is based on the idea that parents have rights, too. And one of the rights to which parents presumably are entitled is that of assisting their children to become superior to other children. What is the point of acquiring wealth, the critics of equal programs ask, if it cannot be used to confer special advantages on one's children?

There is relatively little to add in the way of further elucidation of these differing positions. To choose among them we must make a very fundamental value judgment: do we desire the penultimate end (and related side effects) to which a strict adherence to equal programs would lead, or do we prefer the penultimate end (and related side effects) to which acceptance of the parental rights view would lead?

Should We Have Equal Educational Outcomes?

Issue 8:_____|

According to a second interpretation of equal education, the educative process should result in equivalent learning outcomes and/or other, more distant, educational outcomes. This could mean that all members of a society should attain a minimal set of common learnings or, in a more stringent interpretation, that the members of the society should not be differentiated with respect to the educational outcomes they achieve. The educational programs necessary to induce equivalent learning outcomes themselves would probably not be equivalent, since less able students might require special forms of education (compensatory education). Nonequivalent programs, therefore, could be used to facilitate the attainment of equivalent learning outcomes.

Some persons who hold the view that the educative process should result in equal outcomes have taken that position after becoming disillusioned with what has been achieved by simply providing equal access to education and/or equal educational programs. It becomes apparent that the latter two policies as applied to the school system cannot result in equal outcomes unless all students are equally capable of learning and equally motivated, to name only two relevant factors. If students are unequal in either respect, equal access and equal programs only insure that there will be "fair" competition. As previously observed, equal access and equal programs merely equalize the opportunities of students to become unequal. (Note 4)

Arguments for Equal Outcomes

One of the strongest advocates of equal educational outcomes is James Coleman, author of the Coleman report, discussed in Chapter 6. In describing the purpose of his study, Coleman has stated that he was mainly concerned with the outcomes of the educative process. For him "equality of educational opportunity" would exist only if the schools were capable of overcoming any educational handicaps a child might bring with him when he entered school. In other words, equal education means equal outcomes.

What is important to a young adult, Coleman writes, is "not how 'equal' his school is, but rather whether he is equipped at the end of school to compete on an equal basis with others, whatever his social origins. From the perspective of society . . . what is important is not to 'equalize the schools' in some formal sense, but to insure that children from all groups come into adult society so equipped as to insure their full participation in this society. Another way of putting this is to say that the schools are successful only insofar as they reduce the dependence of a child's opportunities upon his social origins. . . . Thus, equality of educational opportunity implies, not merely 'equal' schools, but equally effective schools, whose influences will overcome the differences in the starting point of children from different social groups."[11]

Another advocate of equal educational outcomes is Edmund Gordon, who expresses the view that certain minimum outcomes must be attained by all students: "[If] the purpose of education in a democratic society . . . is to broaden opportunities for meaningful participation in the mainstream of society through the development of necessary skills and credentials, then educational opportunity is unequal unless it serves that purpose for all learners. At any point in the history of a society, the minimum educational goals are defined by the prerequisites for meaningful participation or for economic, social, and political survival. The educational experience can and should enable many persons to go far beyond the development of such survival skills, but it cannot be considered to have provided equality of opportunity unless it enables nearly all to reach the survival or participation level. . . . Democratically administered educational programs combined with enlightened educational practices should insure that basic competencies are universally achieved. Equality of educational opportunity would mean the achievement of at least these basic competencies in all pupils save the 3 percent to 5 percent who are truly mentally defective. To make the opportunity equal, the school would have to develop and use whatever methods, materials, or procedures are required by the special style, special ability, or special background the child may bring. That the school may not yet know what and how to do this is a part of the problem. That it accept the challenge to pose the question and actively pursue solutions is the issue at hand. Equal educational opportunity de-

[11]James S. Coleman, "Equal Schools or Equal Students," in *Policy Issues in Urban Education,* eds. Marjorie B. Smiley and Harry L. Miller (New York: Free Press, 1968), pp. 453–454.

mands that, where what children bring to the school is unequal, what the school puts in must be unequal and individualized to insure that what the school produces is at least equal at the basic levels of achievement."[12]

The approach of providing unequal educational inputs in order to equalize educational outputs is usually termed "compensatory education." Daniel Levine has argued for the adoption of this type of education. "Our commitment to providing the best possible education for all students," Levine writes, "is impossible to achieve if we ignore the fact that minority-group students and/or students from low-status homes cannot deposit their special problems at the entrance when they enter the school. We might wish it were otherwise, but those teachers who say they try to 'teach children' without reference to their background are teaching papier-mâché figures, and not human beings; no wonder we fail to reach so many students. . . . If a student's background has not prepared him for working quickly and within narrow time limits, we must make some allowance for this fact. If he has never been encouraged to work independently on intellectual tasks, his teachers should offer more supervision and guidance to help him over his problems. If presenting him with a thick textbook is threatening because it symbolizes a long history of previous failures, by all means we should choose detachable materials which he may feel he can complete in a reasonable amount of time. And so on."[13]

Arguments Against Equal Outcomes

Strong arguments have also been expressed against the idea of equal educational outcomes. Some advocates of nonequal educational outcomes have an elitist conception of society; this view is represented in the following statement by Professor Pillans: "There is an early training, moral and intellectual, which it is desirable to secure to the great body of the people, whether agricultural or manufacturing. Now, it is abundantly obvious, that the object to be kept in view

[12]Edmund W. Gordon, "Toward Defining Equality of Educational Opportunity," in *On Equality of Educational Opportunity*, eds. Frederick Mosteller and Daniel P. Moynihan (New York: Vintage Books, 1972), pp. 431–433.

[13]Daniel U. Levine, "Issues in the Provision of Equal Educational Opportunity," *Journal of Negro Education*, 37 (1968): 12–13.

in such early tuition is, to take advantage of the brief period of docility which intervenes between the age of helpless infancy and that period of life when the sinews are sufficiently knit for hard and continuous labour, and when the profit of the child's handiwork becomes available for the support of the parent, or for its own. This interval, so precious because so brief, amounts often, in large manufacturing towns, to not more than a single twelvemonth, and almost everywhere it is a period of lax and irregular attendance; and yet it is all the time that can be depended upon for training the children of the working classes to such habits, tastes, and feelings, as may render them honest, industrious, intelligent, and happy. . . . A very different treatment, however, is required, and with higher objects in view, for the classes of society whom birth, or fortune, or extraordinary talent, exempt from manual [labour] and drudgery, and who are to earn their livelihood, and improve or adorn their condition, by the feats of the head rather than by the labour of the hand. The studies of this class of youth are extended over a much longer period than those of the labouring population. Time is allowed for following out a systematic course of training, through various stages of progress, and for a series of years; and it is a training as distinct in its nature as it is different in its aim."[14]

Other exponents of the view that equal educational outcomes are not always desirable have argued that education should be aimed at developing the full potentialities of each person. Thus unequal programs would be provided to attain unequal outcomes. One advocate of this position is John Gardner, who states his view as follows: "Our kind of society demands the maximum development of individual potentialities at *every level of ability*. . . . The traditional democratic invitation to each individual to achieve the best that is in him requires that we provide each youngster with the particular kind of education which will benefit *him*."[15]

Peter Schrag offers the argument that differentiated educational outcomes are necessary in a pluralistic society. "What does equality mean in education?" Schrag asks. "Does it mean that the average Negro should be doing as well as the average white, and

[14]Quoted in Leslie M. Brown, ed., *Aims of Education* (New York: Teachers College Press, 1970), pp. 130–131. These comments were made in 1835.

[15]John W. Gardner, *Excellence: Can We Be Equal and Excellent Too?* (New York: Harper Colophon Books, 1962), pp. 74–75. (Emphasis in the original.)

that the resources devoted to his education should be improved until he does? Or does it point to some sort of parity in resources? Or to something else? Coleman himself said that . . . 'equality of educational opportunity implies not merely "equal" schools but equally effective schools, whose influences will overcome the differences in starting point of children from different social groups.' Pedagogically and politically, Coleman's suggestion is pleasant, impossible, and probably undesirable. Pleasant because it has a nice democratic ring; impossible because the haves in the society won't allow it to happen; undesirable because it assumes that all social and cultural differences should be equalized away, that Negro children (or Chinese or Jews) have nothing to offer *as Negroes* except problems. . . . It is likely that we can achieve a greater measure of equality—to narrow the gap between the advantaged and the disadvantaged. More effective preschool programs, and a general extension of the social responsibility of the school for children from deprived homes, may make the classroom more effective. But the matter of achieving genuine equality is another question."[16]

Schrag goes on to concede that "there is a common culture that demands certain levels of verbal and social ability. The question slowly emerging from the current debates, however, is whether that ability must become a universal virtue. Should we be concerned only with the preparation of economic functionaries and the development of conventional academic skills, or also with the growth of human beings whose dignity is not necessarily dependent on middle-class standards of success? Is an understanding of algebraic functions any more desirable than the ability to paint or dance? (The mandated requirements for many jobs—nursing, for example—include verbal abilities that are higher than those the job[s] actually require; the stipulated credentials are not necessarily related to the characteristics the jobs demand.) Are we establishing norms that tend to under-value characteristics that all of society could well use, and for which certain children might be especially well prepared, or do we have to make *all* children into replicas of the middle class? . . . Perhaps," he concludes, "we have to recognize the principle of pluralism not only in a cultural context but in an educational one as well."

[16]The quotations in this paragraph and in the one which follows it are from Peter Schrag, "Why Our Schools Have Failed," *Commentary*, March, 1968, pp. 33, 36–37. (Emphasis in the original.)

Discussion of Equal Outcomes Arguments

As Schrag's statement makes clear, the basic reason for his opposition to the goal of equal educational outcomes is a desire for a
pluralistic rather than a unitary society. Once again, therefore, we
are confronted with the question of pluralism, which arose during
the consideration of whether the locus of governmental control over
the schools should be national or local, and whether there should be
public financial support of private schools (see Chapter 3).

Is it possible to resolve this question of pluralism? Only, it
would seem, if we are prepared to make another fundamental value
judgment comparable to the one about parental rights, which was
discussed in connection with the equal programs arguments. The
notion of pluralism asserts that a group of parents characterized by
such features as a common ethnic identity has the predominant
right to determine the learning outcomes of its children. Thus, for
example, it may be contended that black parents as a group have the
right to educate their children differently from the way white parents as a group do. Those who oppose pluralism argue, in effect, that
it is the society as a whole that has the predominant right to prescribe the learning outcomes that the children of that society should
achieve, irrespective of the claims of particular groups within the
society.

In fact, there are those who suggest that the societal unit is itself "pluralistic" from a world perspective, and that mankind as a
whole should constitute the basis on which the educational objectives of the world's children are determined.[17] What we must do,
therefore is to choose between the educational means-ends chain
that has pluralistic learning outcomes as one of its intermediate
ends and the educational means-ends chain that has a societally-
determined common set of learning outcomes as one of its intermediate ends.

It would probably be relatively easy to use the schools for the
attainment of a minimum set of common learning outcomes, and
even the strongest supporters of pluralism might wish to have certain learning outcomes achieved by all members of society. Just
what these common learning outcomes should be, however, would
still need to be decided.

[17]See John A. Laska and William C. Bailey, "Education for International Understanding—What Do We Really Want?" *International Education,* Fall, 1972, pp. 70–73.

On the other hand, it is questionable whether the school system can be used as a means for accomplishing the larger goal of creating a more equal society. Although James Coleman seems to believe the schools could be "equally effective" in overcoming "the differences in starting point of children from different social groups," Christopher Jencks has reached an opposite conclusion. "Even if we reorganized the schools," Jencks writes, "there is no reason to suppose that adults would end up appreciably more equal as a result." Jencks' "primary concern is with equalizing the distribution of income," and it does seem reasonable to accept his contention that the schools cannot equalize all of the factors that account for differences in incomes (some of these factors are inherited characteristics, of course, as well as differential learning outcomes).[18]

If the schools are unable to bring about a significantly more equal society, what is to be done if that is our goal? Jencks suggests that "if we want to equalize the distribution of income, then, we need a more direct approach. . . . As long as egalitarians assume that public policy cannot contribute to economic equality directly but must proceed by ingenious manipulations of marginal institutions like the schools, progress will remain glacial. If we want to move beyond this tradition, we will have to establish political control over the economic institutions that shape our society."

But, as Jencks points out, "relatively few people view income inequality as a serious problem." He proposes the following course of action: "If egalitarians want to mobilize popular support for income redistribution, their first aim should be to convince people that the distribution of income is a legitimate political issue. Americans now tend to assume that incomes are determined by private decisions in a largely unregulated economy and that there is no realistic way to alter the resulting distribution. Until they come to believe that the distribution of income is a political issue, subject to popular regulation and control, very little is likely to change. In this connection it is worth noting that until a generation ago, Americans also believed that the rate of economic growth depended on private decisions and that it could not be controlled by the government. Today, virtually everyone assumes that the federal government is responsible for the state of the economy. . . . The time may now be ripe for a

[18]The quotations by Jencks in this paragraph and in the two which follow it are from *Inequality: A Reassessment of the Effect of Family and Schooling in America* (New York: Basic Books, 1972), pp. 255, 261, 263–265.

similar change in attitudes toward income inequality. We need to establish the idea that the federal government is responsible not only for the total amount of the national income, but for its distribution. If private decisions make the distribution too unequal, the government must be held responsible for improving the situation."

SUMMARY

This chapter is concerned with the question of whether we should have equal education. There are at least two ways that the term "equal education" may be interpreted. It may refer to (1) the provision of equal educational opportunity, or (2) to the achievement of equal outcomes by means of the educative process.

As a result of the school desegregation decision of the Supreme Court in 1954, the only major obstacles in the way of attainment of equal access to schooling in the United States are the academic requirements for admission that most universities impose and the economic factors that prevent some students from attending the schools of their choice. The first of these problems, however, is also essentially financial (or would be if criterion-referenced examinations were used in the issuance of school certificates), since equal access might induce more people to attend school. Therefore, the issues of equal access to schooling and economic support of students come down to the question of whether society is willing to pay the costs.

The question of whether all schools and educational programs of a particular type should be of equivalent quality is probably the most sensitive one confronting the present-day American school system. This issue has two dimensions: the question of whether we should provide equivalent financial resources to all publicly supported primary and secondary schools and the question of whether the student composition of our schools should be ethnically balanced. In the case of the latter question, the problem of whether we should have mandatory busing of students is particularly sensitive.

Some persons argue that the educative process should result in equal outcomes. They are opposed to both equal access and equal programs, therefore, since these two conceptions of equality of educational opportunity only serve to give students an equal opportunity to become unequal. The proponents of equal outcomes generally favor the use of unequal educational programs (compensatory education) in order to equalize educational outcomes. On the other hand, some who believe that unequal outcomes are permissible also favor unequal programs, since they believe that each person should be provided with an educational program that will help him to achieve his full potentiality.

GENERAL NOTES AND BIBLIOGRAPHY

1. CONCEPT OF EQUAL EDUCATION. For a discussion of different interpretations of equal education that closely parallels the conceptualization used in this chapter, see Torsten Husén, *Social Background and Educational Career: Research Perspectives on Equality of Educational Opportunity* (Paris: OECD, 1972), pp. 13–39. The concept of equality is analyzed from a philosopher's point of view in R. S. Peters, *Ethics and Education* (Glenview, Ill.: Scott, Foresman, 1967), pp. 45–70. See also B. Paul Komisar and Jerrold R. Coombs, "The Concept of Equality in Education," *Studies in Philosophy and Education* 3 (1964): 223–244, and Mary Warnock, "The Concept of Equality in Education," *Oxford Review of Education* 1 (1975): 3–8. For general treatments of the problems of equal education, see: Charles A. Tesconi and Emanuel Hurwitz, *Education for Whom?* (New York: Dodd, Mead, 1974); Bryan R. Wilson, ed., *Education, Equality and Society* (New York: Barnes and Noble, 1975); Murray Milner, *The Illusion of Equality* (San Francisco: Jossey-Bass, 1972); and John D. Owen, *School Inequality and the Welfare State* (Baltimore: Johns Hopkins University Press, 1974).

2. EQUAL ACCESS TO EDUCATION. The general problem of access to the university is dealt with in many recent sources, including: Frank Bowles, *Access to Higher Education* (Paris: UNESCO, 1963); *The Second Newman Report: National Policy and Higher Education* (Cambridge, Mass.: MIT Press, 1973); Martin Trow, *Problems in the Transition from Elite to Mass Higher Education* (Berkeley, Calif.: Carnegie Commission on Higher Education, 1973); S. A. Kendrick and Charles L. Thomas, "Transition from School to College," *Review of Educational Research* 40 (1970): 151–179; A. G. Watts, *Diversity and Choice in Higher Education* (London: Routledge and Kegan Paul, 1972); Julius Menacker, *From School to College: Articulation*

and Transfer (Washington, D.C.: American Council on Education, 1975).

The policy of open admissions is analyzed in Jack Rossmann, *Open Admissions at City University of New York* (Englewood Cliffs, N.J.: Prentice-Hall, 1975); Earl J. McGrath, ed., *Universal Higher Education* (New York: McGraw-Hill, 1966); K. Patricia Cross, *Beyond the Open Door* (San Francisco: Jossey-Bass, 1971).

A number of sources deal specifically with the financial aspects of equal access. See, for example, the following: Carnegie Commission on Higher Education, *Higher Education: Who Pays? Who Benefits? Who Should Pay?* (New York: McGraw-Hill, 1973); R. Fein and G. Weber, *Financing Medical Education* (New York: McGraw-Hill, 1971); W. L. Hansen and B. A. Weisbrod, *Benefits, Costs and Finance of Higher Education* (Chicago: Markham, 1969); D. B. Johnstone, *New Patterns for College Lending: Income Contingent Loans* (New York: Columbia University Press, 1972). For the view that at present state support of public higher education actually results in the payment of subsidies from low income groups to high income groups, see George M. Vredeveld, "Income Inequality and Subsidizing Higher Education," *Costs and Benefits of Education,* ed. Robert D. Leiter (Boston: Twayne, 1975), pp. 116–150.

3. EQUAL EDUCATIONAL PROGRAMS. For a discussion of the inequalities of school finance, see: James W. Guthrie et al., *Schools and Inequality* (Cambridge, Mass.: MIT Press, 1971); John E. Coons, William H. Clune and Stephen D. Sugarman, *Private Wealth and Public Education* (Cambridge, Mass.: Harvard University Press, 1970); John F. Hughes and Anne O. Hughes, *Equal Education: A New National Strategy* (Bloomington: Indiana University Press, 1972); Arthur E. Wise, *Rich Schools, Poor Schools: The Promise of Equal Educational Opportunity* (Chicago: University of Chicago Press, 1968); Gail R. Wilensky, *State Aid and Educational Opportunity* (Beverly Hills, Calif.: Sage, 1970); Robert D. Reischauer and Robert W. Hartman, *Reforming School Finance* (Washington, D.C.: Brookings Institution, 1973); Joel S. Berke, *Answers to Inequity: An Analysis of the New School Finance* (Berkeley, Calif.: McCutchan, 1974); John Pincus, ed., *School Finance in Transition: The Courts and Educational Reform* (Cambridge, Mass.: Ballinger, 1974); and Betsy Levin, ed., *Future Directions for*

School Finance Reform (Lexington, Mass.: Lexington Books, 1975).

For an overview of the issue of school integration, see: David W. Beggs and S. Kern Alexander, eds., *Integration and Education* (Chicago: Rand McNally, 1969) and *Twenty Years After Brown: Equality of Educational Opportunity* (Washington, D.C.: U.S. Commission on Civil Rights, 1975). Numerous empirical studies have been conducted to determine the effects of the heterogeneous grouping of students compared to homogeneous grouping. A review of this literature is provided in Nancy H. St. John, "Desegregation and Minority Group Performance," *Review of Educational Research* 40 (1970): 111–133. The legal aspects of school integration are covered in David L. Kirp and Mark Yudof, *Educational Policy and the Law* (Berkeley, Calif.: McCutchan, 1974).

4. EQUAL EDUCATIONAL OUTCOMES. Many general sources cited in Note 1 are relevant to this topic. In particular, see Milner, *The Illusion of Equality.* The topic of compensatory education is treated in Edmund Gordon and Doxey Wilkerson, *Compensatory Education for the Disadvantaged* (New York: College Entrance Examination Board, 1966), and Francesco Cordasco, *The Equality of Educational Opportunity: A Bibliography of Selected References* (Totowa, N.J.: Rowman and Littlefield, 1973).

One of the principal arguments for unequal educational outcomes is the view that differences in educational access, educational programs, learning outcomes, and incomes are justified by differences in academic ability. See: R. J. Herrnstein, *I.Q. in the Meritocracy* (Boston: Atlantic-Little, Brown, 1973); Leon Kamin, *The Science and Politics of I.Q.* (New York: Wiley, 1974); Alan Gartner, Colin Greer and Frank Riessman, eds., *The New Assault on Equality: IQ and Social Stratification* (New York: Perennial Library, 1974).

EDUCATIONAL GOALS: FINAL ENDS AND INTERMEDIATE OUTCOMES

CHAPTER 9

The question of which learning outcomes we should attempt to achieve through education must now be considered. Exactly what should a person learn as the result of the educative process? Should he learn to appreciate poetry, or should he become vocationally competent? Should he be taught to be absolutely patriotic, or should he learn to question what the government says and does? These are among the types of questions that need to be discussed.

A total of three generally recognized approaches to the determination of learning objectives shall be examined. The first of these approaches consists of an attempt to identify the ultimate and/or penultimate end of education, and from this final end to deduce the learning outcomes required for its achievement. The second approach focuses on the intermediate outcomes of the educational means-ends chain. It entails an identification of the important activities in which human beings engage; after this has been done, the learning outcomes required for the effective performance of these activities are ascertained. The third approach starts at the beginning of the educational means-ends chain and involves an attempt to formulate learning objectives through a justification of the curriculum.

The major foci or starting points of these three approaches are represented in the following simplified diagram of the educational means-ends chain:

APPROACH III .   APPROACH II   . APPROACH I
             .   .

Curriculum ⟶ . Learning ⟶ Effective Citizens, ⟶. Penultimate⟶
           . Outcomes   Effective Parents, . End
           .   etc.   .

                                          ⟶Happiness
                                          (Ultimate
                                          End)

This diagram is similar to the one in Chapter 4. It differs in that one more element is added to the chain in order to show better the focus of the second approach. Also, the element "Learner Involvement" has been omitted, since this factor is not usually considered in the third approach. Each of the three approaches will be discussed as a major educational controversy in Issues 9, 10, and 11.

These issues shall be used as a means of elucidating the particular approaches involved. The first two will be considered in this chapter; the third approach will be discussed in Chapter 10.

What Should Be the Ultimate and/or Penultimate End of Education?

Issue 9:

The justification of policy statements about desirable learning outcomes has occupied the attention of a great number of writers on education, going back to the earliest times. Several of these writers have attempted to describe a desirable ultimate and/or penultimate end and then demonstrate how it can be achieved by an appropriate means of education. The writings which express this approach to the formulation of learning objectives constitute a voluminous body of literature and probably the most distinguished set of writings on any topic in education. Among the authors represented are such notable figures as Plato, Aristotle, Plutarch, Cicero, St. Augustine, Erasmus, Martin Luther, John Locke, Immanuel Kant, Alfred North Whitehead, John Dewey, Bertrand Russell and Jacques Maritain. Together their writings form a body of literature that any educator would be proud to consider his own; moreover, it is a body of literature that supports the claim of educational studies to be an area of basic human inquiry and concern.

Plato

The major source of Plato's views on the goals of education is his book the *Republic*. Because this book represents the first attempt by a Western writer to explain and justify fully his position on the goals of education, it ranks as an educational classic. In fact, Plato's *Republic* and Rousseau's *Emile*—which, as we have noted, has outstanding significance for its original treatment of teaching method—are regarded by many authorities as probably the two greatest works on education ever written.

The *Republic* is written in the form of a dialogue in which the central character is Socrates. In the discussion that ensues between the various participants, Socrates presents his ideas on the characteristics of an ideal society. He believes that "a state comes into existence because no individual is self-sufficing; we all have many needs." Socrates also maintains that "no two people are born exactly alike. There are innate differences which fit them for different occupations." In the interests of greater efficiency, therefore, Socrates concludes that "more things will be produced and the work be more easily and better done, when every man is set free from all other occupations to do, at the right time, the one thing for which he is naturally fitted."[1]

Socrates says that the determination of who possesses the qualities necessary to be a ruler will be on the basis of rigorous performance tests. Socrates describes these tests as follows: "We shall have to watch [the prospective rulers] from earliest childhood and set them tasks in which they would be most likely to forget or to be beguiled out of [their] duty. We shall then choose only those whose memory holds firm and who are proof against delusion. . . . We must also subject them to ordeals of toil and pain and watch for the same qualities there. . . . If we find one bearing himself well in all these trials and resisting every enchantment . . . such a one will be of the greatest service to the commonwealth as well as to himself. Whenever we find one who has come unscathed through every test in childhood, youth, and manhood, we shall set him as a Ruler to watch over the commonwealth."

Socrates believes that a system of education will be necessary

---

[1]Plato *Republic* (trans. Francis Cornford) 369b–c, 370b–c. Sources for quotations of Socrates in succeeding paragraphs are: 413c–414a, 376e, 532a, 536d, 537d, 540a–c, 414a–b, 419–421c.

for the citizens of his imaginary society. He asks: "What is this education to be, then? Perhaps we shall hardly invent a system better than the one which long experience has worked out, with its two branches for the cultivation of the mind and of the body. And I suppose we shall begin with the mind, before we start physical training."

The "two branches" of the traditional educational program to which Socrates refers here are the study of music and physical training (gymnastic). As Cornford (Plato's translator) explains, the study of "music" encompassed a much broader range of studies than is now associated with the term. Music "included all the arts over which the Muses presided: music, art, letters, culture, philosophy." Richard L. Nettleship, in discussing the meaning of "gymnastic," points out that it encompassed "the whole system of diet and exercise which, varying with the customs of different [Greek] states, had for its common object the production of bodily health and strength and the preparation for military service."[2]

Socrates also suggests that a special educational program will be necessary for the rulers of his ideal state. He declares that "the summit of the intelligible world is reached in philosophic discussion by one who aspires, through the discourse of reason unaided by any of the senses, to make his way in every case to the essential reality and perseveres until he has grasped by pure intelligence the very nature of Goodness itself. This journey is what we call Dialectic." Socrates proposes that the study of arithmetic and geometry be included in the education of children in order to "pave the way for Dialectic." Then, "some of those who are now twenty years old will be selected for higher privileges. The detached studies in which they were educated as children will now be brought together in a comprehensive view of their connexions with one another and with reality. . . . When they reach thirty they will be promoted to still higher privileges and tested by the power of Dialectic, to see which can dispense with sight and the other senses and follow truth into the region of pure reality." About five years will then be given to the study of Dialectic, followed by a period of fifteen years devoted to practical experience.

"Then," Socrates continues, "when they are fifty, those who have come safely through and proved the best at all points in action

[2]Richard L. Nettleship, *The Theory of Education in the Republic of Plato* (Chicago: University of Chicago Press, 1906), p. 28.

and in study must be brought at last to the goal. They must lift up the eye of the soul to gaze on that which sheds light on all things; and when they have seen the Good itself, take it as a pattern for the right ordering of the state and of the individual, themselves included. For the rest of their lives, most of their time will be spent in study; but they will all take their turn at the troublesome duties of public life and act as Rulers for their country's sake, not regarding it as a distinction, but as an unavoidable task. And so, when each generation has educated others like themselves to take their place as Guardians of the commonwealth, they will depart to dwell in the Islands of the Blest. . . . And you must not forget that some of them [the Rulers] will be women. All I have been saying applies just as much to any women who are found to have the necessary gifts."

Socrates gives explicit attention to the incentive structure that will be established for the Guardians of his ideal society. (Socrates uses the term "Guardian" sometimes to refer to the Rulers, and sometimes to refer both to the Rulers and to the Auxiliaries, who are the persons "who will enforce the decisions of the Rulers.") The Guardians "will be honored in life, and after death receive the highest tribute of funeral rites and other memorials." But the Guardians will be required to forgo material and monetary rewards for their services.

One of the participants in the discussion with Socrates points out that the life of a Guardian would not seem to be a very happy one, at least by conventional standards. Socrates responds to this objection, and in so doing identifies the ultimate end of his ideal state, which is to maximize the happiness of the entire society: "Though it would not be surprising if [the Guardians] were perfectly happy . . . our aim in founding the commonwealth was not to make any one class specially happy, but to secure the greatest possible happiness for the community as a whole. . . . So we must consider whether our aim in establishing Guardians is to secure the greatest possible happiness for them, or happiness is something of which we should watch the development in the whole commonwealth. If so, we must compel these Guardians and Auxiliaries of ours to second our efforts; and they, and all the rest with them, must be induced to make themselves perfect masters each of his own craft. In that way, as the community grows into a well-ordered whole, the several classes may be allowed such measure of happiness as their nature will compass."

Aristotle

Aristotle, who once was a student of Plato, was also very much aware of the need to justify the ends and means of education. He declared in his *Politics* that "no one knows on what principle we should proceed—should the useful in life, or should virtue, or should the higher knowledge, be the aim of our training; all three opinions have been entertained. Again about the means [of education] there is no agreement."[3]

Aristotle gave considerable attention in his writings to the identification of an ultimate or final end. In the following selection he discusses the nature of a final end and concludes that happiness is the universal ultimate end: "Since there are evidently more than one end, and we choose some of these (e.g. wealth, flutes, and in general instruments) for the sake of something else, clearly not all ends are final ends; but the chief good is evidently something final. Therefore, if there is only one final end, this will be what we are seeking. . . . Now such a thing happiness, above all else, is held to be; for this we choose always for itself and never for the sake of something else, but honour, pleasure, reason, and every virtue we choose indeed for themselves (for if nothing resulted from them we should still choose each of them), but we choose them also for the sake of happiness, judging that by means of them we shall be happy. Happiness, on the other hand, no one chooses for the sake of these, nor, in general, for anything other than itself. . . . Happiness, then, is something final and self-sufficient, and is the end of action."[4]

But Aristotle was aware that simply defining the ultimate end of human life as happiness is not enough. Happiness might be achieved through a variety of means; therefore, if the ultimate end is to be of assistance in the formulation of the curriculum, it is necessary to know what must be done to reach the ultimate end of happiness—that is, we must determine our penultimate end. He concludes that happiness can best be achieved through the exercise of reason (the contemplative life). "That which is proper to each thing," Aristotle argues, "is by nature best and most pleasant for each thing; for man, therefore, the life according to reason is best

---

[3]Aristole *Politics* (trans. Benjamin Jowett) 1337a–b.
[4]Aristotle *Nicomachean Ethics* (trans. W. D. Ross) 1097a–b.

and pleasantest, since reason more than anything else *is* man. This life therefore is also the happiest. . . . The activity of God, which surpasses all others in blessedness, must be contemplative; and of human activities, therefore, that which is most akin to this must be most of the nature of happiness. This is indicated, too, by the fact that the other animals have no share in happiness, being completely deprived of such activity. For while the whole life of the gods is blessed, and that of men too in so far as some likeness of such activity belongs to them, none of the other animals is happy, since they in no way share in contemplation. Happiness extends, then, just so far as contemplation does, and those to whom contemplation more fully belongs are more truly happy, not as a mere concomitant but in virtue of the contemplation."[5]

Aristotle's views on the curriculum are related to his conception of the ultimate end and the means for its attainment. "There is," he maintains, "a sort of education in which parents should train their sons, not as being useful or necessary, but because it is liberal or noble. . . . To be always seeking after the useful does not become free and exalted souls." Aristotle believes that "pleasure and happiness and enjoyment of life . . . are experienced, not by the busy man, but by those who have leisure. . . . It is clear then that there are branches of learning and education which we must study merely with a view to leisure spent in intellectual activity, and these are to be valued for their own sake; whereas those kinds of knowledge which are useful in business are to be deemed necessary, and exist for the sake of other things. And therefore our fathers admitted music into education, not on the ground either of its necessity or utility, for it is not necessary, nor indeed useful in the same manner as reading and writing, which are useful in money-making, in the management of a household, in the acquisition of knowledge and in political life, nor like drawing, useful for a more correct judgement of the works of artists, nor again like gymnastic, which gives health and strength; for neither of these is to be gained from music. There remains, then, the use of music for intellectual enjoyment in leisure; which is in fact evidently the reason of its introduction, this being one of the ways in which it is thought that a freeman should pass his leisure."[6]

[5]Ibid., 1178a–b. (Emphasis in the original.)
[6]*Politics* 1338a–b.

Individual or Social Penultimate Ends?

A survey of a large number of policy statements referring to the penultimate ends of education would show two major divergent emphases. One emphasis found in many statements is on the development of a particular type of society as the condition (penultimate end) essential for the attainment of the ultimate end. Such a society might be a world society, a democratic society, or a communist society, for example. The task of education would be to prepare the individual to fit into or create a desired society. The preceding selections from Plato are illustrative of this approach.

An alternative emphasis found in other statements about the penultimate ends of education is on the development of the individual, without particular concern for the nature of the society in which the individual is to function. The type of individual development envisioned in these statements may vary. It may have an intellectual character, as in the preceding excerpts from Aristotle; it may be religious; or it may be an extremely flexible notion of developing each individual to the maximum of his potential.

Individualistic and social conceptions of the penultimate ends of education are still being offered. The following statement by Sir Percy Nunn, for example, expresses an extremely individualistic point of view. The author believes that each person should be provided with educational opportunities; however, he stipulates that the individual should be responsible for the formulation of his own educational aims: "Nothing good enters into the human world except in and through the free activities of individual men and women, and . . . educational practice must be shaped to accord with that truth. . . . There can be no universal aim of education if that aim is to include the assertion of any particular ideal of life; for there are as many ideals as there are persons. Educational efforts must, it would seem, be limited to securing for every one of the conditions under which individuality is most completely developed—that is to enabling him to make his original contribution to the variegated whole of human life as full and as truly characteristic as his nature permits; the form of the contribution being left to the individual as something which each must, in living and by living, forge out for himself."[7]

[7]Quoted in Leslie M. Brown, ed., *Aims of Education* (New York: Teachers College Press, 1970), pp. 9–10.

Contrasting with the preceding viewpoint is John Dewey, who in his essay, "My Pedagogic Creed," argues that education should be used as the means to achieve social progress and reform. "The only true education" Dewey insists, "comes through the stimulation of the child's powers by the demands of the social situations in which he finds himself. Through these demands he is stimulated to act as a member of a unity, to emerge from his original narrowness of action and feeling, and to conceive of himself from the standpoint of the welfare of the group to which he belongs. . . . I believe that education is the fundamental method of social progress and reform. . . . Education is a regulation of the process of coming to share in the social consciousness; and the adjustment of individual activity on the basis of this social consciousness is the only sure method of social reconstruction. . . . The teacher is engaged, not simply in the training of individuals, but in the formulation of the proper social life. Every teacher should realize the dignity of his calling; he is a social servant set apart for the maintenance of proper social order and the securing of the right social growth."[8]

Ivan Illich

A major shortcoming of many writers who use the ultimate/ penultimate ends approach for the determination of educational goals is their failure to demonstrate convincingly that the ends they propose are actually realizable through the means they advocate. Instead of citing the facts of empirical research studies in support of their assertions, these authors generally base their arguments on assumptions derived from personal experience or, even worse, merely from speculation. The ancient writers may certainly be excused for their omission of research evidence; however, this deficiency is as characteristic of John Dewey and Bertrand Russell (both twentieth century authors) as it is of Plato and Aristotle.

There are some writers, however, who are concerned with the ultimate/penultimate ends of education as well as with the problem of whether the means (of education) are appropriate for specified ultimate or penultimate ends. Usually these writers are critical of the

[8]Quoted in Reginald D. Archambault, ed., *John Dewey on Education: Selected Writings* (Chicago: University of Chicago Press, 1974), pp. 427, 437, 439.

existing educational means-ends chain, either because it does not lead to the preferred ultimate and/or penultimate end, or because it is too effective in the attainment of remote ends not desired by them. While these writers do not necessarily make use of empirical research studies, they are at least sensitive to the importance of empirical data pertaining to the educational means-ends chain. Moreover, in their arguments, they often are willing to utilize such evidence as they possess about the efficacy of the educational means-ends chain.

An excellent example of a writer who fits the above description is Ivan Illich, a contemporary critic of education. Illich describes his penultimate end as follows: "I believe that a desirable future depends on our deliberately choosing a life of action over a life of consumption, on our engendering a life style which will enable us to be spontaneous, independent, yet related to each other, rather than maintaining a life style which only allows us to make and unmake, produce and consume—a style of life which is merely a way station on the road to the depletion and pollution of the environment."[9]

Illich is very much aware of the need to select appropriate means to reach desired ends, particularly institutional mechanisms. "The future depends," he declares, "more upon our choice of institutions which support a life of action than on our developing new ideologies and technologies." Illich is highly critical, however, of the capability of the present school system to attain his penultimate end: "All over the world the school has an anti-educational effect on society: school is recognized as the institution which specializes in education. The failures of school are taken by most people as a proof that education is a very costly, very complex, always arcane, and frequently almost impossible task. School appropriates the money, men, and good will available for education and in addition discourages other institutions from assuming educational tasks."

What Illich considers to be the undesirable effects and side effects of conventional schooling are described: "From the beginning of this century, the schools have been protagonists of social control on the one hand and free cooperation on the other, both placed at the service of the 'good society,' conceived of as a highly organized and smoothly working corporate structure. Under the impact of intense

[9]The quotations in this paragraph and in the three which follow it are taken from Ivan Illich, *Deschooling Society* (New York: Harper and Row, 1971), pp. 8, 52–53, 66–67, 75.

urbanization, children became a natural resource to be molded by the schools and fed into the industrial machine." Even some of the critics of the school system, in Illich's view, believe that "they have an obligation to the young, especially to the poor, an obligation to process them, whether by love or by fear, into a society which needs disciplined specialization as much from its producers as from its consumers and also their full commitment to the ideology which puts economic growth first."

Illich's solution to the problem posed by the deleterious effects of the conventional school system is to "deschool" society. By this he means the elimination of obligatory curriculum and school system credentialing; he does not advocate the abolition of all educational agencies. In fact, he proposes that abundant educational opportunities be made freely available. "A good educational system," he explains, "should provide all who want to learn with access to available resources at any time in their lives; empower all who want to share what they know to find those who want to learn it from them; and, finally, furnish all who want to present an issue to the public with the opportunity to make their challenge known. Such a system would require the application of constitutional guarantees to education. Learners should not be forced to submit to an obligatory curriculum, or to discrimination based on whether they possess a certificate or a diploma."

Additional Views on the Ultimate/Penultimate Ends of Education

We could provide numerous examples in this section of statements on the ultimate and/or penultimate ends of education. But rather than briefly summarize the views of these writers, it would seem far better to suggest to the reader that he consult directly the writings involved. As was mentioned earlier, these constitute probably the most eloquent and stimulating body of literature on any topic in education. Many of these writings are worthy of perusal simply for their literary merits alone. The reader is, therefore, urged to become familiar with them on a first-hand basis, if he or she has not already done so. Numerous published collections that provide representative samples of the great writings on education are also available, as are many interpretive works which deal with the ideas of their authors. (Note 1)

Comments on Issue 9

The ultimate/penultimate ends approach to the formulation of learning objectives has the distinct advantage of requiring its users to consider what the final end of the educative process should be. Unless this is done, a satisfactory justification of a policy statement concerning desired learning outcomes cannot be provided.

As has already been mentioned, however, many writers using this approach have failed to explicate fully the relationships between the means of education and a proposed ultimate/penultimate end. We would expect that someone who presents a policy proposal about an ultimate/penultimate end of education would be very knowledgeable about the empirical relationships between educational means and ends. This person would also be expected to be as much an empirical researcher (or user of research studies) as he is a philosopher (or user of philosophical studies). Yet, in fact, many who advocate an ultimate or penultimate educational objective do not provide much supporting research evidence regarding the means for its achievement; nor if such evidence is presently unavailable do they request that it be collected (and, until this evidence becomes available, advance their policy proposals on a tentative basis). It is also interesting to note that those persons who are concerned with the conduct of empirical research on education tend to confine their efforts to the part of the educational means-ends chain that is closest to the initial means; with some exceptions, they rarely apply their research skills to policy questions involving the ultimate or penultimate ends of education.

The existing empirical data on the effects of schooling are exceedingly sparse (as mentioned in Chapter 7), notwithstanding the enormous sums of money spent for the operation of the school system. It is difficult to imagine the executives of an automobile manufacturing company, for example, having relatively little accurate data on the number of cars they sold each year or on the customers' reactions to these cars. Yet as far as the school system is concerned, there is a deficiency of reliable information about its effects.

While recognizing that the determination of learning objectives is fundamentally a judgmental activity, it is very important for us to increase our empirical knowledge of the effects of various learning outcomes if we are to improve the process of formulating learning objectives. To support this contention, suppose for a moment that each person determined his own learning objectives. In this situation there would be no problem of reconciling different value judgments, since each person would be the only one involved in determining the learning outcomes that he or she should achieve. Each person would, however, require information identifying: (1) the total number of possible learning outcomes he might achieve, and (2) the empirical consequences that would follow from each of these various outcomes. If this information were possessed, each person could choose among the available alternatives.

Of course, in reality it would be impossible to obtain information of the completeness described above. But obviously the more information on alternative learning outcomes and the consequences of these alternatives that an individual has, the greater the likelihood is that he will be able to make a good decision. Even if several persons are involved in the decision-making process, information about means-ends relationships can sometimes be an essential factor in resolving a disagreement.

It is probable that, because sufficient attention has not been given to the available empirical evidence pertaining to the educational means-ends chain, the writers who use the ultimate/penultimate ends approach have (with such exceptions as Illich) ignored the credentialing function of the school system and its effects on the teaching function. Is the existing school system accomplishing the educational tasks assigned to it? Does the conventional school system through its unintended effects have costs which outweigh its benefits? Or is it possible that the nonteaching functions of the school system (such as the selecting and sorting of students) are those which we really value, whether we realize it or not, with the result that our discussion about the schools as a means to an ultimate/penultimate end is at best misleading and at worst a deception? These are some of the fundamental questions about the relationship between schooling and educational goals that have for too long been neglected. The need to raise them becomes clear, however, as soon as the educational means-ends chain is studied closely.

Another criticism of the application of the ultimate/penultimate ends approach is that it has produced relatively imprecise identifications of desirable learning outcomes. While this problem is no doubt mainly due to the failure of users of this approach to make extensive use of empirical research, another factor is probably that the task of explicating and justifying a penultimate/ultimate end is exceedingly demanding, leaving little opportunity for a detailed discussion of required learning outcomes.

Which Human Behaviors and Capabilities Should Be Developed Through Education?

Issue 10: _____

Instead of trying to identify the ultimate and/or penultimate end of education and then work back to derive the appropriate learning outcomes (which, as indicated above, may result in imprecise identifications of these outcomes), a second group of writers has focused on a much narrower portion of the educational means-ends chain. The users of what we shall call the "basic human activities" approach to the determination of learning objectives first attempt to discover what the basic activities in which human beings engage throughout their lifetimes are. Then an analysis of these basic human activities is made to ascertain which behaviors and capabilities are involved in the effective performance of the activities. Since behaviors and capabilities developed through education are learning outcomes, it is a relatively simple matter for the users of the basic human activities approach to specify the learning outcomes they consider desirable.

As a group the writers who use the basic human activities approach are less concerned than the first group with demonstrating that the acquisition of a human behavior or capability leads to a desirable ultimate end, either because they believe the basic activity to which the learning outcome relates is obviously necessary or because the activity can be justified on the basis of several remote ends. For example, the basic activity of being an effective worker might be defended because it will lead to a better society, because it will yield intrinsic satisfaction, or because it will enable a person to increase his or her income level.

Nevertheless, although those who use the basic human activities approach do not provide as complete a justification of their policy statements as the writers we examined in the preceding section, there are some definite advantages in their approach. The writers using this approach provide detailed statements of the learning outcomes they consider desirable; consequently, their policy proposals have maximum utility as a guide to the establishment of the curriculum. Also, these writers are much more interested in the use of empirical research than are those of the previous group.

Herbert Spencer

Although several earlier writers also attempted to identify the human behaviors and capabilities which they believed should be developed through education, Herbert Spencer (1820–1903) is one of the best examplars of this approach. In his essay "What Knowledge Is of Most Worth?" Spencer explicitly states that "we must settle which things it most concerns us to know" before we can make a rational decision about the curriculum. He is critical of those persons who do not decide upon their educational goals in this systematic way: "If there needs any further evidence of the rude, undeveloped character of our education, we have it in the fact that the comparative worths of different kinds of knowledge have been as yet scarcely even discussed—much less discussed in a methodic way with definite results. . . . Men read books on this topic, and attend lectures on that; decide that their children shall be instructed in these branches of knowledge, and shall not be instructed in those; and all under the guidance of mere custom, or liking, or prejudice; without ever considering the enormous importance of determining in some rational way what things are really most worth learning. It is true that in all circles we hear occasional remarks on the importance of this or the other order of information. But whether the degree of its importance justifies the expenditure of the time needed to acquire it; and whether there are not things of more importance to which the time might be better devoted; are queries which, if raised at all, are disposed of quite summarily, according to personal predilections."[10]

In making decisions about which learning outcomes should be required, Spencer argues that we need some standard. He believes that a generally acceptable basis for determining the value of a given learning outcome is its utility in the performance of human activities. According to Spencer, "every one in contending for the worth of any particular order of information, does so by showing its bearing upon some part of life. . . . When the teacher of writing has pointed out how great an aid writing is to success in business—

[10]The quotations from "What Knowledge Is of Most Worth?" in this paragraph and in the five which follow it are from Herbert Spencer, *Education* (New York: Appleton, 1897), pp. 29, 26–27, 30–31, 32–34, 93–94. (Emphasis in the original.)

that is, to the obtainment of sustenance—that is, to satisfactory living; he is held to have proved his case. And when the collector of dead facts (say a numismatist) fails to make clear any appreciable effects which these facts can produce on human welfare, he is obliged to admit that they are comparatively valueless. All then, either directly or by implication, appeal to this as the ultimate test."

Thus, "How to live?" is for Spencer the essential question: "Not how to live in the mere material sense only, but in the widest sense. The general problem which comprehends every special problem is— the right ruling of conduct in all directions under all circumstances. In what way to treat the body; in what way to treat the mind; in what way to manage our affairs; in what way to utilize all those sources of happiness which nature supplies—how to use all our faculties to the greatest advantage of ourselves and others—how to live completely? And this being the great thing needful for us to learn, is, by consequence, the great thing which education has to teach. To prepare us for complete living is the function which education has to discharge; and the only rational mode of judging of any educational course is, to judge in what degree it discharges such function."

Spencer believes that his criterion must be "applied consciously, methodically, and throughout all cases" in the determination of the curriculum. He even seems to suggest that empirical research should be used to give us the data we require: "It must not suffice simply to *think* that such or such information will be useful in after life, or that this kind of knowledge is of more practical value than that; but we must seek out some process of estimating their respective values, so that as far as possible we may positively *know* which are most deserving of attention."

Spencer identifies five areas of human life which he considers to be of major significance and then classifies these activities in order of their importance: "The actions and precautions by which, from moment to moment, we secure personal safety, must clearly take precedence of all others. . . . That next after direct self-preservation comes the indirect self-preservation which consists in acquiring the means of living, none will question. . . . As the family comes before the State in order of time—as the bringing up of children is possible before the State exists, or when it has ceased to be, whereas the State is rendered possible only by the bringing up of children; it follows that the duties of the parent demand closer attention than those of the citizen. . . . And. . .that part of human

conduct which constitutes good citizenship, is of more moment than
that which goes out in accomplishments or exercise of the tastes;
and, in education, preparation for the one must rank before preparation for the other."

The conclusion Spencer reaches is that science is the most valuable form of knowledge. "This is the verdict," he declares, "on all
the counts. For direct self-preservation, or the maintenance of life
and health, the all-important knowledge is—Science. For that indirect self-preservation which we call gaining a livelihood, the
knowledge of greatest value is—Science. For the due discharge of
parental functions, the proper guidance is to be found only in—
Science. For that interpretation of national life, past and present,
without which the citizen cannot rightly regulate his conduct, the
indispensable key is—Science. Alike for the most perfect production
and present enjoyment of art in all its forms, the needful preparation is still—Science; and for purposes of discipline—intellectual,
moral, religious—the most efficient study is, once more—Science.
The question which at first seemed so perplexed, has become, in the
course of our inquiry, comparatively simple. We have not to estimate the degrees of importance of different orders of human activity, and different studies as severally fitting us for them; since we
find that the study of Science, in its most comprehensive meaning, is
the best preparation for all these orders of activity."

Franklin Bobbitt

An early attempt to obtain empirical data about the utilization
of learning outcomes and to combine this with an assessment of the
desirability of those outcomes is represented in the work of Franklin Bobbitt, a professor of educational administration at the University of Chicago during the early part of the twentieth century. Bobbitt contends that education should "prepare men and women for
the activities of every kind which make up, or which ought to make
up, well-rounded adult life." He also believes that an important task
of the educational policy maker is to analyze the "actual activities of
mankind" and from this analysis determine the various types of
learning outcomes essential to the performance of these activities.
An evaluation would also be made of the adequacy of learning outcomes in meeting the requirements of various human activities.

Those needs and shortcomings identified would provide the basis for deciding the educational role of the schools.[11]

Bobbitt assumes that the purpose of education is to prepare a person to perform effectively the various activities of adult life. His basic approach to the determination of educational goals is well summarized in the following excerpt:

> It is helpful to begin with the simple assumption, to be accepted literally, that education is to prepare men and women for the activities of every kind which make up, or which ought to make up, well-rounded adult life; that it has no other purpose; that everything should be done with a view to this purpose; and that nothing should be included which does not serve this purpose.
>
> Education is primarily for adult life, not for child life. Its fundamental responsibility is to prepare for the fifty years of adulthood, not for the twenty years of childhood and youth.
>
> When we know what men and women ought to do along the many lines and levels of human experience, then we shall have before us the things for which they should be trained. The first task is to discover the activities which ought to make up the lives of men and women; and along with these, the abilities and personal qualities necessary for proper performance. These are the educational objectives.

To obtain relevant data, Bobbitt proposes that the curriculum planner prepare activity analyses for each of the various basic human activities. These analyses should be carried on, he suggests, until the curriculum planner "has found the quite specific activities that are to be performed." Bobbitt believes that empirical research will be required in completing the analyses: "As the analyses approach the units that are minute, numerous, and interrelated with each other, and especially when accuracy demands quantitative definition, careful scientific assembling of the facts becomes necessary. . . . It is unfortunate that so little scientific analysis has yet been possible in most fields of human action. Nobody knows with definiteness, for example, what specific things the good citizen should do. Little scientific analysis of civic activities has yet been made. In matters of personal hygiene, our knowledge is somewhat more complete; but there are no authoritative analyses of communi-

[11]The quotations in this paragraph and in the four which follow it are from Franklin Bobbitt, *How to Make a Curriculum* (Boston: Houghton Mifflin, 1924), pp. 7–10, 33–36, 67.

ty health activities which can be accepted for guidance in listing objectives of health education. Recreational analyses have not been made. We do not know accurately what specific activities parents should perform in the upbringing of children; or what activities should make up the religious life; or the field of unspecialized practical arts."

Bobbitt suggests that the identification of consequences attributable to inadequate learning outcomes may be as helpful in the activity analyses as the identification of consequences resulting from desired learning outcomes. He explains this procedure: "In locating the objectives that require special emphases, especially in general education, the diagnostic method of discovering the personal and social shortcomings to be overcome is more fruitful. Let one discover the mistakes commonly made in English expression, and these will point to the aspects of the English training that are to be specially emphasized. Find health errors that are common, and one can discover the health abilities that will prevent these errors. Locate civic deficiencies in the adult world, and they point to the attitudes, powers of judgment, habits, and other civic matters to be emphasized. The recreational shortcomings of our population show the kinds of preventive and protective training needed."

Bobbitt's proposal for activity analyses has never been fully implemented, nor has a complete curriculum based on this approach ever been instituted. However, Bobbitt does offer some suggestions on the kinds of changes in the school curriculum that might be brought about if activity analyses were conducted: "When things are included in the educational program for occupational purposes, they will be placed only in the occupational courses, and taken only by those who are consciously taking their occupational training. For example, activity-analyses will show that trigonometry is called for by the activities of the engineer; that it is not called for by the activities of typists, physicians, or milliners; nor by the general activities of persons outside of their occupations. As a consequence, trigonometry will be prescribed as occupational training in the courses for engineers, but not in courses for the other occupations named; nor for general education. . . . The absurdity of this confusion of vocational and general is obvious when one clearly distinguishes the two. The error, however, is common because of a frequent haziness of ideas relative to the constituents of the general and of the vocational, and of the relations of the one to the other. Thus trigonometry is often included in the high school for vocational purposes and then opened to everybody for general education. There is similar confusion of vocational and general in the administration of algebra, physics, drawing, practical arts, Spanish, economic geography, and many other matters."

Florence Stratemeyer

Another example of the method of determining educational goals through the analysis of basic human activities is in the work of Florence Stratemeyer and her colleagues. Her approach consists in the identification of what she terms "persistent life situations" and the analysis of these situations for their implications regarding desirable learning outcomes. She defines a persistent life situation as one which recurs "in the life of the individual in many different ways as he grows from infancy to maturity."[12]

Stratemeyer points out that "every individual is concerned to some degree with such fundamentals as keeping well, understanding himself, making a living, getting along with others, adjusting to the natural environment, dealing with social and political structures and forces, developing a sustaining philosophy or set of values. These and other concerns tend to persist throughout life, although the circumstances through which they are met vary with the individual's background and maturity."

Stratemeyer gives several concrete examples of persistent life situations and indicates what they would entail for the curriculum: "The little child faces persistent life situations in the area of health, primarily in adjusting to family and school health patterns, and develops simple understandings which serve as a basis for his actions. The adolescent assumes a much larger responsibility for his own health. His concerns and activities include such problems as those of his weight and skin condition which are important to attractive appearance, of the routines required for membership on the athletic team, of whether or not to begin to smoke. He needs more knowledge as well as more fully developed concepts of the relationship of good health to effective living. The adult takes on a wide va-

---

[12]The quotations in this paragraph and in the four which follow it are from Florence B. Stratemeyer et al., *Developing a Curriculum for Modern Living* (2nd ed.; New York: Bureau of Publications, Teachers College, 1957), pp. 115–116, 119, 122, 718–719.

riety of family responsibilities and, at times, his health activities may relate to the national and world scene. . . . Persistent life situations, as learners face them, become the fabric from which the curriculum develops. First-grade Billy learning that plants will die without water; tenth-grade Jane sharing her talent with the committee building stage sets; Dorothy in grade four discovering that she cannot serve as treasurer unless she is a better mathematician; Jim and a committee of eighth-graders talking with officials about a school bank; Grace in the tenth grade struggling with the conflict between the values held by her family and those governing the activities of her crowd—these are situations central in living in our society as they are reflected in the activities of learners."

According to Stratemeyer, the curriculum will always be flexible. "Part of the teacher's role is to identify the experiences through which values and understandings can be most clearly and meaningfully developed for given learners. . . . The safeguard against omitting or slighting important aspects of growth lies in the range and variety of persistent life situations with which all persons inevitably deal. When the members of a school faculty have worked together to prepare an analysis of the persistent problems of living . . . each teacher has an objective basis against which to study the growth of his group. This does not mean that every persistent life situation identified in this analysis as important need have a place in the daily work of each group. The teacher would use such an analysis as a check, not a prescription."

Thus Stratemeyer favors the use of empirical research to facilitate the identification and analysis of persistent life situations: "Charts of the persistent life situations learners face can be developed through research or tested for their accuracy by classroom experimentation. This represents an important area in which teachers' judgments or generalized statements about learners should be supported by data. Studies can be made of the ways in which persistent life situations appear for particular age groups, for the gifted, and for slow learners. . . . The procedures of research offer possibilities for helping teachers to study individuals and groups, to identify the immediate and recurring situations with which they are and should be dealing, to gain insight into ways of working with learners on these problems, and to evaluate the effectiveness of the guidance provided pupils as they meet the persistent problems of living which are a part of their everyday experiences." (Note 2)

Comments on Issue 10

The basic human activities approach to the formulation of learning objectives permits its users to arrive at a precise identification of learning outcomes. Also, because it is very specific about the learning outcomes that are desired, it allows its users to make specific recommendations about the curriculum. These are highly desirable characteristics, which prompts us to inquire whether the present curriculum has been determined on the basis of this approach. Before we deal with this important question, however, let us examine some of the criticisms that have been made of the basic human activities approach. One of these has a familiar sound. Saylor and Alexander, in discussing the basic human activities approach, wonder whether all significant learning outcomes can be specified in terms of observable behavior. "Competency-based curriculum plans," they contend, "have much utility for some objectives but are futile for others."[13]

The appropriate response to this criticism, of course, would be the same one given in Chapter 6 in the discussion of performance objectives and grading: the very fact that someone is using the educative process means that he must have some kind of goal in mind pertaining to the achievement of a learning outcome. Whether the attainment of this learning outcome results in observable behavior change is another matter: some outcomes do and some do not. If an educator has an imprecise and relatively nonobservable learning outcome in mind such as "the development of music appreciation," this does not mean that he should not attempt to achieve it. But if it cannot be satisfactorily determined that this outcome has been attained, the educator should not try to grade students on the basis of it.

On the other hand, even if a learning outcome does not produce some observable change in behavior, an educator may recommend that a student participate in certain learning situations (or even require the student's participation) if he believes—either as the result of personal experience or the experiences of others—that the learning situation will probably bring about the desired outcome. In this case a certificate of attendance could be issued if a school system credential were required.

[13]J. Galen Saylor and William M. Alexander, *Planning Curriculum for Schools* (New York: Holt, Rinehart and Winston, 1974), p. 204.

In fact, as an approach to educational goals formulation, analyzing basic human activities would be very beneficial to an educator dealing with an imprecise and relatively nonobservable learning outcome, such as music appreciation. Data could be collected on what this outcome means to different people, how it manifests itself, what further outcomes follow from it, and how it is evaluated by those who have attained it. The most efficacious way of achieving the outcome might also be determined from an inquiry into the learning experiences of these persons. All of these data would be very helpful in attempting to further specify the outcome of music appreciation and evaluating its desirability, and in trying to develop more effective ways of achieving the goal. Hence we would disagree with Saylor and Alexander and insist that the basic human activities approach can be used with all learning outcomes. Of course, neither Spencer, Bobbitt or Stratemeyer would confine their educational objectives to observable behaviors. Only certain critics have interpreted their approach this way.

It has also been suggested that the basic human activities approach might produce a static curriculum; it would seem, however, that just the opposite would be the case. Systematically assessing how learning outcomes are actually used would provide a type of feedback that is not now available to educational policy makers on the adequacy of the curriculum, thereby enabling these policy makers to make changes and adjustments in the curriculum as necessary. The approach would thus promote flexibility and change, rather than maintenance of the status quo. To be sure, education must prepare individuals for a future world whose learning requirements might be very different from the present; hence any goals formulated without due consideration of this factor may be inadequate. But this is a problem which affects all policy makers, not just those in education: any policy maker needs to utilize the best available data concerning trends of change, future projections, and the like.

It is agreed, however, that the proponents of the basic human activities approach often have failed to give adequate attention to the ultimate and/or penultimate end of education. Spencer, Bobbitt and Stratemeyer make some assumptions about which intermediate ends are desirable, but they do not seem sufficiently aware of their obligation to justify these intermediate ends in terms of an ultimate end. These authors frequently ignore the difference between empirical facts and value judgments; they seem to think that discovering facts through activity analysis will also result in a knowledge of what should be done. Bobbitt, for example, declares that "the actual abilities at their best show us what they ought to be" and that "the abilities are to be determined on the basis of human needs."[14]

But the concept of a "need"—as Hirst and Peters have pointed out—implies a value judgment: "If we say that a child needs something—love for instance, or a bath—we are making a diagnostic type of remark about him. We are suggesting (i) that he lacks something—love, a bath (ii) that what he lacks is desirable in some way. It is necessary *for* some desirable condition, the determination of which is a matter of ethical valuation rather than of psychological research."[15]

Nevertheless, the basic human activities approach provides an excellent way to think about educational objectives. It allows for a comparison of evidence about the learning outcomes the schools are actually achieving with our views about what the schools ought to be accomplishing. If a close correspondence is found between these two sets of outcomes, then we have reason to be satisfied; if not, then we have a very practical reason for suggesting changes in the curriculum.

Has the basic human activities approach been systematically applied to the determination of the learning objectives of the school system? It seems obvious that the answer to this question is "no." The clearest evidence of this contention is found in the fact that the primary and secondary school curriculum has been largely unchanged since the establishment of the first schools by the ancient Greeks and Romans. This curriculum is still mainly concerned with teaching reading, writing, and mathematical skills; and it is still mainly organized on the basis of academic fields of knowledge (English literature, mathematics, foreign languages, physical sciences, and the social sciences) rather than on the basis of the human activities that are intended to be served. If the suggestions of Spencer and Bobbitt were accepted, major portions of the curriculum would be devoted to the preparation of effective parents, effective citizens, and so forth, and presumably labeled as such. But, except for vocational programs, this is not how the primary and secondary school curriculum is structured. Instead of designating the major components of the curriculum on the basis of the functions they are ex-

[14]Bobbitt, *How to Make a Curriculum,* pp. 38–40.
[15]P. H. Hirst and R. S. Peters, *The Logic of Education* (London: Routledge and Kegan Paul, 1970), p. 33. (Emphasis in the original.)

pected to perform, curricular categories that denote academic fields of knowledge are mainly used.

Given the fact that the functions of the curriculum cannot be inferred from its designations, school system policy makers should be able to give us a precise statement of the intermediate and remote ends being served by the existing curriculum. What, for example, is the intermediate end of the study of plane geometry? If it is held by school system policy makers that plane geometry produces logical thinkers, what is the evidence for this view? Which portion of the curriculum is devoted to preparation of effective parents, and what is the evidence that this end is being accomplished? However, satisfactory answers to questions of this type are rarely if ever offered.[16] Hence it would seem a reasonable supposition that parts of the present curriculum may be irrelevant to the performance of basic human activities. (The question of the relevance of the curriculum will be examined further in Chapter 10.)

SUMMARY

Many writers have offered their views on which learning outcomes the educative process should try to accomplish. One approach to the formulation of educational objectives involves an attempt to identify the ultimate and/or penultimate end of education; once this is established, the curricular means to that end may be deduced.

Plato and Aristotle are among those educational writers who have based their justification of learning outcomes on an ultimate or penultimate end. Plato's *Republic* ranks as an educational classic because it constitutes the first comprehensive explanation and justification of a society-wide system of education. Aristotle, whose extant writings on education are less complete than Plato's, identified rational contemplation as the appropriate end of education. He also identified an appropriate curricular means for the achievement of that end: the study of liberal arts.

Some writers explicitly justify their educational goals on the basis of an ultimate or penultimate end. They consider the development of a particular type of society to be an essential condition for

---

[16]It has previously been pointed out that data on the effects of schooling are very limited. See Chapter 7 and the earlier discussion in this chapter.

the attainment of their ultimate end; other writers emphasize individual development.

In contrast with the writers who emphasize an ultimate and/or penultimate end in their justification of proposed learning outcomes, another group of writers utilize the "basic human activities" approach. These writers focus their attention on identifying learning outcomes that fulfill important human needs. Because these writers are concerned primarily with the immediate outcomes of education, they tend to be more specific in their identification of desirable outcomes, thus allowing for a more useful guide to curriculum formulation. A well-known illustration of this approach can be found in Herbert Spencer's essay, "What Knowledge Is of Most Worth?" Spencer concludes that a knowledge of science would be most useful, because science affords the best preparation for complete living.

On examining the present school curriculum, few indications that the basic human activities approach has been used in its formulation are found. The labels by which portions of the curriculum are designated, for example, usually refer to fields of academic knowledge rather than to human activities. Also, school system policy makers are generally unable to supply a precise statement of the ends served by the present curriculum, nor can they produce evidence to show that the curriculum actually accomplishes these outcomes. It must be concluded, therefore, that portions of the present curriculum may be irrelevant.

GENERAL NOTES AND BIBLIOGRAPHY

1. ULTIMATE/PENULTIMATE ENDS APPROACH. Statements on the ultimate/penultimate ends of education are surveyed in a number of sources. See, for example, Edward J. Power, *Evolution of Educational Doctrine: Major Educational Theorists of the Western World* (New York: Appleton-Century-Crofts, 1969); Adrian M. Dupuis, *Philosophy of Education in Historical Perspective* (Chicago: Rand McNally, 1966); S. J. Curtis and M. E. A. Boultwood, *A Short History of Educational Ideas* (3rd ed.; London: University Tutorial Press, 1961); Paul Nash, A. M. Kazamias and H. J. Perkinson, eds., *The Educated Man* (New York: Wiley, 1965); Richard L. Derr, *A Taxonomy of Social Purposes of Public Schools* (New York: McKay, 1973); Ger-

ald Lee Gutek, *Philosophical Alternatives in Education* (Columbus, Ohio: Charles E. Merrill, 1974).

The educational views of Plato and Aristotle are examined in the following sources: R. C. Lodge, *Plato's Theory of Education* (London: Kegan Paul, Trench, Trubner, 1947); Richard L. Nettleship, *The Theory of Education in the Republic of Plato* (Chicago: University of Chicago Press, 1906); John Burnett, ed., *Aristotle on Education* (London: Cambridge University Press, 1967); William K. Frankena, *Three Historical Philosophies of Education: Aristotle, Kant, Dewey* (Glenview, Ill.: Scott, Foresman, 1965); Robin Barrow, *Plato, Utilitarianism and Education* (London: Routledge and Kegan Paul, 1975). For an analysis of the ideas of Ivan Illich and a bibliography, see John Ohliger and Colleen McCarthy, *Lifelong Learning or Lifelong Schooling? A Tentative View of the Ideas of Ivan Illich with a Quotational Bibliography* (Syracuse, N.Y.: Syracuse University Publications in Continuing Education, 1971).

2. BASIC HUMAN ACTIVITIES APPROACH. The concept of "need" is analyzed in R. D. Archambault, "The Concept of Need and Its Relation to Certain Aspects of Educational Theory," *Harvard Educational Review* 27 (1957): 38–62; B. Paul Komisar, "'Need' and the Needs-Curriculum," in *Language and Concepts in Education,* eds. B. Othanel Smith and Robert H. Ennis (Chicago: Rand McNally, 1961), pp. 24–42; R. F. Dearden, "'Needs' in Education," in *A Critique of Current Educational Aims,* eds. R. F. Dearden, P. H. Hirst and R. S. Peters (London: Routledge and Kegan Paul, 1975), pp. 48–62. A contemporary application of the basic human activities approach to educational goals formulation is called "needs assessment." See Fenwick W. English and Roger A. Kaufman, *Needs Assessment: A Focus for Curriculum Development* (Washington, D. C.: Association for Supervision and Curriculum Development, 1975).

For additional sources on the basic human activities approach, see: Wayne C. Booth, ed., *The Knowledge Most Worth Having* (Chicago: University of Chicago Press, 1967); P. S. Wilson, "In Defence of Bingo," *British Journal of Educational Studies* 15 (1967): 5–27; R. S. Peters "In Defence of Bingo: A Rejoinder," *British Journal of Educational Studies* 15 (1967): 188–194. James M. Gibson and James C. Hall, *Damn Reading! A Case Against Literacy* (New York: Vantage Press, 1969) offers an interesting argument against literacy as a human need. The procedure advocated by Franklin Bobbitt is discussed in the following sources: Mary L. Seguel, *The Curriculum Field: Its Formative Years* (New York: Teachers College Press, 1966); Elliot W. Eisner, "Franklin Bobbitt and the 'Science' of Curriculum Making," *School Review* 75 (1967): 29–47; Philip W. Jackson, "Shifting Visions of the Curriculum: Notes on the Aging of Franklin Bobbitt," *Elementary School Journal* 75 (1975): 116–133.

EDUCATIONAL GOALS: CURRICULUM AND THE EDUCATIVE SOCIETY

CHAPTER 10

Issue 11 considers a third widely used approach for the determination of which learning outcomes we should try to accomplish. This approach, which shall be called the "curriculum approach," focuses on the issue of what curriculum we should have.

The formulation of learning objectives will be further discussed in Issue 12. In answering the question of whether an educative society should be established, we shall attempt to relate the control of education to the determination of educational goals, thereby joining the two major topics presented in this book.

What Curriculum Should We Have?
Issue 11:

Another way of asking the question "Which learning outcomes should we try to accomplish?" is to inquire "Which learning experiences should we provide?" or "What curriculum should we have?"

A number of controversies have arisen with respect to choice of curriculum. Some of these controversies do not pertain to the formulation of learning objectives, because they are concerned with the relative effectiveness of different learning experiences in reaching an already agreed upon learning outcome. For example, the issue of whether we should use the phonics or whole-world approach in the teaching of reading falls into this category, since proponents of both points of view in the controversy agree on the desired goal (the acquisition of reading skills); they only differ in this case on which set of learning experiences would be more effective in reaching the designated goal.

Another basic type of curriculum controversy does pertain to the determination of learning objectives, however. In this type of controversy an advocate of one curriculum may disagree with the advocate of an alternative curriculum because of a dispute over the relative desirability of the learning outcomes that would be achieved through use of the respective curricula. Or two persons may disagree over whether the learning outcomes to which a given curriculum leads should even be attained at all.

Of the three generally recognized approaches to the formulation of learning objectives, application of the curriculum approach probably has been least successful in identifying the total set of learning outcomes that we should try to accomplish. The reason for this is quite simple: most curriculum controversies are concerned with very specific questions (example: Should the schools provide driver education?); relatively few persons have asked questions about the entire curriculum. With this caveat in mind, we shall examine three of the broadest questions that have been raised about the curriculum. The first question deals with the issue of whether the schools should indoctrinate, the second deals with the practicality of the curriculum, while the third question addresses the relevancy of the curriculum. (Note 1)

Indoctrination or a Rational Examination of Values?

Deciding whether the school system should indoctrinate the learner into an acceptance of certain values or whether the learner should be exposed to different points of view to enable him to form his own value judgments is an exceedingly complex issue. If we indoctrinate, presumably we impose our ideas (values) on someone; if we do not indoctrinate, we allow the other person to choose his own ideas. This controversy encompasses the problem of how the schools should deal with values that are grounded in a particular religious belief.

In the following excerpt, Philip Phenix takes the position that the principal purpose of the curriculum is to foster a religious commitment: "The central task of education is *religious conversion.* . . .

Whatever its visible forms, the important goal is the re-directing of life which takes place when a person is delivered from finite attachment and acquisitiveness to the active love of the good. To accomplish this change is the supreme end of all teaching and learning. . . . Studies which increase the power to exploit the earth and other people, which arm one for the struggle for privilege, which prepare one to pursue his advantage more successfully, destroy rather than edify a person. The sovereign test of all education is whether or not it is religious, that is, whether or not it tends toward conversion of the person to unconditional commitment to truth and right."[1]

Phenix believes that "this central religious task is inherent in all teaching, regardless of the field of study. It is the end which should govern instruction in mathematics and in literature, in mechanical arts and in modern dance, in biochemistry and in law. Every study, theoretical and applied, elementary and advanced, formal and informal, is an appropriate vehicle for teaching the one fundamental lesson of loyalty to what is true, excellent, and just. Every institution of education—the home, the school, the church or temple, the industrial shop or laboratory, the museum or library, the mass media—can be and ought to be an agency of religious instruction."

A basic reason Phenix gives for his curriculum proposal is that without religious education our civilization will deteriorate. "If a wall of separation is erected between religion and the state (and its schools), that wall," he contends, "will prove to be a tomb in which church, state, and schools will decay with a civilization which has lost its soul. Schools which are purged of all religious concerns become agencies for the propagation of irreligion or idolatry—for the feeding of selfish ambitions or training for subservience to secular utopias. If religion is understood in its elemental sense, and not merely in its sectarian expressions, it is entirely practicable for the public schools to educate religiously without violating any ideals of religious freedom, without partisanship for any historical tradition, and without transgressing the principle of persuasion, not compulsion, in all matters of faith. . . . This is the one supreme purpose which unites all the lesser purposes of education: to engender reverence."

[1]The quotations in this paragraph and in the two which follow it are from Philip Phenix, "The Religious Element in Education," *Educational Forum* 26 (1961): 15–16, 21–22. (Emphasis in the original.)

William Frankena takes a position directly opposed to that of Phenix. Frankena argues that while some values should be fostered through the public schools, these should not include spiritual or religious values: "Is there a place for [spiritual] values in the public schools? . . . As I see it, public education cannot be concerned to promote spiritual values." Frankena explains that by "spiritual values" are meant "specifically religious values."[2]

Frankena addresses the contention that "religion is indispensable both to the good and to the moral life. If this contention is true without qualification, then . . . public education must disown the endeavor to advance either the good life or the moral. . . . [However,] like the phrase 'spiritual values,' the thesis of the indispensability of religion is very unclear and emotionally charged. Those who maintain it rarely make clear just what they mean by 'religion,' just what they mean by 'indispensable,' or just what they think religion is indispensable to. Let us begin with a partial clarification of the term 'religion.' In discussions of the treatment of religion in state-supported institutions 'religion' is sometimes used to mean any kind of ultimate creed, and sometimes to mean only such ultimate creeds as are typified by Judaism, Christianity, or Islam. In the former sense, even atheism and naturalism are religions; in the latter, however, they are anti-religions. I propose that we use 'religion' in the latter or narrower sense, and have so been using it. Then the thesis that religion is necessary to the good and the moral life does not mean merely that *some* kind of ultimate commitment is required. This, I think, may be admitted. The thesis means, rather, that a specifically theistic kind of ultimate commitment is required. And, in this sense, it is not obviously true."

Frankena considers the specific claim that religion is indispensable for the good life. He goes on to discuss the question of "whether there are any important values or ingredients in the good life which are not dependent on any religious belief. To many people it seems clear that there are such goods as knowledge, artistic creation and appreciation, friendship, love, freedom, sense of achievement, etc., which do not have any religious faith as a necessary condition of their attainment or enjoyment. . . . It may be that the val-

---

[2]The quotations in this paragraph and in the two which follow it are from William Frankena, "Public Education and the Good Life," *Harvard Educational Review* 31 (1961): 418–421. (Emphasis in the original.)

ues mentioned gain an additional dimension if they are woven into a religious life, but it is at any rate plausible to hold that they do or at least may bring a genuine worthwhileness into the life of an unbeliever as well. . . . If this is so, then it is also plausible to maintain that religion is not so indispensable to the good life that only a religious institution can minister to such a life. For then it is possible that there is a part or aspect of the good life for which a neutral institution such as the state may be concerned, even if there is also another part or aspect of it which is beyond the care or competence of such an institution."

Some persons advocate that the schools should not become involved in the inculcation of values. What the schools should do instead, it is argued, is to develop the ability to think rationally about values. However, young children do not seem to have the capability to engage in moral reasoning or to be instructed successfully in the process of reasoning about ethical questions. R. S. Peters has summarized this difficulty as follows: "Given that it is desirable to develop people who conduct themselves rationally, intelligently and with a fair degree of spontaneity, the brute facts of child development reveal that at the most formative years of a child's development he is incapable of this form of life and impervious to the proper manner of passing it on."[3]

William Frankena describes an approach to moral education which would take account of the irrationality of young children. His solution is to structure the curriculum in two stages. The first stage would employ a nonrational approach, while the second would be devoted to a rational consideration of values. Two alternatives would be possible for the first, nonrational stage. One plan involves "indoctrination, or the use of example, habituation, suggestion, exhortation, propaganda, and sanctions like blame and punishment in such a way as to inculcate certain rules or virtues and with the purpose of ensuring behavior that conforms with these rules, not of preparing the way for reflection and spiritual freedom." The second alternative for the first stage "involves the use only of those nonrational methods, such as example, environmental influence, and positive statement of rules or ideals, which are consistent with the goals [of

[3]R. S. Peters, "Reason and Habit: The Paradox of Moral Education," in *Moral Education in a Changing Society,* ed. W. R. Niblett (London: Faber and Faber, 1963), p. 54.

the second stage] of cultivating a moral viewpoint and of promoting autonomy and reflectiveness."[4]

Frankena's proposal for a rational consideration of values in the second stage or phase of the curriculum raises another important question: Should the schools treat various sensitive and controversial matters that, strictly speaking, are outside the area of values (for example, the empirical facts about evolution, sex, politics, and the metaphysical question of the existence of God), but which might impinge upon values held to be very important by some members of society? In dealing with this problem, a number of specific issues would have to be resolved, including the following:

(1) Should sex education be provided? If so, what topics should be covered, and to what age groups should it be provided? Should any views on sexual morality be taught?
(2) In the teaching of history, should information about the government and government leaders be presented which might be interpreted adversely (for example, all of the facts concerning the treatment of Indians and blacks in the United States)?
(3) In the teaching of literature, should works that some persons regard as being pornographic be studied?
(4) Should the theory of evolution be taught? In what way?
(5) Should the political motives of contemporary government leaders (national and local) be identified and analyzed?
(6) What should be regarded as "social problems," and how should these be treated in the curriculum?
(7) How should a teacher deal with the topic of communism?
(8) Should philosophy be taught? If so, how should metaphysical questions, such as whether or not God exists, be handled?

One of the factors that must be considered in trying to answer these questions is the age of the student. Sterling McMurrin, for example, believes that "there clearly are some things that should be aired and examined, that have, nevertheless, no place in the instruction of young children, either because no real gain would result or because the consequence might be genuine intellectual or moral

---

[4]William Frankena, "Moral Education, Philosophical View Of," in *Encyclopedia of Education,* ed. Lee C. Deighton (New York: Macmillan, 1971), 6:396.

harm. . . . This is not to say that children should be protected from the facts of life, the truth about themselves and the world in which they live, or that their capacities for objective appraisal and critical insight should not be encouraged and cultivated. Far from it. . . . But this does not mean that the teacher is justified, for instance, in bringing before third- and fourth-grade children controversial issues for the consideration of which they may lack adequate knowledge, experience, and intellectual and emotional maturity. . . . Obviously there is a point in the educative process, and it is usually earlier than the more conservative elements in any society are willing to admit, when somewhat sensitive issues in matters of politics, economics, or general human behavior not only can but should be made the focus of expository, analytical, and critical study with all sides carefully examined and objectively appraised."[5]

McMurrin's statement is by no means a complete answer to the problems we are considering, however. He does not say, for instance, whether all sensitive and controversial topics should be included in the school curriculum. It also seems that he assumes those sensitive and controversial topics which are selected for consideration in the schools can be handled "objectively," but exactly what does this mean? That some issues are chosen for examination while others are left out is a good example of a value judgment. Moreover, in the "objective" examination of any topic, value judgments must be made on what should and should not be presented.

There is no escape from the conclusion that the distinction between "indoctrination" and the "rational examination of values" is in one sense a spurious one. Everything that we decide to do or not do with respect to the curriculum entails a value judgment, and to the extent that the curriculum affects the student, these value judgments are imposed upon him. Even if the student is told that he ought to think rationally about values, the value "rational examination of values" is being imposed on him. Although there are major differences in the kinds of values imposed, in how this is done (positively or aversively), and with regard to whether the values are deliberately or inadvertently inculcated, the fact remains that schooling does impose values. "If we want to avoid imposing anything on our children," George Counts has written, "we should alter the architectural style of the [school] building every day. . . . [Even] our

[5]Sterling M. McMurrin, "Academic Freedom in the Schools," *Teachers College Record* 65 (1964): 660–661.

arithmetic textbooks transmit to the younger generation countless social, political, and moral ideas—for the most part a white middle-class culture."[6]

Practical Studies or the Liberal Arts?

One of the most enduring educational controversies is whether the curriculum should be given a practical emphasis or not. In other words, should the curriculum be oriented toward occupational preparation and similar practical concerns, or should the emphasis be on liberal arts? Aristotle's views on the need for liberal (nonvocational) education have already been discussed. An important statement on the opposite view of this issue has been provided by Bertrand Russell, who examines the specific question of whether the classics or science should be studied.

One of the claims that has been made in this controversy, Russell points out, "is that the classics are ornamental and science is useful." But after a consideration of what is meant by the term "useful," Russell concludes that this part of the issue is "unreal." He contends that "in the widest and most correct sense of the word, an activity is 'useful' when it has good results. . . . The essence of what is 'useful' is that it ministers to some result which is not merely useful. Sometimes a long chain of results is necessary before the final result is reached which can be called simply 'good.' A plough is useful because it breaks up the ground. But breaking up the ground is not good on its own account: it is in turn merely useful because it enables seed to be sown. This is useful because it produces grain, which is useful because it produces bread, which is useful because it preserves life. But life must be capable of some intrinsic value. . . . Somewhere we must get beyond the chain of successive utilities, and find a peg from which the chain is to hang; if not, there is no real usefulness in any link of the chain. When 'useful' is defined in this way, there can be no question whether education should be useful. Of course it should, since the process of educating is a means to an end, not an end in itself."[7]

[6]George S. Counts, "Should the Teacher Always Be Neutral?" *Phi Delta Kappan* 51 (1969): 188.
[7]The quotations in this paragraph and the three which follow it are from Bertrand Russell, *On Education* (London: George Allen and Unwin, 1926), pp. 19–25.

Russell thus admits that the question of whether education should or should not lead eventually to some desirable end is not in dispute. "The real issue," he explains, "is: should we, in education, aim at filling the mind with knowledge which has direct practical utility, or should we try to give our pupils mental possessions which are good on their own account?"

In attempting to answer the question he has posed, Russell argues that "most modern well-to-do Englishmen and Americans, if they were transported by magic into the age of Elizabeth, would wish themselves back in the modern world. The society of Shakespeare and Raleigh and Sir Philip Sydney, the exquisite music, the beauty of the architecture, would not console them for the absence of bath-rooms, tea and coffee, motor-cars, and other material comforts of which that age was ignorant. . . . I do not think it would be fair to meet this attitude by the mere assertion that mental goods are of more value than such as are purely physical. I believe this assertion to be true, but not the whole truth. For, while physical goods have no very high value, physical evils may be so bad as to outweigh a great deal of mental excellence."

Russell believes, however, that through modern science and technology, it is now possible "to create a world where everybody shall have a reasonable chance of happiness. Physical evil can, if we choose, be reduced to very small proportions. It would be possible, by organization and science, to feed and house the whole population of the world . . . to combat disease, and to . . . prevent the increase of population from outrunning improvements in the food supply. The great terrors which have darkened the sub-conscious mind of the race, bringing cruelty, oppression, and war in their train, could be so much diminished as to be no longer important. All this is of such immeasurable value to human life that we dare not oppose the sort of education which will tend to bring it about. In such an education, applied science will have to be the chief ingredient. Without physics and physiology and psychology, we cannot build the new world. We can build it without Latin and Greek, without Dante and Shakespeare, without Bach and Mozart. That is the great argument in favour of a utilitarian education. I have stated it strongly, because I feel it strongly."

Russell has made an important point which warrants consideration. He emphasizes that the entire curriculum must be practical or relevant—that is, whatever learning experiences are provided must produce learning outcomes that are in some sense utilitarian.

But it would be wrong to equate "useful" with "vocational." For vocationally-oriented learning outcomes by themselves cannot sufficiently prepare a person to fulfill the various roles he or she will occupy as an adult; learning outcomes that will contribute to making an effective parent, effective citizen, and so forth are also necessary. This means that we must confront the problem raised by Herbert Spencer: the relative importance of the basic human activities for which education is a preparation must be determined, and then the curriculum must be adjusted accordingly.

Is the Curriculum Relevant?

Under the pseudonym of J. Abner Peddiwell, Harold Benjamin wrote an entertaining satire, entitled *The Saber-Tooth Curriculum*, on the relevancy of the curriculum. It recounts the efforts of a paleolithic educator named New-Fist to establish the first educational system for the children of his tribe. Benjamin describes the curriculum devised by New-Fist and explains the rationale behind it. This, incidentally, is an excellent illustration of the application of the basic human activities approach:

> New-Fist proceeded to construct a curriculum for reaching [his educational] goal. "What things must we tribesmen know how to do in order to live with full bellies, warm backs, and minds free from fear?" he asked himself.
> To answer this question, he ran various activities over in his mind. "We have to catch fish with our bare hands in the pool far up the creek beyond that big bend," he said to himself. . . .
> Thus New-Fist discovered the first subject of the first curriculum—fish-grabbing-with-the-bare-hands.
> "Also we club the little woolly horses," he continued with his analysis. . . .
> So woolly-horse-clubbing was seen to be the second main subject in the curriculum.
> "And finally, we drive away the saber-tooth tigers with fire," New-Fist went on in his thinking. . . .
> Thus was discovered the third subject—saber-tooth-tiger-scaring-with-fire.[8]

Many years passed; during that time profound changes took place in the environmental situation of the tribe, owing to the onset

[8]Harold Benjamin [Peddiwell], *The Saber-Tooth Curriculum* (New York: McGraw-Hill, 1939), pp. 28–29.

of a glacial period. One change occurred to the stream which flowed through the tribe's territory. The stream became muddy, and through natural selection the fish became very adept at eluding the most expert fish-grabber. Another change affected the little woolly horses. They moved out of the tribe's territory and were replaced by antelopes that "were so shy and speedy and had so keen a scent for danger that no one could approach them closely enough to club them." Still another change affected the saber-tooth tigers. The air became damper, and most of the saber-tooth tigers succumbed to pneumonia. "So there were no more tigers to scare the paleolithic community. . . . Yet this danger to the people was lost only to be replaced by another and even greater danger, for with the advancing ice sheet came ferocious glacial bears which were not afraid of fire, which walked the trails by day as well as by night, and which could not be driven away by the most advanced methods developed in the tiger-scaring courses of the schools."[9]

The tribe adapted to changes by developing new techniques to cope with the environment. For example, one tribesman discovered the technique of fishnet-making and using in order to catch fish; another formulated a procedure for constructing and using antelope snares; a third invented the technique of catching bears in bear pits.

It was then obvious to some radical thinkers that the existing curriculum—which had not been altered—was irrelevant to the new needs of the community. They raised questions about the schools. The response they received is described in the following way:

> "Fishnet-making and using, antelope-snare construction and operation, and bear-catching and killing," [the radicals] pointed out, "require intelligence and skills—things we claim to develop in schools. They are also activities we need to know. Why can't the schools teach them?"
>
> But most of the tribe, and particularly the wise old men who controlled the school, smiled indulgently at this suggestion. "That wouldn't be *education*," they said gently.
>
> "But why wouldn't it be?" asked the radicals.
>
> "Because it would be mere training," explained the old men patiently. "With all the intricate details of fish-grabbing, horse-clubbing, and tiger-scaring—the standard cultural subjects—the school curriculum is too crowded now. We can't add these fads and frills of net-making, antelope-snaring, and—of all things—bear-killing. Why, at the very thought, the body of the great New-Fist, founder of our pa-

[9]Ibid., pp. 33–37.

leolithic educational system, would turn over in its burial cairn. What we need to do is to give our young people a more thorough grounding in the fundamentals. Even the graduates of the secondary schools don't know the art of fish-grabbing in any complete sense nowadays, they swing their horse clubs awkwardly too, and as for the old science of tiger-scaring—well, even the teachers seem to lack the real flair for the subject which we oldsters got in our teens and never forgot."

"But, damn it," exploded one of the radicals, "how can any person with good sense be interested in such useless activities? What is the point of trying to catch fish with the bare hands when it just can't be done any more. How can a boy learn to club horses when there are no horses left to club? And why in hell should children try to scare tigers with fire when the tigers are dead and gone?"

"Don't be foolish," said the wise old men, smiling most kindly smiles. "We don't teach fish-grabbing to grab fish; we teach it to develop a generalized agility which can never be developed by mere training. . . . We don't teach tiger-scaring to scare tigers; we teach it for the purpose of giving that noble courage which carries over into all the affairs of life and which can never come from so base an activity as bear-killing. . . .You must know that there are some eternal verities, and the saber-tooth curriculum is one of them!"[10]

Although this satire was published in 1939, Benjamin seems to have been extremely perceptive in identifying the type of argument that is often given on behalf of the traditional curriculum. As Benjamin suggests, the defenders of the traditional curriculum are very likely to advocate even more rather than less of the "fundamentals."

Such an argument was advanced by Arthur Bestor. He raises and provides his answer to the following question: "Do the societal needs of the present day call for an indefinite extension of the functions and responsibilities of the school—an extension that would involve remaking the curriculum? One cannot answer by pointing to the many problems of society that are not being adequately met. The adequacy with which social problems are handled by any society depends largely upon the appropriateness of the agencies that are developed to meet them, the exactitude with which the means devised are adapted to the ends in view."[11]

Bestor's position is that the educational role of the schools

[10]Ibid., pp. 41–44. (Emphasis in the original.)
[11]The quotations in this paragraph and in the one which follows it are from Arthur Bestor, "Education and the American Scene," in *Education in the Age of Science,* ed. Brand Blanshard (New York: Basic Books, 1959), pp. 66–67, 70–71. (Emphasis in the original.)

should be a relatively limited one. "The argument that the public day school in twentieth-century America must assume responsibility over wide-ranging areas of social concern apart from intellectual training is, at bottom, an argument that other agencies of society are not capable of, and cannot be made capable of, dealing with the problems involved. This argument I find completely unconvincing. . . . The glowing spark of intellectual independence, which social conditioning is most apt to quench, can be kept alive in the school if the development of critical intelligence remains its overriding objective. Freedom to think—which means nothing unless it means freedom to think differently—can be society's most precious gift to itself. The first duty of a school is to defend and cherish it. . . . The public day school—supported by taxes derived from the community, subject to immediate community pressure, recognizably an agent of local government and of the state—lacks any such power to resist conformism, unless it takes the high ground that its proper task is to develop critical, independent, well-informed judgment by means of disciplined intellectual training. Not the indiscriminate molding of attitudes desired by the community, but the deliberate molding of a specifically *intellectual* attitude, is the function and the responsibility of a publicly supported school in a society that wishes to preserve its vital freedoms."

A similar concern with enhancing the traditional role of the schools has become evident recently in the United States. Groups of parents have organized to express their disenchantment with present school practices and to call for a return to fundamentals. What is the reason for this, if (as Benjamin has indicated) it is probably the fundamentals which make the curriculum irrelevant? It may be hypothesized that these parents are aware that a thorough knowledge of fundamentals can help their children gain a higher standing on the norm-referenced examinations that are utilized within the school system and which govern admission to the more prestigious universities; they favor the traditional curriculum, therefore, because it is "relevant" for this limited purpose.

Benjamin's satire does not stress the role of the traditional curriculum in the selecting and sorting of students. But the Schoolboys of Barbiana—who present their criticism of the Italian school system in their book *Letter to a Teacher*—are very conscious of this function. The authors are a group of eight boys who had attended a special, privately run school for dropouts in Barbiana, Italy. The schoolboys were thirteen to sixteen years old when they wrote the book. The basic argument of the book is contained in the excerpt which follows. The authors are eager for educational opportunities, but they vigorously oppose the irrelevancy of the curriculum and the sorting and selection to which it contributes (in this excerpt the "Miss" and "you" refer to the teacher; the "I" represents all of the authors):

Dear Miss,

You won't remember me or my name. You have flunked so many of us.

On the other hand I have often had thoughts about you, and the other teachers, and about that institution which you call "school" and about the kids that you flunk.

You flunk us right out into the fields and factories and there you forget us. . . .

Languages are created by the poor, who then go on renewing them forever. The rich crystallize them in order to put on the spot anybody who speaks in a different way. Or in order to fail him at exams.

You say that little Pierino, daddy's boy, can write well. But of course; he speaks as you do. He is part of the firm.

On the other hand, the language spoken and written by Gianni is the one used by his father. . . . Your own language could become a convenience in time. But meanwhile, don't throw him out of school.

"All citizens are equal without distinction as to language," says the Constitution, having Gianni in mind.

But you honor grammar more than constitutions. And Gianni never came back, not even to us.

Yet we can't get him off our mind. We follow him from a distance. We heard that he doesn't go to church any more, or to any political meetings. He sweeps up in a factory. During his free time he follows like a puppet whatever is "in." Saturday, dancing; Sunday, the ballpark.

But you, his teacher, don't even remember his existence. . . .

Examinations should be abolished. But if you do give them, at least be fair. Difficulties should be chosen in proportion to their appearance in life. If you choose them too frequently, it means you have a trap-complex. As if you were at war with the kids.

What makes you do it? Is it for the good of the students? . . .

While cramming for the exams we would steal a couple of hours every day to read the paper, overcoming our stinginess. Because nothing is found in the newspaper that could help us pass your exams. This proves again how little there is in your school useful for life. . . .

One woman teacher ended her lessons before the First World War. She stopped exactly at the spot where school could tie us to life. In the whole year she never once read a newspaper to her class. . . .

If schooling has to be so brief, then it should be planned according to the most urgent needs. . . .

If all of you knew that, by any means possible, you had to move every child ahead in every subject, you would sharpen up your wits to find a way for all of them to function well.

I'd have you paid by piecework. So much for each child who learns one subject. Or, even better, a fine for each child who does not learn a subject.

Then your eyes would always be on Gianni. You would search out in his inattentive stare the intelligence that God has put in him, as in all children. You would fight for the child who needs you most, neglecting the gifted one, as they do in any family. You would wake up at night thinking about him and would try to invent new ways to teach him—ways that would fit his needs. You would go to fetch him from home if he did not show up for class.

You would never give yourself any peace, for the school that lets the Giannis drop out is not fit to be called a school.[12]

The conclusion reached in Chapter 9 that the existing curriculum has not been greatly influenced by the basic human activities approach needs to be considered in conjunction with the views advanced by Benjamin and the Schoolboys of Barbiana. It seems fair to suggest that the present curriculum is in some degree irrelevant to the attainment of those learning outcomes involved in the performance of essential human activities. This is not to say that a subject such as plane geometry is without value, but it is to suggest that the time spent in the study of plane geometry may be preventing students from acquiring more important learning outcomes. The situation in the schools is somewhat equivalent to that of a hospital staff's spending much of its time elaborately washing, grooming and feeding their patients and occasionally dispensing aspirin tablets to take care of the illnesses of the patients. Washing, grooming and feeding patients in a hospital are not totally unwarranted functions, but they are justifiable only if they contribute to the primary task of helping the patients to get well.

On the basis of the priorities it exemplifies, therefore, it may be argued that portions of the present school curriculum are irrelevant. The curriculum is concerned in many instances with the accomplishment of relatively unimportant learning outcomes, while those learning experiences which might be expected to accomplish the most important learning outcomes are either altogether lacking or are available only to a limited extent. One needs only to visit an

[12]Schoolboys of Barbiana, *Letter to a Teacher* (New York: Vintage Books, 1971), pp. 3, 12–13, 15, 20–22, 76–77.

average American secondary school to become aware of the inordinate amount of time devoted to learning relatively trivial facts of, say, history, English literature, and advanced mathematical skills in algebra and geometry; on the other hand, little if any time is devoted to instructing students in how to deal with the important problems they will confront as adults.

How can the apparent irrelevancy of portions of the existing primary and secondary school curriculum be explained? There would seem to be two possible explanations. First, there are important vested interests, represented mainly by teachers who have been trained in the academic fields of knowledge. Since these teachers are presumably deeply committed to the fields in which they have been trained, they would very likely resist any effort to eliminate these fields from the curriculum or to decrease their importance.

The preceding explanation does not, however, appear adequate to account for the lack of serious challenge to the present curriculum. If a hospital did not go beyond dispensing aspirin tablets, then a very strong criticism of its activities would be quickly forthcoming, regardless of how dedicated the hospital staff was to bathing, grooming and feeding patients. The second explanation of why many persons seem reasonably content with the existing curriculum is that the schools are now performing a variety of useful functions (some of which are described in Chapter 7), so that it is not always evident that the schools may have serious deficiencies with respect to the fulfillment of their teaching function. Furthermore, the selecting and sorting function of the present school system is probably facilitated by an irrelevant curriculum! If the curriculum is irrelevant, only those students who are the quickest learners, who have an above-average ability to conform to the expectations of others, who are docile, and who are clever in figuring out how to cope with a frustrating situation, will be likely to succeed. This suggestion should not be too surprising, because it is consistent with the fact that the school system utilizes norm-referenced rather than criterion-referenced grading.

As stated in Chapter 6, once we become aware of the extremely significant implications of the evaluation procedures utilized by the school system, there are two options open to us: either the selecting and sorting function of the schools can be recognized as their principal activity, or teaching can be reaffirmed as the central function of the school system by instituting criterion-referenced grading and related changes.

Comments on the Curriculum Approach

Our survey of selected writings that advocate use of the curriculum approach has revealed the value of this approach. The question "What curriculum should we have?" invariably results in a discussion of the desirability of particular kinds of learning experiences. As a guide to what teachers should do, such writings can be extremely useful. Also, in dealing with learning outcomes that are difficult to identify as observable performances, the curriculum approach represents what is probably the best way of arriving at a specification of appropriate learning experiences. These advantages of the curriculum approach are illustrated in the first two questions examined in this section: the problem of indoctrination versus the rational examination of values, and the question of whether emphasis should be placed on practical studies or the liberal arts.

The curriculum may also be used as the starting point in discussing the educational means-ends chain. In this case the analysis is similar to what it would have been if the ultimate/penultimate ends approach or the basic human activities approach had been applied, although the initial question involved is different. The writings of Harold Benjamin and the Schoolboys of Barbiana on the relevance of the curriculum exemplify this procedure.

The curriculum approach and the two approaches examined in Chapter 9 have a somewhat restricted focus on the educational means-ends chain. A more comprehensive approach would be one which recognizes the distinction between the goals of education (which logically must be expressed in terms of learning outcomes) and the functions of schooling (which may or may not entail a principal emphasis on the attainment of desired learning outcomes). Such an approach would also recognize the need to involve prospective learners in appropriate learning situations, the relationship of the schools to other educational agencies, and the effects of the societal incentive structure on learner performances. We shall call a society which utilizes a comprehensive approach to the formulation of educational objectives an *educative society*. As our final question, the merits of this alternative shall be considered.

Issue 12: Should We Have an Educative Society?

An educative society is one that has chosen to maximize the participation of its members in desirable learning experiences. Therefore, in an educative society explicit attention is given to all major factors involved in or that affect the educative process.

Primacy of the Teaching Function

One of the factors explicitly considered by an educative society is the relationship between the goals of education and the functions of schooling. The conventional school system performs manifold functions; some are manifest while others are latent. In an educative society, however, all functions of its educational agencies have been made manifest.

Since an educative society places a very high value on learning, the principal function (actual as well as declared) of the school system is the provision of desirable learning experiences. Any other functions performed by the school system must be compatible with its teaching function. Since norm-referenced grading detracts from the effective performance of the teaching function, the school system in this type of society relies upon criterion-referenced examinations or it omits student evaluation entirely.

The credentials issued by the school system would consist of statements identifying the specific learning outcomes that have been accomplished (certificates of achievement), and/or statements identifying the specific learning experiences to which the student had been exposed (certificates of attendance). In many instances it will probably be feasible to specify the learning outcomes that have been achieved, but in other cases these outcomes will defy precise identification. Where this is so, the types of learning experiences required to produce the imprecisely defined outcomes will be indicated.

Costs and Benefits of Using Student Control Techniques

Deciding that the schools should be primarily oriented toward inducing the attainment of specified learning outcomes by students still leaves the educative society with a basic problem. This is the problem of getting the prospective learner to become involved with the educative process. Another fundamental characteristic of the educative society, therefore, is that explicit attention is given to the costs and benefits of using various learner control techniques.

In an educative society—as is true of every human society— some persons (very young children, for example) are the recipients of deliberate learning experiences whose outcomes they have not chosen; we shall call any such person an "educational recipient." In every society there are also some persons who make decisions about the learning experiences that others will receive; we shall call such a person an "educational policy maker." How does an educational policy maker get an educational recipient to participate in the educative process?

One course of action the educational policy maker might consider is whether to utilize the technique of access control. This control technique is involved in every educational situation in which someone or something other than the learner is the source of the desired learning experience; obviously this condition applies in most educational situations. Therefore, some provision usually must be made to bring the learner into contact with relevant learning experiences. For example, the sources of learning experiences can be geographically distributed in proximity to the learner, the buildings and rooms in which the learning experiences are provided (if that is the case) can be kept open to permit the learner to enter, and potential recipients can be subsidized for the costs they might incur in gaining access to desired learning situations. The use of access control assumes that—within the prevailing societal incentive structure—persons are motivated to learn, but that the educational policy maker can influence what is learned by controlling the accessibility of certain learning experiences.

The learner may decide not to participate in a given learning situation, however, even if it has been made conveniently accessible. Another course of action that the educational policy maker might consider, therefore, is whether to use the control technique of positive motivation to induce the learner to participate. This procedure would entail giving recipients a reward for participating in specified learning situations or for achieving designated learning outcomes. For example, a recipient might be informed that he would be given an attractive position of employment if he demonstrated that he had achieved certain learning outcomes. The educational policy maker could also offer the learner money if he participates in a stipulated learning situation; he could tell the learner about the important social advantages that will be derived from attaining certain learning outcomes; and so forth.

As a third possible course of action, the educational policy maker might consider the use of aversive motivation. Through the use of this control technique, educational recipients can be compelled to participate in stipulated learning situations and to achieve specified learning outcomes. For example, students could be told that they must continue to attend a certain school until they have demonstrated the attainment of prescribed learning outcomes; or a student could be threatened with the loss of a teacher's esteem if he did not participate in a stipulated learning situation.

In an educative society, the decision about which of these three learner control techniques to use with respect to a given learning outcome or learning situation is based on an evaluation of the costs and benefits entailed in using them. The educational policy maker must determine which learning outcomes are sufficiently valuable to warrant the costs involved in adopting any of these three courses of action. Giving easier access to certain learning experiences is probably the least costly of the three courses of action, although there would be some economic costs involved (particularly if recipients are to be subsidized for the costs they incur in gaining access to learning situations). Use of positive motivation probably represents the most expensive of the three options; monetary costs of providing aversive inducements are lower than the costs of positive inducements, although the psychic costs to recipients (engendered by the fear of unpleasant consequences) are obviously greater. The policy maker must also consider the effectiveness of a given technique in relation to its costs.

These costs-benefits assessments are explicitly undertaken in an educative society for all of the learning outcomes which the policy makers want the recipients to achieve and for all of the learning situations in which learner participation is desired. By comparing the costs of using the three learner control procedures (access control, positive motivation, and aversive motivation) with an assessment of the benefits to be gained, it will be possible for the educational policy makers to arrive at a specification of educational ends and means. They should be able to state which learning outcomes and/or learning situations are desirable and why they are so regarded (in terms of the ultimate or penultimate end to which they lead). They also should be able to stipulate which learning outcomes are so valuable as to warrant the use of aversive motivation, which ones can be achieved through positive motivation, and which ones can be attained merely through access control.

Establishment of an Educational System

Since the school system is only one of several educational agencies, it is possible to have a higher-order system in which the activities of the school system are coordinated with those of other educational agencies. We shall call such a higher-order system an *educational system*. Since an educative society is concerned with maximizing appropriate educational opportunities for all members of the society, it possesses an educational system rather than just a school system.

If an educational system were to be established in the United States, the activities of the school system would be explicitly coordinated with the educational activities of the mass media, apprenticeship programs, and so forth. The extent of the coordination among educational agencies is governed by a consideration of costs and benefits. Obviously it could be very costly (both monetarily and in loss of individual initiative, to name just two costs) to direct all of a society's educational activities from one central policy making office. The minimum requirement to have an educational system is that the school system be operated with an explicit awareness of what other educational agencies in the society are or are not doing, with such adjustments as are deemed appropriate being made in the activities of the school system and the other educational agencies.

Recently several authors have discussed the possibility of establishing a "learning society." This concept can be interpreted to be very close to our notion of an educational system. A learning society provides lifelong learning opportunities in a large number of settings, both inside and outside the school system.

Theodore Hesburg, Paul Miller and Clifton Wharton describe the characteristics of a learning society in the following excerpt:

> Something is clearly wrong in the way the society has conceived and structured the formal processes of learning. In the future, the United States should be conceived of as a learning society. Educational policy planning should begin with a comprehensive framework that addresses the needs of the entire population, from infancy through adulthood. The entire population should be seen as a national resource comprising a society in which continuous, purposeful learning is not only talked about but carried out in a great variety of settings

and formats. . . . In the learning society, formal education would be spread throughout one's lifetime. This reflects a recognition that people learn more readily when they see a clear need to do so, and also that some learning is more appropriate to one age than to another. It makes little difference where or how learning takes place, whether it occurs in the classroom or on a job, at age twenty, fifty, or seventy, as long as it does take place, and under circumstances appropriate to the learner. Education for adults as well as for children should be centered on the needs of the learner. . . . Under a system of lifelong learning, all institutions would share responsibility for helping people to educate themselves. Employers, for example, should give greater recognition than they do to the potential of the workplace as a prime site for vocational upgrading and personal fulfillment through well-designed educational programs. Church-related groups, families, labor unions, and the media all have unused potential for purposeful learning. In the future, all the major institutions of society should be conscious of their educational functions and take deliberate, planned steps to improve them. . . . Educational means must be multiplied and made more accessible than is now the case. . . . Education should become the responsibility of all components of organized society.[13]

The authors of the preceding selection emphasize the necessity for a national policy as the foundation for the learning society: "When the able adult population of the nation is viewed as a vast learning force whose development is in the national interest, the basis for public policy becomes clearer. First, the provision of opportunities for lifelong learning has nationwide implications, since the development of human skill is closely related to the social and economic advancement of the entire country. The integration of learning with life and careers cannot be effectively accomplished on an ad hoc basis, dependent on the person's ability to pay, or solely upon self-interest. Rather, lifelong learning should be guided by public policies that encourage the systematic integration of learning opportunities with the needs of people at different stages of life." (Note 2)

Appropriate Societal Incentive Structure

An educative society is one that is concerned with whether the members of the society make use of desirable learning outcomes in

[13]The quotations in this paragraph and in the one which follows it are from Theodore M. Hesburgh, Paul A. Miller, and Clifton R. Wharton, *Patterns for Lifelong Learning* (San Francisco: Jossey-Bass, 1973), pp. 4–8, 14.

their behavior. Thus a fourth characteristic of an educative society is the attention it has given to creating an incentive structure that will induce members of the society to perform in accordance with the learning outcomes fostered by the educational system. Very few writers on educational goals have discussed the societal incentive structure (Plato and Skinner are two important exceptions); yet unless this factor is taken into account it is possible that many learning outcomes will have been achieved in vain or will not be achieved at all.

An educative society periodically assesses the societal incentive structure and determines the costs and benefits of modifying it. Even if no action is taken to change the existing incentive structure, the educative society explicitly recognizes its importance in bringing about the utilization of the learning outcomes produced by the educational system.

Why Should We Have an Educative Society?

Probably the major reason an educative society should be created is that such a society would maximize available opportunities for desirable learning experiences. Through education, which is a fundamental societal process, human beings can be helped to develop their capabilities and potentialities as human beings. It is the process through which we can begin to create a better world in which to live. In short, it is the process that allows full expression to be given to our idealistic aspirations for mankind.

Should the school system be permitted to give its primary attention to selecting and sorting students instead of to educating them? Or should the conventional school system be changed? If we favor an educative society, then we believe that the school system should make teaching its primary responsibility. The choice is very fundamental. Yet the "villain" in the present school system is an exceedingly unobtrusive one—the practice of norm-referenced grading. A choice to eliminate norm-referenced grading will demonstrate a commitment to the teaching function of the school system. This is the first decision that must be made if we are to have an educative society.

The second decision that must be made if we are to have an educative society is to give explicit attention in the formulation of policy to all of the basic factors entailed in the educative process, particularly when making costs-benefits assessments. If we are to achieve an educative society, the costs and benefits of utilizing different control techniques to secure learner cooperation in the attainment of these learning outcomes must be publicly identified. The educative society also has an educational system rather than a school system, because educational policy makers are explicitly aware of the role of the schools vis a vis other educational agencies. Finally, in an educative society explicit consideration is given to the effects of the societal incentive structure on the utilization of desirable learning outcomes engendered by the educational system.

The fact that an educative society gives explicit consideration to the major factors that are involved in or that affect the educative process does not mean that all educative societies would formulate the same educational policies. Some educative societies might be conservative, others might be liberal. The concept of an educative society is compatible with almost any political/economic ideology. It is possible, for example, that the members of one educative society may prefer to make extensive use of aversive motivation to achieve desired learning outcomes, whereas in another society greatest reliance may be placed on access control and positive motivation. One educative society may favor a considerable amount of centralized direction of the educational system, but another might prefer a decentralized approach. Thus the only uniformity among educative societies would be their common concern with the maximization of desirable educational experiences.

Elimination of Norm–Referenced Evaluation

As previously indicated in the discussion of teacher control, abolishing norm-referenced evaluation will probably help teachers achieve recognized professional status. Teachers will be able to concentrate their efforts on helping students to learn, since this will be the principal function of the schools (instead of rank-ordering students).

The aversive character of the present teacher-student relationship will also disappear. Elimination of norm-referenced evaluation means that flexible rather than fixed time limits can be used. Students will thus be reinforced when they acquire desired learning outcomes (ratio reinforcement); the teacher will not need to perform the aversive function of "task stimulator," which is necessary in a situation of fixed-interval reinforcement. Even if society decides that students must be compelled to learn (for their own good or for the good of society), the aversiveness of this situation would not require the teacher to be the task stimulator—the teacher would still be the one who helps the student to learn. The aversive stimuli, in this case, would be provided by society, not by the teacher.

If norm-referenced evaluation is replaced by criterion-referenced grading, employers will have a much better knowledge of the learning outcomes that have been achieved by prospective employees. On the other hand, if employers do not really care about the attainment of specified learning outcomes, and instead have been relying on existing school certificates as a screening device to identify quick learners, conformists and so forth, then it is time for this latent function to be made manifest. Schooling is very expensive; if employers want to know who is a quick learner, for example, tests could be devised to reveal who possesses this natural talent, with much less cost required from students and society.

Although the adoption of criterion-referenced evaluation would probably significantly reduce the amount of competition between students, selection on the basis of school certificates would not be eliminated. Since the school system might still issue credentials, then presumably some students would obtain credentials that are not acquired by other students. For example, some students might decide to make the effort required to achieve the learning outcomes stipulated for a medical doctor, whereas other students might choose not to make this effort. As a result, school credentials would still be a factor in the allocation of students to social roles. However, the determination of whether the student eventually obtains a credential would be his or her own, not that of the system; since there are no fixed time limits, the student would not be afraid of being "flunked out" or given low grades.

Nevertheless, it may be argued that people do not learn the same amounts, and that it would be nice to know who has learned the most. As we have already noted, however, the rank-ordering of students is not a declared purpose of the school system. Other helping institutions in our society are not obligated to provide an official rank-ordering of their clients. The churches, for example, try to help everyone attain the benefits provided by religion; they are not involved in official rank-ordering. Similarly, hospitals try to help all of their patients get well; they do not officially rank-order their patients on the basis of the time taken to regain their health. Why must the schools engage in official rank-ordering instead of helping all students to attain specified learning outcomes?

In recent years in the United States, some universities abolished norm-referenced grading, but more recently a trend has been observed to restore the norm-referenced system. An explanation given for this trend is that students want norm-referenced grading. But it would appear that they want it because graduate schools are reluctant to admit students with no record of norm-referenced grading and because certain employers (such as law firms) want to know a graduate's rank-in-class. So students have a very practical reason for their willingness to submit to norm-referenced grading. However, if such practical reasons do not exist, the credential-holder is generally reluctant to provide information on his standing vis a vis other persons. When one visits a medical doctor's or dentist's office, for example, diplomas and licenses certifying attainment of designated competencies may be prominently displayed, but information on where the professional stood in his licensing examinatin is not given. It is known that the professional has met the prescribed standards of his profession, and that is all. Surely if it is sufficient in such important occupations as physician and dentist to assure the prospective user of the professional's services that relevant learning outcomes have been achieved, it should be sufficient for prospective employers to be given comparable information in school system credentials.

Also, the negative side effects of norm-referenced evaluation should be remembered, particularly the effect on the self-concept of persons who consistently receive low or failing grades. Do we want these persons to acquire the belief that they are incompetent and stupid—that they are destined to fulfill only inferior roles in adult life? Norm-referenced evaluation in the schools could cause exactly this type of reaction. Most people who attend school believe that they have had a "fair chance"; if they are not very successful in the competition for high grades, this is attributed to personal inadequacies rather than to norm-referenced evaluation. It should be realized that, when norm-referenced evaluation is used, half of the persons graded will be below average.

Since norm-referenced grading is currently practiced in the American school system, it must be asked why this is so. Are there reasons for the official rank-ordering of students that we have not yet examined? Some teachers may like norm-referenced evaluation because it gives them a powerful means for motivating students. Therefore, as long as teachers in the present system of fixed-interval reinforcement are obliged to stimulate student effort, some will probably wish to retain norm-referenced evaluation. Furthermore, an evaluation procedure that utilizes fixed-interval reinforcement is much more convenient to administer than one that entails ratio reinforcement. But norm-referenced grading also seems to be acceptable to many students and parents. The explanation for this appears to be that students and parents simply are not aware of the deleterious effects of this practice, nor are they familiar with the criterion-referenced alternative. Students and parents believe that a teacher is designating absolute rather than relative levels of performance when he awards an "A" or a "C."

Knowing the difference between norm-referenced and criterion-referenced evaluation, however, then leaves the question of whether the rank-ordering of students should be eliminated or continued. If the principal purpose of the schools is to foster the attainment of specified learning outcomes, then norm-referenced grading must be rejected, since this evaluation procedure is not appropriate for the achievement of specified learning outcomes. If norm-referenced evaluation is retained as a preferred function of the schools, then we must be willing to acknowledge publicly that the rank-ordering of students has a higher priority than the teaching function.

Explicit Consideration of Other Relevant Factors

Other major factors involved in or that affect the educative process—the costs and benefits of using different control techniques to bring about student participation, the relationship between the schools and other educational agencies, and the appropriateness of the societal incentive structure—should be explicitly considered. The reason that more explicitness is needed is that it will lead to greater efficiency in the conduct of educational activities.

If it is known precisely which learning outcomes are desired, for example, a more successful curriculum can be designed. Of course, there is a limit on how explicitly the major relevant factors in the educative process can be considered, because obtaining the requisite data entails costs. It would seem that the relationship of explicitness to efficiency would be obvious; however, it does not appear that the United States has even begun to approach the point where the additional costs of explicit attention to relevant educational factors would outweigh the additional benefits. Indeed, as far as several of these basic factors are concerned, almost no explicit consideration has yet been undertaken.

The field of educational studies will play an important supportive role in the effort to give explicit consideration to the major relevant factors in the educative process. Therefore, greater emphasis needs to be given to the further development of this field. (Note 3)

CONCLUDING COMMENTS

One of the criticisms that might be raised against the idea of an educative society is the objection that in such a society the national government directs all educational activities. This is not correct, however. To have an educative society would necessitate general societal planning of education (in the sense of explicitly considering or being aware of all basic factors), but the national government could decide to delegate the responsibility for detailed formulation of educational policy to the local level, as is presently the case in the United States.

It may also be objected that education is a control technique, and that any form of control is bad. Hence to increase the number of educational opportunities by establishing an educative society would be bad. It is agreed, of course, that education is a control technique, but it can be argued that some forms of control may be good. The basic reason that people have decided to control the learning process (that is, to have education rather than inadvertent learning) is that they recognize the importance of the learning process in the development of human beings. Without learning, a human organism would never become recognizably human. Rather than allow learning to take place only through chance occurrences, therefore, human beings have decided to control this vital process to insure that desired learning outcomes are achieved, and that they are achieved efficiently rather than inefficiently.

The problem, then, is not whether to have education, but whether to maximize the opportunities for desirable educational experiences. If we do not believe that the learning process can be controlled without undue risk of its being used for the wrong ends, then we should not have any education. But all societies do make use of education. Therefore, if norm-referenced grading has been rejected, all societies can become educative societies, because to become an educative society means only that the use of the educative process must be planned. We could quite conceivably prepare a comprehensive educational plan and decide to make no changes in the use of the educative process, on the grounds that the costs of making changes would outweigh the benefits. Such a society would still be an educative one, however, because it would have rationally considered whether desired learning outcomes and situations were specified as precisely as they should be, whether the costs and benefits of using learner control techniques in relation to these learning outcomes and situations had been adequately assessed, whether the role of the school system vis a vis other educational agencies should be modified, and whether the existing societal incentive structure was appropriate. Even if no changes are made in present practices, an educative society will have become rationally cognizant of all the fundamental educational policy decisions that need to be made.

Advocating the establishment of an educative society is not necessarily done to bring about change, but to enable each society to derive the most from its use of the educative process. If all of the alternatives for the educative process have not been rationally examined, then a strong possibility exists that a society may be ignoring some important benefits.

Surely education is the most important process available to us for improving the quality of human life. We should, therefore, use it as effectively as possible.

SUMMARY

Issue 11 raises the question "What curriculum should we have?" Three relatively broad problems have been selected for discussion in this chapter: (1) indoctrination; (2) practicality of the curriculum; and (3) curriculum relevancy.

Indoctrination involves the imposition of someone's values on someone else. Should the schools do this? Or should the schools be neutral with respect to values, confining themselves to the rational examination of values? Also, there is the question of what the schools should do in dealing with matters that do not directly involve values but which are nonetheless sensitive and controversial, such as teaching about communism and sex. There does not seem to be a way for the schools to avoid transmitting values; even the decision to examine values rationally represents the imposition of the value "rational examination of values" on the student.

At least since the time of Aristotle we have been faced with the question of how practical the curriculum should be. As Bertrand Russell points out, however, all aspects of the curriculum need to be practical in the sense of being instrumental to the attainment of a desirable end.

Some users of the curriculum approach have dealt with the relevance of the curriculum. In a satirical book entitled *The Saber-Tooth Curriculum,* Harold Benjamin suggests that once it has been established a curriculum tends to endure, with its defenders often imputing to it the attribute of being the best way to obtain general intellectual training, even though it lacks immediate relevance. On balance, there are strong indications that the present school curriculum is irrelevant to the accomplishment of learning outcomes entailed in the performance of essential human activities. As an explanation for the continued toleration of this situation, it is noted that the schools perform many useful functions, and one of these— the selecting and sorting function—is probably even assisted by an irrelevant curriculum. However, once aware of the possibility that portions of the curriculum may be irrelevant, it must be decided whether we want to assert the primacy of the teaching function of the school system or whether we want to recognize selecting and sorting as its major function.

Issue 12 treats the question of whether or not to have an educative society. In considering this issue, we must take a more comprehensive view of the educative process than is usually achieved through the three approaches to the formulation of educational aims previously discussed.

An educative society is defined as one which embodies the following four characteristics: (1) The actual as well as the declared purpose of the schools (educational system) is to facilitate the attainment of desired learning outcomes. (2) The costs and benefits of using the techniques of access control and motivational control with respect to student involvement in the educative process are explicitly assessed. This analysis entails a specification of desired learning experiences and/or learning outcomes and a specification of which learner control techniques (at what cost) are warranted by the benefits involved. (3) An educative society has an educational system, which is created by coordinating the activities of the school system with those of other educational agencies. (4) An educative society is explicitly aware of the importance of the societal incentive structure in inducing members of the society to utilize learning outcomes acquired through the educational system. It periodically assesses the appropriateness of the incentive structure and determines the costs and benefits of modifying it.

It is only through a comprehensive approach to the formulation of learning objectives—such as establishing an educative society—that each person will be able to achieve those learning outcomes that both he or she and the educational policy makers regard as desirable.

The first decision that must be made to establish an educative society in the United States is to eliminate norm-referenced grading. This must be done to give priority to the teaching function of the schools. The second decision involves giving explicit consideration to all of the basic factors in the educative process. Thus, the costs and benefits of utilizing different learner control techniques must be publicly assessed. Society must also be explicitly aware of the role the schools should have in relation to other educational agencies. Finally, explicit attention needs to be given to the effects of the societal incentive structure on the utilization of desired learning outcomes.

Education is the most important process available to mankind for the improvement of human life. The establishment of an educative society is advocated because it will enable each society to derive maximum benefits from the educative process.

GENERAL NOTES AND BIBLIOGRAPHY

1. CURRICULUM APPROACH. Some basic procedures and assumptions involved in a justification of curriculum are discussed in Israel Scheffler, "Justifying Curriculum Decisions," *School Review* 66 (1958): 461–472 and James McClellan, "Why Should the Humanities Be Taught?" *Journal of Philosophy* 55 (1958): 997–1008. Several general assessments of the curriculum and discussions of its rationale are provided in Robert M. McClure, ed., *The Curriculum: Retrospect and Prospect* (Chicago: National Society for the Study of Education, 1971).

Two interesting attempts to offer a justification for the entire curriculum are J. P. White, *Towards a Compulsory Curriculum* (London: Routledge and Kegan Paul, 1973) and Dennis Lawton, *Class, Culture and the Curriculum* (London: Routledge and Kegan Paul, 1975).

This chapter examines only three specific curriculum questions. Two of the many books that deal with other specific curriculum questions are Jim Haskins, ed., *Black Manifesto for Education* (New York: Morrow, 1973) and H. B. Griffiths and A. G. Howson, *Mathematics: Society and Curricula* (London: Cambridge University Press, 1974).

The terms "curriculum evaluation" and "educational evaluation" refer to the assessment of a curriculum (instructional program) from either of two different points of view: (1) the efficacy of the curriculum in achieving agreed-upon goals, or (2) the desirability of accomplishing those goals that the curriculum is presently achieving. See Robert L. Baker, "Curriculum Evaluation," *Review of Educational Research* 39 (1969): 339–358. The entire April, 1970, issue of this magazine is devoted to educational evaluation. For several empirical studies of curriculum reform, see William A. Reid and Decker F. Walker, eds., *Case Studies in Curriculum Change: Great Britain and the United States* (London: Routledge and Kegan Paul, 1975).

Different aspects of the indoctrination issue are explored in the following sources: Antony Flew, "What Is Indoctrination?" *Studies in Philosophy and Education* 4 (1966): 281–306; James F. Doyle, ed., *Educational Judgments* (London: Routledge and Kegan Paul, 1973); Glenn Langford and D. J. O'Connor, eds., *New Essays in the Philosophy of Education* (London: Routledge and Kegan Paul, 1973); Norman J. Bull, *Moral Education* (Beverly Hills, Calif.: Sage, 1969); Richard S. Peters, *Reason and Compassion* (London: Routledge and Kegan Paul, 1973); William G. Carr, ed., *Values and the Curriculum* (Washington, D.C.: National Education Association, 1970); Louis Raths, M. Harmin and S. Simon, *Values and Teaching* (Columbus, Ohio: Charles E. Merrill, 1966); Robert H. Ennis, "Is It Impossible for the Schools to Be Neutral?" in *Language and Concepts in Education*, eds. B. Othanel Smith and Robert H. Ennis (Chicago: Rand McNally, 1961), pp. 102–111; Sterling M. McMurrin,

"Academic Freedom," in *Encyclopedia of Educational Research*, ed. Robert L. Ebel (4th ed.; New York: Macmillan, 1969), pp. 1–7.

Two recent sources which provide a justification for liberal arts (often referred to as "general education") are Brand Blanshard, *The Uses of a Liberal Education* (LaSalle, Ill.: Open Court, 1973) and Sidney Hook, Paul Kurtz and Miro Todorovich, eds., *The Philosophy of the Curriculum: The Need for General Education* (Buffalo, N.Y.: Prometheus Books, 1975). For reviews of literature on liberal education and vocational education, see Edward B. Blackman, "General Education," in *Encyclopedia of Educational Research*, ed. Ebel, pp. 522–537, and George L. Brandon, "Vocational and Technical Education," in *Encyclopedia of Educational Research*, ed. Ebel, pp. 1506–1522.

The relevance of the curriculum is discussed in Arthur Daigon and Richard A. Dempsey, *School: Pass at Your Own Risk* (Englewood Cliffs, N. J.: Prentice-Hall, 1974); Kingsley Price, "On Educational Relevance and Irrelevance," in *Educational Judgments*, ed. Doyle, pp. 212–231; Neil Postman and Charles Weingartner, "What's Worth Knowing?" in *Radical School Reform*, eds. Beatrice Gross and Ronald Gross (New York: Simon and Schuster, 1969), pp. 161–172; Mario D. Fantini and Gerald Weinstein, "Making Contact with the Disadvantaged," in *Radical School Reform*, eds. Gross and Gross, pp. 172–178; S. Samuel Shermis, "Educational Critics Have Been Wrong All Along: Long Live Tradition!" *Phi Delta Kappan* 55 (1974): 403–406.

2. LEARNING SOCIETY. For additional references on the learning society concept, see Torsten Husén, *The Learning Society* (London: Methuen, 1974); Robert M. Hutchins, *The Learning Society* (New York: Mentor Books, 1969); Carnegie Commission on Higher Education, *Toward a Learning Society* (New York: McGraw-Hill, 1973); Charles S. Benson and Harold L. Hodgkinson, *Implementing the Learning Society* (San Francisco: Jossey-Bass, 1974); W. Kenneth Richmond, *Education and Schooling* (London: Methuen, 1975); Edgar Faure et al., *Learning to Be* (Paris: UNESCO, 1972); Roger Hiemstra, *The Educative Community: Linking the Community, School, and Family* (Lincoln, Neb.: Professional Educators Publications, 1972).

3. THE FUTURE OF EDUCATIONAL STUDIES. It is hoped that the field of educational studies can play an important part in the creation of an educative society in the United States and in other countries of the world. Adequate knowledge must be obtained about the educative process and the educational system; the field of educational studies is devoted to the scholarly investigation of this process and institution.

A scholar engaged in the study of education needs a conceptual and analytical framework to identify the critical gaps in available knowledge about education and to carry out research. And, if the scholar is also a teacher, he or she requires a conceptual and analytical framework in presenting the body of knowledge about education to students.

However, many educational researchers and teachers of foundations of education owe their primary allegiance to an academic discipline outside of education. Their approach to the study of educational phenomena is through conceptual and analytical frameworks of these outside disciplines, rather than by means of a framework that is distinctively educational in its focus. While it is certainly desirable to have a number of different frameworks utilized in the study of something as important as education, it does seem astounding that only a small number of scholars consider themselves as belonging to the discipline of educational studies. The formulation of economic policy would not be too well done if the only scholars involved were those who identified primarily with the disciplines of, say, psychology, sociology, and political science!

It would probably be relatively easy to drop the outside labels currently used to designate the component areas of the foundations of education and substitute truly educational labels. For example, one of the major subdivisions of the field could be called "control of education" instead of "politics of education" and "educational psychology." Another major component could be designed "functions of education" rather than "educational sociology" and "economics of education." And a third subdivision could be labeled "goals of education" in place of "educational philosophy." These three segments would undertake specialized studies of the educative process and the educational system. The comprehensive study of contemporary educational (school) systems on a world-wide basis could be called "comparative education" (the label presently used), while the comprehensive study of the historical development of educational (school) systems could be designated "development of education," rather than "history of education."

These, or similar changes are imperative. The existing designations for the component areas of the foundations of education foster a dependence on disciplines outside of education, which can only hinder the development of a discipline of educational studies.

INDEX

Davidoff, Linda, 229
Davidoff, Paul, 229
Davies, Ivor K., 177n
De Boer, Peter, 123, 124n , 155
Definitions: nature of, 5
  problems in formulating, 16
Degrees, academic: Origins of
  134-135
  See also Credentialing
Deighton, Lee C., 101n, 124n, 155n,
  275n
Descriptive study, 42
Dewey, John, 148, 250
Dialectic, 245
Dingman, C. Wesley, 100, 101n
Dunkel, Harold B., 15n
Dyke, Doris, 167n

Ebel, Robert L., 181n, 219n
Education: defined, 7, 16-17
  problems in applying definition
  of, 7-10
  as product, 9
  and schooling, 12-13
  See also Control; Goals of
  education
Education Commission of the
  States, 199
Educational agencies: examples of,
  13, 18-19
Educational evaluation, 301
Educational studies, field of, 4, 15,
  45, 297, 302-303
Educational system: defined, 290
Educative process. See Education
Educative society: arguments
  concerning, 292-298
  characteristics of, 287-292
  defined, 287
Eells, Walter C., 135n
Effect, Law of, 126, 128
Empirical generalization. See
  Empirical statement, general
Empirical research: role of, in
  resolving policy disagree-
  ments, 27
  value of, 50
  See also Case study; Correlation
  method; Descriptive study;

Experimental method;
  Historical method; Predictive
  study
Empirical statement: characteristics of, 49
  confirmation of, 31-33, 49
  defined, 28
Empirical statement, general, 32,
  42-43
Empirical statement, particular, 32
Equal access to education:
  arguments concerning,
  216-223, 239-240
  factors involved in, 214, 239-240
Equal education: different
  conceptions of, 213, 239
  See also Equal access to
  education; Equal educational
  programs; Equal educational
  outcomes
Equal educational outcomes:
  arguments concerning,
  231-238, 241
  factors involved in, 231, 241
Equal educational programs:
  arguments concerning,
  225-230
  factors involved in, 223, 240
Examinations, 148, 189
  role of, in grading, 135-136
  validity of, 136-137
Experimental method, 35-37, 50,
  182

Factual statements, 30
Fargo, George A., 130n
Faris, Robert E. L., 61n
Final end. See Ultimate end
Financing of schools. See School
  finance
Fischer, Louis, 88
Flanders, Ned A., 181n
Folger, J. K., 219n
Formal discipline. See Mental
  discipline
Franke, Wolfgang, 189
Frankena, William K., 194, 273-275
Free market principle, 70, 82
Friedenberg, Edgar, 167